MW00399745

Longing for a Better Country

365 Daily Readings on Life before Jesus

by

G. Duane Nieuwsma

Longing for a Better Country: 365 Daily Readings on Life before Jesus
Copyright © 2016 G. Duane Nieuwsma
Published by Christian Leaders Press, Monee, Illinois
www.ChristianLeadersInstitute.org
Address inquires to author, PO Box 217, Dorr, MI, 49323

All rights reserved

Printed in the United States of America
Cover Art: George Peebles

All Scripture quotations, unless otherwise indicated, are taken from the *Holy Bible, New International Version®, NIV®*. Copyright © 1973, 1978, 1984, 2011 by Biblica, Inc.™ Used by permission of Zondervan. All rights reserved.

Scripture quotations marked (ESV) are from *The Holy Bible, English Standard Version® (ESV®)*, copyright © 2001 by Crossway, a publishing ministry of Good News Publishers. Used by permission. All rights reserved.

ISBN-13: 978-1517645885
ISBN-10: 1517645883

Dedication

for my family
immediate—and extended
related by blood—and adopted in Christ
now in the race—and still eluding *The Hound of Heaven**
*(from Francis Thompson's poem of the same name)

Acknowledgments

Thanks to the professors, students, friends, colleagues, and congregations who allowed me to practice on them and helped me grow in my own faith.

Thanks to all who have taken my questions and supported and encouraged me in this work.

Special thanks goes to:

- Barb, the love of my life, for her support and insights,
- Rev. Art Schoonveld, for his friendship and feedback,
- Meredith Nieuwsma, for her invaluable editorial help,
- George Peebles, for his painting that evokes the *better country* and for permission to use it on the cover.

Preface

Hebrews 12:1 commends the faith and perseverance of the ancient heroes of the faith as examples for us to follow in the race of our own lives. All of these: Abel, Abraham, Moses, and many more, according to Hebrews, "were still living by faith when they died. They did not receive the things promised; they only saw them and welcomed them from a distance…They were **longing for a better country**—a heavenly one." (Heb. 11:13, 16).

The human race had once lived in a very good country—the Garden of Eden—in which Adam and Eve served their Creator perfectly. But sin destroyed that paradise, and afterwards their descendants sought to regain what they had lost. That attempt was with God's full approval; he even took the initiative to reestablish what sin had wrecked. Genesis 3:15 records the first hint of what God would do for Adam and Eve's descendants.

In the stories that follow, especially those having to do with Abraham and his offspring, we see progress toward that goal. God called Abraham to be in a special relationship with himself and gave him a three-fold promise: many descendants, a homeland for them, and an assurance that they would be a blessing to the world. It was essentially the promise of a better country—a place where God's rule would be clearly seen in the hearts and lives of the people he planted there. That kingdom would be a testimony and blessing to the rest of the world.

The movement toward the fulfillment of that promise, as detailed in the narratives of the Old Testament, is not a smooth one. Although God gave Abraham's descendants a homeland, time and again they violated their pledge to love and serve God alone. Instead, they repeatedly gave themselves to the service of false gods. After punishment and correction by God, the people would repent and again live as God wanted them to, but their obedience never lasted.

Still, the faithful among God's people, some of whom are identified in Hebrews 11, kept looking forward to the complete fulfillment of his promises, even throughout the worst time in their history: their time of exile from their God-given homeland.

Increasingly, their hope became tied to a future Messiah who would lead them back to the life for which God had destined them. Hebrews and the other books of the New Testament identify Jesus as this Messiah and as the one who fulfilled all of the desires of the Old Testament saints for a better country.

The stories and teachings of the Old Testament are part of the spiritual history of all Christians and are essential for helping us understand what God wanted from the beginning. They illuminate the rebellious tendencies that still compromise our love and obedience to God, and they are a testament to God's unfailing faithfulness, love, and grace. In these Scriptures we already see what the New Testament makes much clearer: the hand and purposes of God that would culminate in the gift of his son to the world—Jesus—whom Christians confess as their only hope for this life and the next.

Time and space prohibits an examination of every Bible story about life before Jesus. But my hope is that the readings and reflections presented here will both edify the readers and stimulate further interest in God's revelation in the Old Testament. What God says here is worth the effort it takes for us to come to a better understanding of what he has revealed about himself and his plan for us. By the power of the Holy Spirit who inspired the Scriptures and who continues to speak through them, God cannot fail to convey his continuing promises and desires for each person who, by his grace, has a heart for serving him.

Therefore, since we are surrounded by such a great cloud of witnesses, let us throw off everything that hinders and the sin that so easily entangles. And let us run with perseverance the race marked out for us, fixing our eyes on Jesus, the pioneer and perfecter of faith (Heb. 12:1-2a).

∞∞∞∞∞∞∞∞∞∞∞∞∞∞∞∞∞∞

My suggestion is that you begin each day's study with a prayer that God will open your heart to what he wants to teach or reinforce in your life. Then, before you look at the meditation, read the Scripture passage that it's based on. Each day's reading also includes a relevant verse or two from the Old or New Testament. May God Bless You!

January 1

In the Beginning, God

Genesis 1:1–2:3

Of old you laid the foundation of the earth,
and the heavens are the work of your hands.
Psalm 102:25 (ESV)

Religions of the ancient world typically thought that their gods were just part of the world in which they lived, a very important and powerful part to be sure, but not with an existence before or outside of the world. The Bible, however, makes the radical claim that the world and all that is in it is the creation of one—Almighty God—who has an existence distinct from the universe he created. But we can know something about God, for the works of his hands reflect his interests and character.

Beyond that, we have God's own revelation of beginnings in the book of Genesis. Without the Creator everything is formless, empty, and dark. But with the progressive work of God a world appears; it is populated with beings who live and interact with each other and their Creator in orderly, dynamic, and purposeful ways.

From the very beginning, therefore, we see that God is not simply a supernatural Incredible Hulk or Force, blindly wielding power, but one who demonstrates consummate artistry, ultimate power, and tender care. This knowledge is a starting point to help us understand our own personality and purpose. It also serves as a firm foundation for lives prone to fear and anxiety. This foundation is strengthened immeasurably by the unfolding story of God's continuing involvement with his creation, and especially with humankind.

Praise God that, despite the rebellions that threaten to undo his good creation, the one who made us still wants us to come to know him. As the apostle Paul told the people of ancient Athens, God wants us to "reach out for him and find him" and to know that "in him we live and move and have our being" (Acts 17:27–28).

January 2

The Creation Declares the Glory of God

Psalm 19:1–6

Worthy are you, our Lord and God, to receive glory
and honor and power, for you created all things,
and by your will they existed and were created.
Revelation 4:11 (ESV)

The opening verses of Psalm 19 not only testify in poetry to the truth that God created the universe, but also say that he deserves all honor and praise for it. We cannot help but notice that the universe is incredibly intricate and orderly. But every day new things are being discovered that stretch the limits of what we previously thought. Lord Kelvin, brilliant mathematician and physicist of a former time, said in an address at the British Association for the Advancement of Science in 1900, "There is nothing new to be discovered in physics now. All that remains is more and more precise measurement." That seems foolish now, but is it any more foolish than the claim with which the late astronomer Carl Sagan opened his book "Cosmos": "The Cosmos is all that is or ever was or ever will be"?

To the contrary, there is strong evidence of order and design in the cosmos, evidence to all but the most closed minds that what we see cannot be simply the result of chance. Some people think that everything can be explained scientifically by evolution, and therefore, that this impression of purposeful order is a mistake. But the notion of the sufficiency of science is itself an expression of faith. Nor can any amount of scientific investigation nullify the sense of order and design in the cosmos. And where order is present, there is purpose.

Native intelligence can't tell us much about this purpose. But it is sufficient to leave us unexcused from seeing in the wonder of creation, a Creator who is above and distinct from it and who deserves our worship (see Rom. 1:20). In addition to that, we have the self-revelation of God in Scripture, which confirms that the whole creation declares the glory of God.

January 3

Image Bearers of the Creator

Genesis 1:26–30

When God created man, he made him in the likeness of God.
Male and female he created them, and he blessed them.
Genesis 5:1b–2a (ESV)

A popular notion today is that humans are nothing special in the world of living beings, but that we are merely one expression of the animal world and do not deserve special consideration, responsibilities, or privileges. However, God's Word has a different message; God gives special blessings and responsibilities to only one of his creatures, to his male and female image bearers.

While all that is involved in this may not be entirely clear, we can see ways in which humankind uniquely reflects God's image:

- We are creative beings, called and equipped to use our abilities to serve and honor God by fulfilling our God-given mandate in his world. Creativity misused in the pursuit of other ends becomes a curse both for ourselves and for God's world.
- We are moral beings with a clear sense of right and wrong. Therefore we can be held accountable for choosing the wrong.
- We are able to be purposeful in our thinking, reflecting, communicating, organizing, governing, and forming relationships in ways that are exponentially greater than any of God's nonhuman creatures are able to do.
- We know, deep in our hearts, that death was not meant to be. It is natural in the sense that it is pervasive; every living thing eventually dies: plants, animals, and humans. Yet, only humans reflect on the strangeness of this. Even though we have never experienced things any other way, and in truth can't even imagine how things could be different, we see death as foreign and intrusive. Ecclesiastes 3:11 sheds some light on the reason for this: "[God] has also set eternity in the human heart; yet no one can fathom what God has done from beginning to end."

Together, these aspects of the image of God in us compel us to seek to live in ways that are both temporally and eternally meaningful.

January 4

Giving God the Worship He Deserves

Psalm 8

Oh come, let us worship and bow down;
let us kneel before the LORD, our Maker!
Psalm 95:6 (ESV)

This Psalm attests to what Genesis says about humans being created in God's image by identifying humankind as the crown of God's creation. With the exception of angels, we, of all creatures in the universe, are the highest representatives of conscious life. One consequence of this is that God has given us authority to rule over the rest of creation. This, of course, is only by the permission and according to the will of the one who gave us this responsibility; our task is to manage and develop God's creation.

To do that properly, we need to know something of our master's desires. Here is where we see a most important aspect of what it means to be an image bearer of God—the need to worship. Psalm 8 was written for worship but, particularly in the way it begins and ends, we see the correct focus of human worship: "LORD, our Lord, how majestic is your name in all the earth!"

From the beginning, human beings have been incurably religious, manifesting in every time and place the desire to worship someone greater than themselves. Humans alone have the desire and ability to do this. We serve our Creator and offer him thoughtful and wholehearted praise because of who he is and what he has done, continues to do, and promises for the future.

Jesus said that such worship was essential to pleasing God; hence his emphasis on the Great Commandment (Mark 12:30–31): "Love the Lord your God with all your heart and with all your soul and with all your mind and with all your strength." And what follows from this is "Love your neighbor as yourself." These two parts of the commandment are inseparable; those who truly love God must also love and support others who are in his service.

January 5

Male and Female

Genesis 1:27; 2:18–24

But from the beginning of creation, "God made them male and female."
"Therefore a man shall leave his father and mother and hold fast
to his wife, and the two shall become one flesh."
Mark 10:6-8a (ESV)

The way Genesis 2 tells the story, the only thing that bothered Adam in Paradise was his loneliness. When he talked, there was no one who could understand or communicate with him. He could train a dog to help manage the sheep, but there was no one who had his own intelligence and who could help him with his oversight and development tasks in God's good world.

That's when God created Eve as Adam's partner, someone suitable to work with him to manage God's world. Man and woman were essentially equal before God, with shared authority. They both realized their accountability to God and their call to work together under him.

In Eve, Adam found what he had not been able to find anywhere else, a partner in work and play. We see this by Adam's response to God's gift. He said, "This is now bone of my bone and flesh of my flesh." In other words: "She is as dear and important to me as is my own life." And Scripture implies that Eve had similar sentiments. You might call these the first wedding vows.

It was a good partnership in the beginning, characterized by communication, cooperation, and commitment. Jesus pointed the Pharisees back to this original harmony as God's norm (Matthew 19:8–9). Divorce, he told them, was an accommodation to hard hearts. He continued, "It was not this way from the beginning."

God made us male and female, responsible to and for each other, meant to be in loving partnership not only with each other, but above all to our Creator who gave us life and put us together for service to him.

January 6

Marriage Essentials—Communication

Genesis 2:18–25

Put on then, as God's chosen ones, holy and beloved, compassionate hearts, kindness, humility, meekness and patience.
Colossians 3:12 (ESV)

Adam and Eve recognized that they were uniquely suited to be together. Each could understand and be understood by the other, able to communicate in a way that they could do with none of the other creatures that God had given them to care for. They probably had some puzzling moments with each other; after all, men and women are neither physically nor emotionally identical. But any mystery was a delight rather than a problem.

Their communication was not simply the ability to pass information back and forth; it was also their ability and willingness to do that with love and respect. In the beginning there was nothing to hinder this communication, no guilt or shame, and no selfishness, insecurity, or distrust. Still today, at the best of times, marriage partners experience something of that loving and respectful communication.

It wasn't long, however, until problems showed up—problems that began in Adam and Eve's lack of communication with their Creator. The unexpressed doubts about his perfect goodness led to disobedience and, then, to feelings of distrust and anger for each other.

Ever since then, how quickly good communication in marriage is hindered by misunderstandings, distrust, anger, and competition. In such a context, spouses stop listening to each other. And what communication occurs is characterized by frustration and anger rather than love. Such talk actually makes things worse instead of better. If you are married or in a relationship, make it your goal to communicate in the ways for which you were created. And don't fail to keep in touch with your Creator, without whom all communication leads to misery.

January 7

Marriage Essentials—Cooperation

Genesis 2:18–25

Whoever would be great among you must be your servant, and whoever would be first among you must be your slave, even as the Son of Man came not to be served but to serve, and to give his life as a ransom for many.
Matthew 20:26b–28 (ESV)

Besides good communication, another marriage essential is that the exercise of authority needs to be cooperative rather than competitive. Eve was created to be Adam's partner, someone suitable to work with him to manage God's world. Their equality didn't mean they looked the same or that they had exactly the same duties in the relationship. Perhaps one was better at something than the other. They weren't identical but they were equal, joined together in service to God.

That doesn't sound quite like the war between the sexes, does it? In our experience, women and men, wives and husbands often fight for power. Married people can make it miserable for each other by their attempts to assert authority over each other. Such power plays started after Adam and Eve messed up their relationship with God by their disobedience. Then they started blaming each other. Adam said, "Her fault." And Eve said, "The serpent's fault."

God described to Eve the way things would be from then on: "Your desire will be for your husband, and he will rule over you." Vying for power, that's the result of sin. It's not the kind of partnership God has in mind for men and women. He still urges another way: the practice of mutual love and cooperation rather than competition and control.

There is wide agreement about the difficulty of obeying the Scriptural admonition to "love your neighbor as yourself." But it may be that the most difficult neighbor to love consistently is a spouse, if only because the more time we spend with people, the more we see their faults. But marriage can school us in the art and practice of love.

January 8

Marriage Essentials—Commitment

Genesis 2:18–25

To the married I give this charge (not I, but the Lord): the wife should not separate from her husband... and the husband should not divorce his wife.
1 Corinthians 7:10–11 (ESV)

God gave Eve and Adam to each other to be permanent companions and partners in managing his world. Jesus confirmed the permanence of marriage: "What God has joined together, let no one separate" (Matt. 19:6).

Jesus did allow for the possibility of marriage breakup because of the disorder and sin in our world, but he clearly wanted people to make their marriages work.

If that is to happen today, those who marry must commit themselves to follow through on what they promise in the ceremony. Commitment is not just an ability to live with pain and a dogged determination to stay together. It is rather a determination to do what it takes to make marriage work as God intends it to work. It is a determination to be faithful, to be kind and loving under stress, not to take advantage of the other's weaknesses, and in cases of failure of any of these, to be forgiving.

A commitment to marriage is a commitment to keep communicating and cooperating in loving and respectful ways. A certain amount of competition or control games are inevitable in any marriage between two sinful people. But commitment means that they watch for these and reject them when they appear. Marriage partners neither seek to control each other nor submit to unhealthy control, remembering that they are to encourage each other in answering God's call to wholehearted service.

Marriage at its very best is a little taste of how good it will be to be with God in heaven. The communication, cooperation and commitment it requires help us see what God has planned for everyone who loves him and serves as his agent in his world.

January 9

Meaningful Work

Genesis 1:26–31; 2:15

Everyone to whom much was given, of him much will be required, and from him to whom they entrusted much, they will demand the more.
Luke 12:48b (ESV)

From the start, the Bible makes clear that humankind has a very special part to play in God's creation. God gave the earth to Adam and Eve to care for. He told them to populate, subdue, and rule over it. The cultural mandate, as this command is called, gives men and women permission and responsibility to use and develop the creation.

According to some people, that's where God went wrong, for too many humans through the years have used this mandate as a license to ravage and exploit rather than responsibly develop. However, that irresponsible development is not biblical servanthood or stewardship. After all, "The earth is the LORD'S, and everything in it" (Psalm 24:1). Jesus illustrated proper stewardship in several stories about faithful and unfaithful servants. And the apostle Paul also emphasized human accountability for how we use the resources that God has trusted us with. He asks, "What do you have that you did not receive?" (1 Cor. 4:7). And he declares, "Each of us will give an account of ourselves to God" (Rom. 14:12).

So then, God's instructions to Adam and Eve made clear that they were to be his agents in caring for his whole creation and everything in it. Ever since, all of humankind is likewise called to represent God's good and sovereign control over his world so that all his creatures might benefit and that the harmony in creation might serve to praise and honor the Creator. All of our time, money, and opportunities are to be used in such a way that no one in all creation can say that they have seen no evidence of God. And so that, in the end, we will be commended by God as good and faithful servants and invited to be at home with God forever.

January 10

The Kind of Religion God Wants

Genesis 1:26–31; 2:15

God is spirit, and those who worship him must worship in spirit and in truth.
John 4:24 (ESV)

In the beginning God called humankind to an intimate relationship with himself and a life that honored his desire for his whole creation to continue to experience the goodness that it originally enjoyed. This is true religion.

There are several varieties of religion that are unacceptable to God:

- Religion that has little to do with everyday life. Some who are Christians in name only give Christ just occasional attention or neglect their accountability for what they do in their personal and public relationships and responsibilities. In Jesus's day, Herod was by all accounts a believer in name only.
- Religion that attends merely to a personal relationship with God and moral interactions with people while neglecting what Scripture calls the weightier matters of the law. Many Pharisees of Jesus's day were very moral but had too small a god and too small a concept of what it meant to care for God's world.
- Religion that focuses on building a tolerant and just society but neglects the one who is at the center of the Scriptures, the one who is the only way, truth, and life and apart from whom there is no salvation. The Sadducees and Zealots of Jesus's day labored for political and social reform but forgot the prerequisite for their participation in God's kingdom: a personal encounter with God and total devotion to him.

Jesus himself is the most excellent example of one who was not only personally above reproach but who, through study of God's word and fellowship with his Spirit, had a good sense of what the Creator had in mind from the beginning—what he wanted from his whole creation and especially the people in it.

January 11

The Trees of Paradise

Genesis 2:8–17

Why do you spend your money for that which is not bread,
and your labor for that which does not satisfy?
Listen diligently to me, and eat what is good.
Isaiah 55:2 (ESV)

There were two special trees in Paradise, the Tree of Life, and the Tree of the Knowledge of Good and Evil. Adam and Eve were prohibited from eating the fruit of only the second. Why? Because the tree of life in the garden represented communion with God, who was shown by his activity in creation to be the one and only source of life. By contrast, the other tree represented rebellion against God and an attempt to establish independence from him.

As long as they ate from the Tree of Life, Adam and Eve showed that they agreed with the conditions under which they lived, namely, that their life could continue only as they continued to depend on the one who created them. To eat from this tree showed gratitude to God and ongoing obedience to him.

If, on the other hand, Adam and Eve ate from the forbidden Tree of the Knowledge of Good and Evil, they would thereby deny their complete and utter dependence on God, saying in effect, "We have just as much right as God does to decide how things will work in the creation." To eat from this tree would show ingratitude to God and rebellion against him.

This was not a period of probation for Adam and Eve, a brief test, which once passed, allowed them to eat of whatever tree they chose. The two trees were mutually exclusive. No one could eat from both; to eat from one was to give up the fruit of the other. These were the conditions for Adam and Eve in Paradise, but they also remain the conditions for every person who ever lived or will live. The trees of the Garden thus reinforce the message of the whole creation story: "There is no life apart from the Giver of life."

January 12

Satan's Alternate Message—Part 1

Genesis 3:1–5

There is no truth in [the devil]. When he lies, he speaks out of his own character, for he is a liar and the father of lies.
John 8:44b (ESV)

Satan is merely called crafty when he is introduced into the story of Paradise. However, his alternate message about the boundaries God imposed upon Adam and Eve was that they were restrictive and life denying rather than permissive and life enhancing. This was an outright lie by the one whom the apostle John would later call "the father of lies." Notice in verses 4 and 5 the lies by which Satan tempted Adam and Eve to distrust their Creator.

1. "You will not certainly die."
2. "Your eyes will be opened."
3. "You will be like God."
4. "[You will know] good and evil."

The first lie directly contradicted the ultimate result that God had said would follow disobedience. Satan promised immortality. Adam and Eve apparently believed it. Since then, of course, we have learned about the death that awaits all living creatures. Nevertheless, Satan's promise of immortality, slightly revised as the doctrine of reincarnation, still seduces many people in our world. This hope of reincarnation, however, is a poor substitute for personal immortality and has no foundation in Scripture.

Satan's second lie was a promise of knowledge that would be better than the knowledge Adam and Eve had already been given by God. This was a temptation for them to believe that God was holding out on them and that they were missing out on something. It was a lie that survives today in the search for esoteric wisdom and religious experience through various occult practices. Many such practices are scams worked on gullible people. But others actually solicit the help of demons to transgress the boundaries God has laid down in his Word—a so-called opening of eyes that leads inevitably to death.

January 13

Satan's Alternate Message—Part 2

Genesis 3:1–5

Woe to those who call evil good and good evil,
who put darkness for light and light for darkness.
Isaiah 5:20a (ESV)

Satan's third lie was that Adam and Eve would be like God. Essentially, Satan was denying the Creator-creature distinction, instead advocating the pantheism that is at the heart of all pagan religions—the idea that the creation itself is divine. If there is such a concept as sin in pantheism, it has nothing to do with disobedience to God or separation between him and humankind. It is rather that one does not realize the divinity in oneself and everything else. Pantheism claims that one of the biggest sins is the failure to worship self. I doubt that there's a bigger temptation that confronts humanity. By nature we love to exercise control over our own lives and actions. Our first parents couldn't resist the temptation; many people today can't either.

Finally, Satan promised that Adam and Eve would be like God specifically in the ability to know good and evil. While it was true that they would come to know something about evil that they did not then know, that knowledge was not at all beneficial. More to the point, Satan's reference to being like God in knowing good and evil was an invitation to moral relativism—the denial of absolute standards for life and morality and the affirmation that people must decide for themselves what is good and what is evil.

A letter posted in a local newspaper affirmed that perspective in this comment: "Parents who impose their morality on their children are abusers." As Satan knew, however, the denial that there are standards of morality, which is really the denial of a distinction between good and evil, is destructive of the very basis of civilization. Under such lawlessness, the very idea of law and lawful behavior or authority becomes unthinkable. This fits perfectly with the goals of Satan, whose desire for humankind was and remains, not paradise, but hell.

January 14

Paradise Lost

Genesis 2:15–17; 2:25–3:7

Sin came into the world through one man, and death through sin, and so death spread to all men, because all sinned.
Romans 5:12 (ESV)

Adam and Eve believed the serpent rather than the one who had given them life. Their sin was not that they wanted to be something like God; after all, God had made them in his image. But it was sin for them to pursue independence from their Creator and the conditions he had established for their happiness.

Satan is not finished with his temptations; he wants all people to repeat this sin in little and big ways. He tempts with half-truths rather than outright lies, suggesting that in following God's way, we're missing out on something. People fall for it every day, swallowing the lie that belief in sin is a mythology that people ought to outgrow, or that it is like breaking the silly and arbitrary rules of some teacher, or that it is the fun things in life that God and self-righteous people don't want us to enjoy. Sin is always made to look like much ado about nothing, that is, until the truth comes out in the end.

The difference in life before sin and after it is pictured in the contrasting images of Genesis 2:25 and 3:7. Adam and Eve began life naked and without shame, and ended up shamed, covering up their nakedness. They began with nothing to hide, either from each other or from God, and they ended up trying to hide everything. Their nakedness became a symbol of their loneliness and fear and recognition of their huge error in reaching out for independence from their Creator.

But for God's grace, we would all remain separated from him in this state of shameful nakedness. But, as the apostle Paul says, "All of you who were baptized into Christ have clothed yourselves with Christ" (Gal. 3:27). Christ reestablishes our connection with our Creator—the paradise for which we were created.

January 15

Blame Games

Genesis 3:8–13

Why do you see the speck that is in your brother's eye,
but do not notice the log that is in your own eye?
Matthew 7:3 (ESV)

Adam was overjoyed when God gave Eve to him. And we have no reason to believe that Eve's feeling about Adam was different. They were together, both because God had made them "one flesh" and because they had the same desire to do the work to which God had called them. But then they agreed to seek independence from their Creator. And after they got caught, the blame games began. Adam blamed Eve, who in turn blamed the serpent. In fact, Adam even implicated God, telling him that the woman—he referred to her impersonally, not as "my wife" or "Eve" but as "the woman"—"The woman you put here with me—she gave me some fruit from the tree, and I ate it" (Gen. 3:12). In other words, "It's not my fault. As a matter of fact, God, it is partly your fault. You gave me the wrong partner, and she tempted me to sin."

Unfortunately, for much of history Eve has been portrayed as the human villain in the Garden of Eden story, and her sex has suffered considerable discrimination and oppression as a result. In reaction, others have sought to excuse Eve because, after all, she was only Adam's helpmate. Neither of these is true. Eve was more than a helpmate; she was Adam's equal, as the NIV correctly puts it, "a helper suitable for him" (Gen. 2:18). And she was not more to blame than Adam; he ate with full knowledge just as she did. Adam and Eve both were accountable, and both were culpable for their sin.

And so are we all, although from early childhood we instinctively shift the blame to others for our own sins. But Jesus and all of Scripture makes clear that the first step of repentance and the first step toward the mending of our relationships, both with God and each other, lies in taking responsibility for our sin.

January 16

God's Gracious Initiative

Genesis 3:8

But God shows his love for us in that
while we were still sinners, Christ died for us.
Romans 5:8 (ESV)

After Adam and Eve consciously disobeyed God and broke communion with him by eating from the forbidden tree and simultaneously ceasing to eat from the Tree of Life, they desperately tried to protect themselves from the presence of God. They were sure that they would die. However, whether they saw it or not, they had an initial sign of God's grace in that they did not immediately return to the dust from which God had formed them. As a further sign of grace, although they doubted at the time that it was grace, God came looking for the sinners.

Of course God knew where they were and why they were hiding, and could have asked them accusatory questions: "How dare you?" Or, "What were you thinking?" Instead, he asked a question designed to let Adam and Eve (and all of us) know what they needed to do now that they had sinned against their Creator. God's "Where are you?" was an implicit call for Adam and Eve to come clean, return to believing and trusting in him, and make a new commitment to obedient living.

To be sure, there would be a price to pay for sin and rebellion. Yet, God was not willing to give up the partnership of caretaking and governance into which he'd installed Adam and Eve at the beginning. Nor was he willing to give up the relationship with himself and each other that he'd created them for.

Today too, God pursues men and women into whatever hiding places sin has led us. He wants us to own up to what we're doing, and then to stop it and walk with him. He wants to restore us to the paradise-relationship from which our first parents fell. In fact, our only hope for forgiveness and our only prospect for life and a future begins with coming out of hiding. Where are you?

January 17

The Aftermath of Sin

Genesis 3:14–24

There is a way that seems right to a man,
but its end is the way to death.
Proverbs 14:12 (ESV)

God had made very clear to Adam and Eve that any rebellion would lead to death. It could not have been otherwise. Separation from the generator and sustainer of life has to result in some form of death, even if God in mercy lessens the sting of it in some way.

For the serpent, whom we've learned to identify as Satan, the result would be eternal alienation from God, represented by the crushed head forecast for him in Genesis 3:15.

For Adam and Eve and the rest of creation the result would be living with continuing signs of the fractures that had occurred in their relationship with God, with each other, and with the cosmos over which God had given them responsibility.

Human procreation would be affected, as would the procreative ability of the ground. Childbirth would be painful, and instead of fruitful plants eagerly sharing their produce, it was the weeds that would effortlessly grow. All work would be so much more difficult and discouraging.

From then on Adam and Eve would vie for power more than cooperate with each other in fulfilling their continuing roles as servants of the Creator. God did not **prescribe** the woman's unhealthy desire for control or man's unhealthy rule over her; he simply **described** the damaging effect of sin on human relationships. God's prescription had been given earlier; it was a prescription for full partnership with mutual love and cooperation rather than competition and control.

By God's grace, Adam and Eve still had a life, but it was far different than the one God had planned for them—the life they had previously enjoyed.

January 18

Signs of Hope

Genesis 3:14–4:2

I, Jesus…am the root and the descendant of David, the bright morning star.
Revelation 22:16 (ESV)

Although Adam and Eve did not recognize it immediately, they had a sign of hope even at the height of their rebellion. Neither they nor the rest of God's creation disintegrated into the nothingness from which they had been made. Eventually, however, they had other reasons for hope: God's reconciling question for them regarding their whereabouts, the clothes God made for them for life outside of Paradise, and the children God eventually gave them.

Their greatest hope for their future, however, was given in God's curse of the serpent in Genesis 3:15. There God promised that the one who had successfully tempted Adam and Eve to overstep the limits of their freedom would forever after find himself at odds with the offspring of the woman. Not only that, but one day her offspring and the serpent would be locked in mortal combat—a combat in which the woman's offspring would be injured, but the serpent would be killed.

In the light of the rest of the biblical story, we understand this to be the first Scripture prophesying the coming of Jesus, whose death Satan would celebrate prematurely. Jesus's death and resurrection delivered a mortal blow to Satan and ensured Christ's final and ultimate victory. In Jesus, therefore, paradise lost has become, and is becoming, paradise regained.

In Jesus the homeless now have a home. And because of Jesus, we can have the power to reject and stay far away from the continuingly forbidden fruit of independence from our Creator and Redeemer. Instead, we may eat from the Tree of Life, thus ensuring our communion with Almighty God and our faithfulness to him.

January 19

Cain and Abel

Genesis 4:1–7

By faith Abel offered to God a more acceptable sacrifice than Cain, through which he was commended as righteous, God commending him by accepting his gifts. And through his faith, though he died, he still speaks.
Hebrews 11:4 (ESV)

The children of Adam and Eve, who had never known intimacy with God in the garden, still felt the internal call to worship the Lord and bring offerings to him. No doubt, Adam and Eve coached them in this. But their desire came from another place too—the image of God in them, damaged but still present, which compelled them to acknowledge their Creator.

Cain and Abel came with different gifts. Each one, naturally, brought to God part of the results of his labor. However, while Cain brought **some** of his harvest, Abel brought the **best** of his. In biblical terms, fat pieces are the choicest parts of the animal, and firstborn are the choicest individuals of the flock or herd. Cain brought his second best; Abel brought the best of the best.

Cain attempted the very same thing that his parents had tried in Paradise—to get by in his service to God. He tried to serve God while at the same time trying to be his own god by establishing his own terms for service. So then, when God looked at Cain he saw a person pretending to worship. Cain's sacrifice was not from the heart, as he himself knew. God reminded him of this with a question, "If you do what is right, will you not be accepted?" (Gen. 4:7).

This is just the first of many times that the Bible makes this point. God doesn't care about pretend sacrifices. No one can fool him with acts of worship that are not real. True sacrifice comes from a heart that genuinely loves God, and then tries to show that in actions that please him and help others he cares for. In other words, real worship begins only when you give God yourself.

January 20

Mastered by Sin

Genesis 4:8–16

We should not be like Cain, who was of the evil one and murdered his brother. And why did he murder him? Because his own deeds were evil and his brother's righteous.
1 John 3:12 (ESV)

Cain's sin against God developed into sin against his brother. God warned him about what would happen if he continued down this path: "Sin is crouching at your door; it desires to have you, but you must master it" (Gen. 4:7). The original problem was one thing; the secondary problem exacerbated it.

Cain's mastery of his sin would have meant self-control at the least. However, in the long run, self-control is not possible where there is no repentance. Self-control can certainly help alleviate fighting among people, but it can never reconcile. Self-control is a product, a fruit of repentance. And so God was really urging Cain to get right with him; if he got his worship right it would also help him to maintain right relations with his brother.

But Cain did not take steps to correct his attitude. Rather he indulged himself and let his anger harden into murderous rage. That's the way sin always goes unless repentance breaks the vicious cycle. The root sin is prideful rebellion against God, and that one sin leads to all others. Cain could not stand it that his worship practices suffered by contrast with those of Abel who conducted himself as a proper imagebearer of God.

Afterwards, God asked Cain, "Where is your brother?" That question was an echo of the "Where are you?" (Gen. 3:9), which God had directed to Adam and Eve after their sin. Cain pled ignorance. Had he been around today he may have claimed temporary insanity. But it is impossible to hide or rationalize murder; the taken life of the victim cries out to God who gave him life. For that matter, no sin or sinner is safe from the eyes of God. Sin must be punished.

January 21

Cain's Harvest

Genesis 4:10–24

You show steadfast love to thousands, but you repay the guilt of fathers to their children after them.
Jeremiah 32:18a (ESV)

What horrible consequences resulted from Cain's refusal to yield himself to God. This was no ordinary murder, as horrific as premeditated murder always is. Nor was it like other murders that happen in our time and place, whether they result from random shootings, domestic violence, burglaries gone bad, or even terrorism. This murder of Abel looked like the end of righteousness on earth. We later learn that Adam and Eve had other sons and daughters, but to this point Scripture mentions only two of their children: Cain, the pretend worshiper, and Abel, the real worshiper. And now that the pretender killed the other, what would become of the world?

As bad as things get in today's world, I'm not sure they ever look this bad. Sometimes Christians may feel entirely alone and forgotten, as probably some in Syria or North Korea do today. And yet, we know that there are places in the world where there is much more hope and evidence of true faith. It was not so in the time of Cain and Abel. The battle between God's people and the serpent's people seemed to be over. So what would now happen?

Cain could have repented. But, apparently he felt sorry only for himself and was content to live apart from the Lord's presence. Cain's offspring were like their father. As imagebearers of God they still had the intelligence and skills to take advantage of the rich resources that remained even in a fallen world; they inventively imitated their Creator in certain ways. However, as exemplified by the actions and boasting of the vengeful bully Lamech, they were morally bankrupt, using their tools and abilities for the wrong purposes. Cain's line followed his example, taking matters into their own hands rather than living as God's servants.

January 22

Servants of God versus Giants of Wickedness

Genesis 4:25–6:8

By faith Enoch was taken up so that he should not see death,
and he was not found, because God had taken him.
Now before he was taken he was commended as having pleased God.
Hebrews 11:5–6 (ESV)

God's gracious answer to the continuing disobedience of Cain's descendants was a sort of re-creation. He reestablished the righteous line through Seth, whose descendants, unlike Cain's, wanted to serve God. The fifth-generation descendant of Seth was Enoch, who walked with God, while Lamech, Cain's fifth-generation descendant, insisted on acting as his own god.

Over time however, even most of the righteous line went astray—at least partly because of the intermarriage between the "sons of God" and the "daughters of men." There is much debate among commentators as to the specific meaning of these terms, but we know this much: wickedness on the earth increased so that people became ever more like Cain and Lamech than like Seth and Enoch. Genesis 6:4 speaks about the heroes of old. But these heroes, no matter what they did to impress their world, were judged by God to be giants of wickedness; they excelled in the art and science of godlessness.

God decided to "uncreate" his world, not as the heartless and cruel act of an uncaring deity, but rather as the logical consequence of his unswerving devotion to his original goal. God had to destroy the polluters of his creation and social order in order to restore it to its original goodness.

In fact, God's judgment is always both the harvest of wickedness and the preparation for righteousness. God's judgment means death for the unrepentant. But for the remnant that is loyal to God, it is preparation for a new life in which sin does not exercise its terrible dominion—a life in which all are the servants they were created to be.

January 23

God's Message in the Flood—Part 1

Genesis 6:9–7:24

As were the days of Noah, so will be the coming of the Son of Man... Therefore you also must be ready, for the Son of Man is coming at an hour you do not expect.
Matthew 24:37, 44 (ESV)

The story of the flood is only somewhat the story of Noah. It is more the story of God's actions to preserve his creation, and particularly, his imagebearers. It is a story both of God's righteous judgment and gracious salvation. As to righteous judgment, it tells us these things:

- God hates wickedness and does not take it lightly when his intentions are disregarded. He is in charge. Since God created the world and its inhabitants, he has the right to judge it for its rebellion.
- God will not yield his will to the desires of those who rebel against him. People often change their minds, especially in the face of opposition. God never does, but always remains committed to his perfect plans and intentions.
- God is powerful enough to have his way. What he created by the force of his will, he can just as easily undo. He who brought order from chaos can just as easily let order degenerate into chaos.
- God does not rush to judgment, but provides adequate opportunity for repentance. As grieved as he was by Noah's generation, God graciously postponed judgment for a time while Noah, whom the apostle Peter calls a "preacher of righteousness" (2 Peter 2:5), gave a word and deed testimony to his world.
- God means for this and every judgment to stand as a warning for future generations until the day of Final Judgment. At that time the faithful will receive honor and position, but the unfaithful will be "cut to pieces and assigned a place with the hypocrites, where there will be weeping and gnashing of teeth" (Matt. 24:51).

January 24

God's Message in the Flood—Part 2

Genesis 8:1–9:17

By faith Noah, being warned by God concerning events as yet unseen, in reverent fear constructed an ark for the saving of his household. By this he condemned the world and became an heir of the righteousness that comes by faith.
Hebrews 11:7 (ESV)

Although the flood means judgment for the wicked, it is equally a gracious story of salvation for the righteous:

- Salvation is by God's initiative. He comes to Noah to instruct him how to escape the coming judgment.
- Salvation is not merit-based, but grace-based. Although Scripture calls Noah a righteous man and says that he walked with God, Noah knew, as did Enoch before him and Abraham after him, that anything good in him was only because of the help and goodness of God who invited him into a relationship with himself. Salvation is always by grace.
- Salvation always comes as God's answer to extreme need and in the midst of judgment; it is not even necessary in any other context.
- Salvation is not merely the saving of individuals from destruction, but the reestablishment of something like the original community that God intended. It puts people in touch with God's original purpose: "Be fruitful and increase in number; fill the earth and subdue it" (Gen. 1:28). Among other things in this post-paradise world, this means that the grace of God which blesses you is also meant to bless both fellow believers and those who have yet to come to a personal knowledge of the saving power of Christ.
- Salvation is a story of grace that endures. The world has deserved flood-style judgment many times since Noah's day. But God has promised to delay such awful judgment until the end, in the meantime preserving his people and giving the world more chances to repent.

January 25

New World—Old Sin

Genesis 9:18–29

Nimrod...was the first on earth to be a mighty man.
He was a mighty hunter before the LORD. Therefore it is said,
"Like Nimrod, a mighty hunter before the LORD."
Genesis 10:8–9 (ESV)

In the course of responding to God's directive to reclaim and cultivate the earth, Noah misused the good products of it. He became drunk and made a fool of himself. Although we don't know whether this happened regularly or it was the only time, Noah's drunkenness was not proper in his role as the new Adam.

However, it is not Noah's action that is primarily in view in this passage; the focus is the response of Ham who chose not to cover up his father's nakedness, but instead to spread the news of it. The implication is that Ham made a joke of it; in any event he showed gross disrespect. Such behavior had been more typical of life before the flood. Ham's behavior was inconsistent with continuing to enjoy the blessing of God.

For disdaining the gracious covenant of God, Ham brought God's curse down upon himself and his descendants. The severity of the curse reflects the severity of the offense against God and God's appointed servant, Noah. Ham had become like another Cain in this world. And his descendants would become like Cain's. As Lamech was the sinner extraordinaire in Cain's line, so was Nimrod in the line of Ham. In fact, Nimrod's name means "let us rebel."

Matthew Henry, relying at least partly on extra-biblical evidence, says in his concise commentary on Genesis 10:8–14: "Nimrod was resolved to lord it over his neighbours. The spirit of the giants before the flood, who became mighty men, and men of renown (Genesis 6:4), revived in him." While the world had been cleansed by the judgment of God, it didn't take long for the same old sin to reappear.

January 26

The Tower of Babel

Genesis 11:1–9

Man in his pomp will not remain; he is like the beasts that perish.
This is the path of those who have foolish confidence;
yet after them people approve of their boasts.
Psalm 49:12–13 (ESV)

Nimrod was apparently the leader of the group who built the city of Babel; one of the centers of his kingdom was Shinar (Gen. 10:10), which was the very location of Babel. The story of what happened here clearly illustrates the return to wickedness in the world that the flood was supposed to have purified.

On the surface there would seem to be nothing wrong in building a city. Such a project might foster a good sense of community. And there's nothing to indicate that God dislikes skyscrapers. But what God does oppose is any attempt to build another kingdom in opposition to his. Yet that's what the builders wanted: a city with its top in the heavens "so that we may make a name for ourselves" (Gen. 11:4).

God is not willing that people should prefer making names for themselves over being his good servants. Nor did he intend for them to fail to take possession of the whole earth in obedience to his command to "be fruitful and increase in number; multiply on the earth and increase upon it" (Gen. 9:7).

Moses would later criticize the Israelites for a similar failure on their way to the Promised Land: "When the LORD sent you out from Kadesh Barnea, he said, 'Go up and take possession of the land I have given you.' But you rebelled against the command of the LORD your God. You did not trust him or obey him. You have been rebellious against the LORD ever since I have known you" (Deut. 9:23-24).

Even if disobedience is less out of pride than out of fear, God is not pleased by it; he expects trust and obedience.

January 27

God's Gracious Choice and Call

Genesis 11:27–12:3

I took your father Abraham from beyond the River
and led him through all the land of Canaan,
and made his offspring many.
Joshua 24:3 (ESV)

God's cleansing of earth with the flood and restart with Noah didn't solve the sin problem that began with Adam and Eve. But, in these verses we see a radical escalation in God's plan to restore his sin-plagued creation. God didn't have much to work with; most, if not all, the people alive at this time were idol worshipers. Abraham and his family were too as Joshua made clear centuries later: "This is what the LORD, the God of Israel, says: 'Long ago your ancestors, including Terah the father of Abraham and Nahor, lived beyond the Euphrates and worshiped other gods'" (Josh. 24:2). (Abraham and his family lived among people who worshiped the moon god.)

If God had been looking for an especially righteous person, he might have gone to the mysterious Melchizedek, to whom we are introduced in Genesis 14. This king of Salem (Jerusalem) was already in Canaan where he was living up to his name, which meant King of Peace. Hebrews 7:1 says that Melchizedek was a priest of God Most High and calls him greater than Abraham.

But God chose unrighteous Abraham, who would respond in belief and by God's grace be credited with righteousness (see Rom. 4:3). This unmerited grace of God would also be extended to Abraham's descendants. Years later Moses would caution Israel not to take credit for their own successes but to give God the credit: "After the LORD your God has driven [your enemies] out before you, do not say to yourself, 'The LORD has brought me here to take possession of this land because of my righteousness'" (Deut. 9:4). It's the very thing every Christian must also remember: "He saved us, not because of righteous things we had done, but because of his mercy" (Titus 3:5).

January 28

God's Promises to Abraham

Genesis 12:1–9

By faith Abraham obeyed when he was called to go out to a place that he was to receive as an inheritance. And he went out, not knowing where he was going. By faith he went to live in the land of promise, as in a foreign land...For he was looking forward to the city that has foundations, whose designer and builder is God.
Hebrews 11:8–10 (ESV)

We don't know how the call to Abraham came, whether audibly or in another way. Nor do we know whether it came once or with insistent repetition. But Abraham heard God's call, believed his promise, and responded in faithful obedience to God's command—he traveled with his wife, nephew, servants, and possessions to the land of Canaan. It was the first step in a lifelong commitment to, and fellowship with, the one who had authority to regulate his movements and the power to bless him.

God's promise to Abraham had three main components:
- to give him many descendants;
- to prosper and protect him and his descendants;
- to make him a great blessing to the world.

The first of these must have astonished Abraham for Sarah was barren and thought to be cursed in a world where the primary evidence of divine blessing and wealth was children to carry on the family name. The second carried the implication of a homeland for him. And the third, Abraham could hardly imagine. Any hope he had would have fallen far short of what really happened.

In view of these promises, Abraham's first official act in the new land was to build an altar to the Lord. From this time on, what he looked for in life was the fulfillment of God's promises. While others worshiped the evidences of the divine in the heavenly bodies and in themselves, Abraham committed himself to the worship of God and staked his future upon God's existence and faithfulness.

January 29

Abraham Made Righteous

Genesis 15:1–7

For by grace you have been saved through faith. And this is not your own doing; it is the gift of God, not a result of works, so that no one may boast.
Ephesians 2:8–9 (ESV)

Abraham had been in the land for some time when God appeared to him in a vision. It was a vision that frightened him, and yet he was glad of the opportunity to question God about the promises he had made. It was especially God's promise about many descendants that troubled Abraham because, after all this time in Canaan, Sarah was still childless. So Abraham naturally wondered if and when God was ever going to fulfill that promise of children. In fact, he had already nearly given up on it and had been making plans to pass on his estate to his chief servant, Eliezer.

So the LORD corrected Abraham, saying that a son from his own body would be his heir. This amazing statement follows: "Abram believed the LORD, and he credited to him as righteousness." Before this, Abraham had rightly obeyed God's call to go to a different land, but as yet he had no righteousness, no ability to stand before God without guilt and as a covenant partner. But now, with Abraham's belief following this repetition of God's original promise, Abraham was credited with righteousness, not as something he earned by believing, but as a gift of God to one who believed.

The Scriptures never tire of stressing this: Righteousness before God cannot be earned; it can only be received by faith as the gracious gift of God. And when received, believing sinners are credited with righteousness. Every other religion of the world emphasizes the need to do creditworthy things. Biblical religion alone says that nothing we do is creditworthy enough to make us righteous; righteousness comes only from God, who then enables us to seek and do what is good.

January 30

The Guarantee of God's Promises

Genesis 15:8–21

Greater love has no one than this,
that someone lay down his life for his friends.
John 15:13 (ESV)

The covenant-making ceremony in Abraham's vision was familiar to him as it was to all who lived in his part of the world. Covenant-makers would typically cut animals in half and then walk together between the pieces to show that as the animal halves were incomplete without each other, so also were the two parties to the covenant. What they would be saying by such a joint action is something like this: "May God make me like these animals if I do not fulfill my part of this covenant." That made this a binding covenant; no one would want to bring the curse of God on their own head and end up like the dead animals.

But here, according to Scripture, it was not the parties to the covenant, God and Abraham, who passed between the pieces, but a smoking firepot and a blazing torch. Both of these were symbolic of the presence of God who would later lead the Israelites through the wilderness by a pillar of smoke and fire.

By passing alone between the divided animals, God made himself responsible for keeping both his part of the covenant and Abraham's. That didn't in any way let Abraham or his descendants off the hook of obedience. But neither Abraham nor his descendants would ever be able to fulfill their covenant obligations unless God made them able. That was to be proven time and again as God stuck with his people despite their repeated covenant-breaking disobediences.

Abraham could be sure that this covenant would last, for the LORD of all the earth guaranteed it. It's the same assurance that the apostle Paul would express: "I know whom I have believed, and am convinced that he is able to guard what I have entrusted to him until that day" (2 Tim. 1:12).

January 31

Covenant Confirmation

Genesis 17:1–14, 23–27

For no one is a Jew who is merely one outwardly, nor is circumcision outward and physical. But a Jew is one inwardly, and circumcision is a matter of the heart, by the Spirit, not by the letter.
Romans 2:28–29 (ESV)

We're not sure when the covenant-making ceremony of Genesis 15 took place, but it was before Abraham reached the age of eighty-six—his age at the birth of Ishmael. Then Abraham had to wait until he was ninety-nine years old for God to confirm the covenant and tell him more about God's expectations of him.

At this time God repeated his earlier promises and reinforced them in the change of names he gave Abram and Sarai. From now on they would be known by the names familiar to us, Abraham and Sarah, which in their meanings was another testimony to God's promise to give them many descendants. In connection with this, God also told Abraham that from now on he and his male descendants would have to be circumcised as a sign of their loyalty to him.

In the earlier ceremony God had emphasized his unbreakable commitment to Abraham by vouching for the fulfillment of both his and Abraham's pledges, even though Abraham's own pledge had at that time been merely implied. Now, however, God specifically required a sign in the flesh to demonstrate commitment.

Circumcision was to involve much more than a physical commitment too. That's why the prophets of Israel later referred to the spiritual reality behind physical circumcision. Jesus himself would emphasize the spiritual reality behind the physical sign when he criticized certain people of his own race: "If you were Abraham's children… then you would do the things Abraham did" (John 8:39). Circumcision was to be a visible reminder and a testimony to the total commitment—body and soul—that God demanded of Abraham and his offspring.

February 1

Abraham, Partner of God

Genesis 18:1-21

You have made him a little lower than the heavenly beings and crowned him with glory and honor. You have given him dominion over the works of your hands; you have put all things under his feet:
Psalm 8:5–6 (ESV)

The LORD said (as if to himself), "Shall I hide from Abraham what I am about to do?" (Gen. 18:17). So far, God had called Abraham, given him a home, and made a covenant with him, all of this putting God's own reputation on the line. It was now time to take Abraham a step farther down the road of partnership with God.

The LORD began to treat Abraham as master of the land and powerful nation long before he became that in fact. He enlisted Abraham in the oversight and governance of the land, talking with him about the sin of Sodom and Gomorrah and sharing what he planned to do about it. It was an object lesson for Abraham, on-the-job-training for ruling. The LORD was modeling the attitude he wanted Abraham to have with his neighbors and in all the circumstances of his life.

God wanted Abraham to appreciate the demands of divine justice. And Abraham did; although he argued for mercy, he knew that Sodom and Gomorrah deserved to be judged by God. But Abraham also had an eye for the righteous who would be destroyed along with the wicked. His heart went out in compassion to them. He did not want them to share the fate of the sinners. In this matter Abraham shared God's own heart.

The just judge is grieved over unrepentant sinners. Jesus would also demonstrate this in a lament over Jerusalem: "Jerusalem, Jerusalem, you who kill the prophets and stone those sent to you, how often I have longed to gather your children together, as a hen gathers her chicks under her wings, and you were not willing. Look, your house is left to you desolate" (Matt. 23:37–38).

February 2

The Prayers of God's Partners

Genesis 18:22–33

I urge that supplications, prayers, intercessions, and thanksgivings be made for all people... This is good, and it is pleasing in the sight of God our Savior, who desires all people to be saved and to come to the knowledge of the truth.
1 Timothy 2:1, 3-4 (ESV)

One motivation for Abraham's prayer was concern for his nephew Lot. More than that, Abraham felt a kinship with all people, known to him or not, who worshiped the one true Lord. Besides, if God were to destroy the righteous together with the wicked, then Abraham must have wondered what that meant for his own future and for the future of all God's promises.

So Abraham prayed with persistence, telling God what was on his heart and mind. With each successive concession, he pushed the LORD farther, and each time found out more about the lengths to which God would go to be merciful. Finally Abraham was content with God's pledge not to destroy Sodom if even ten righteous people were found there.

There is no indication that the LORD was at all displeased by Abraham's requests. It is not persistence that angers God, but self-centeredness and wickedness. In fact, the LORD wanted Abraham to come to him again and again because his cause was God's own. Not that Abraham perfectly knew the mind of God; so far he had only a little first-hand evidence of his mercy. Yet he seized the opportunity afforded by their relationship to take on the responsibility of partnership. And God accepted the requests of his partner as good.

Ever since God created the world he'd been giving people chances to fulfill his intentions. It's still what he wants, so that's also what God's faithful people pray for, saying with him, "Today, if you hear [God's] voice, do not harden your hearts" (Heb. 3:15). That's as good an admonition for our world as it was for Israel's.

February 3

The Sin of Sodom

Genesis 18:20–21; 19:1–9

In the prophets of Jerusalem I have seen a horrible thing: they commit adultery and walk in lies; they strengthen the hands of evildoers, so that no one turns from his evil; all of them have become like Sodom to me.
Jeremiah 23:14 (ESV)

Tradition has it that the sin of Sodom was sexual in nature. This seems clear in the demand the men of the town made to Lot with regard to his visitors: "Where are the men who came to you tonight? Bring them out to us so that we can have sex with them" (Gen. 19:5).

But Sodom's sin was more than this. Besides Jeremiah's comparison of disobedient Israel to Sodom is Ezekiel's (16:49-50): "Now this was the sin of your sister Sodom: She and her daughters were arrogant, overfed and unconcerned; they did not help the poor and needy. They were haughty and did detestable things before me. Therefore I did away with them as you have seen."

In the New Testament, Jude has the most to say about Sodom: "Sodom and Gomorrah and the surrounding towns gave themselves up to sexual immorality and perversion. They serve as an example of those who suffer the punishment of eternal fire" (Jude 7).

Jude goes on to indicate other problems: pollution of their own bodies, rejection of authority, abuse of celestial beings, and slander against whatever they did not understand. They took the way of Cain (envy), Balaam (religion for profit), and Korah (rebellion). Their modern counterparts are "grumblers and faultfinders; they follow their own evil desires; they boast about themselves and flatter others for their own advantage" (Jude 16).

Such are the kind of people who deserve and bring down upon themselves the judgment of God. But for even such as these, with repentance comes mercy. Nor is it ever too late for repentance until death or judgment arrives.

February 4

Unholy Compromise

Genesis 19

Do not be unequally yoked with unbelievers. For what partnership has righteousness with lawlessness? Or what fellowship has light with darkness?
2 Corinthians 6:14 (ESV)

Like Abraham, Lot wanted to be a good host to his visitors. But Lot was not able to be as hospitable as he wanted to be because the wicked men of the city surrounded the house and called for the release of the visitors for the pleasure of the townsmen. Lot's dilemma was connected to an earlier choice he'd made. When he and Abraham parted ways, Lot had chosen the greener pastures of the rich, but wicked, Sodom. It seemed just a little compromise; Lot thought their wickedness would not affect him and his family. But it did. When Lot told his future sons-in-law about the sin of their city, they took his serious words as a joke; their neighbors' conduct was too common to be regarded as especially sinful. So, like everyone who compromises, Lot became unable to live as consistently as his heart and his religion instructed him.

Lot's prayer life was affected too. Abraham had shared the LORD's desire to temper judgment with mercy, and proved by his prayers to be a good partner for God. Lot, with far closer ties to the city, seemed to think only of himself. The angels told Lot to get out—to flee to the mountains and not look back. But Lot asked that he might be permitted to move to another town. He didn't want to lose everything that he'd worked so hard for. However, Lot obeyed and his life was spared. But his future was much unhappier than the future reserved for God's eager partner.

Lot's wife was also affected. She was given the opportunity to leave but couldn't break her ties to the city and its ways. Her looking back was more than a glance; it signified an unwillingness to leave. So she shared the death that the city experienced. Death is the inevitable end to the path of unholy compromise. How much better it is, like Abraham, to partner with God.

February 5

The Partner of God Stumbles

Genesis 20

You have commanded your precepts to be kept diligently.
Oh, that my ways may be steadfast in keeping your statutes!
Then I shall not be put to shame.
Psalm 119:4–6 (ESV)

After God's judgment on Sodom and Gomorrah, Abraham moved south into the territory of Abimilech, king of Gerar. We don't know what prompted his move; maybe it was a drought. But in what happened in Gerar, we see that Abraham was not a perfect man of faith and partner with God. Yes, God had taken him into his confidence and listened to him in the matter of Sodom and Gomorrah. And yes, Abraham had faith that God would ultimately fulfill the promise of a seed. But his actions were not always the most responsible.

Abraham allowed Sarah, who was to bear the promised seed of God, to be taken by Abimilech into his harem. Abraham was trying to avoid irritating the king. However, in his silence, he put his entire future with God at risk. How could God fulfill his promise if Abraham allowed his wife to become the wife of another man?

Providentially and with great patience, God acted to preserve Abraham and Sarah for the purpose he had called them by preventing Abimilech from coming near Sarah, and at the same time making Abimilech's entire harem sterile. Soon the king recognized that he and his household were under God's curse because of Abraham and Sarah. So he quickly sent them away with gifts and a request for prayer that God would lift the curse.

God answered Abraham's prayer for Abimelech. In mercy, and in spite of Abraham's wavering faith, God still accepted Abraham as his partner. Once again he guarded him and Sarah so that they might see the fulfillment of God's promise to them in the birth of a son through Sarah. In fact, that is the next part of the story.

February 6

The Son Named "Laughter"

Genesis 21:1–20

Can you find out the deep things of God? Can you find out the limit of the Almighty? It is higher than heaven— what can you do? Deeper than Sheol—what can you know?
Job 11:7–8 (ESV)

Abraham and Sarah had earlier thought to do their part to make God's promise come true. With Sarah's consent, Abraham had taken her maid as a second wife and had a son by her—Ishmael. Later, when God repeated his promise that Sarah would have a son, Abraham responded by laughing and suggesting to God that he would be satisfied with Ishmael as his heir (Gen. 17:17–18). Sarah, too, had her own moment of laughing incredulity (Gen. 18:9–15). A son born to an old and barren woman was simply too hard to believe.

But who can fathom the mysteries of God? And so, finally, at a mind-boggling age, Sarah gave birth to the promised child. And now she and Abraham saw with their physical eyes what they had previously seen only dimly, and only then with the wavering eyes of faith—the possibility of a future and the promise of a nation begin to take shape.

Abraham named the child *Laughter*, that's what Isaac means. He named the child *Laughter* in memory of his and Sarah's incredulous laughter, and in tribute to the joy that this son of the promise brought to his household. The naming was accompanied by Isaac's circumcision as a sign that he too was an heir to the promise and a son of the covenant with the LORD.

Isaac was proof of God's miraculous presence with Abraham and his family. In the midst of death, Isaac was life and laughter and heir to the blessings promised to Abraham. Isaac's half-brother, Ishmael, would get a blessing of a sort as well. But, Isaac would be the father of the holy nation of Israel—the people of God's choosing and God's everlasting covenant.

February 7

Abraham's Unnatural Offspring

Genesis 18:10–14; 21:1–7

Not all who are descended from Israel belong to Israel... This means that it is not the children of the flesh who are the children of God, but the children of the promise are counted as offspring.
Romans 9:6b, 8 (ESV)

Humanly speaking, Isaac's birth was an unnatural one. He was born, beyond all reckoning, to an old and barren woman. His birth was a bigger deal than even Sarah and Abraham recognized. It was in partial fulfillment of God's pledge to the serpent right after the sin of Adam and Eve had plunged the world into misery: "I will put enmity between you and the woman, and between your offspring and hers; he will crush your head, and you will strike his heel" (Gen. 3:15).

However, Jesus, not Isaac, would be the most important representative of the seed of Adam and Eve. Jesus, his birth also an unnatural one, would actually crush the serpent's head and thereby break the stranglehold that the devil had on God's fallen creation. And through faith in Jesus other unnatural children of the promise would also be born (see Rom. 9:8).

The apostle continues this theme in his letter to the Galatians. The essence of his argument is that since Christ is Abraham's seed and since the inheritance still comes by faith, everyone who has faith in Christ becomes united in him as the true seed of Abraham. "If you belong to Christ," Paul writes, "then you are Abraham's seed, and heirs according to the promise" (Gal. 3:29). And he concludes his letter by pronouncing God's peace on those he calls "the Israel of God" (Gal. 6:16).

This means that all true people of God are Abraham's unnatural offspring—miracle children born only by God's grace and with the promise of a rich inheritance. We are a holy nation in whom the world must see a witness of shalom, contentment, and laughter until the day Christ returns.

February 8

Abraham's Dilemma

Genesis 22:1–2

Search me, God, and know my heart! Try me and know my thoughts! And see if there be any grievous way in me, and lead me in the way everlasting!
Psalm 139:23–24 (ESV)

This is one of the most difficult stories in the entire Bible. It's one of the primary reasons that Marcion, a Christian bishop in the second century, decided that the God of the Old Testament was a different deity than the Father of Christ portrayed in the New Testament. In Marcion's view, God had put Abraham into an impossible situation, forcing him to violate his conscience in order to please God.

However, the church excommunicated Marcion for heresy, correctly holding that we have only one God—the God of all of Scripture. James 1:13 clearly says that God never tempts anyone to sin nor asks people to violate one of his commands in order to obey another. For example, God never forces anyone to choose between the central commands of his law—whether to obey "Love God above all" or "Love your neighbor as yourself." The first is an issue of faith; the second is an issue of morality, but God wants both of them obeyed simultaneously just as Jesus, God's premier representative, always did.

So then, however much Abraham struggled with what God had instructed him to do, it wasn't that he wrestled with the dilemma of whether to violate his conscience or disobey God. Nor was he struggling, as so many of us do, over uncertainty about what God wanted. Abraham's true difficulty was deciding where he would put his faith even at the cost of losing the most important person in the world to him. Abraham knew that God was testing him to see whether his faith and his hope for the future after all these years was now in God's gift of Isaac, or in God himself, as the one who had invited Abraham on this life and death journey.

February 9

Abraham's Decision

Genesis 22:3-8

By faith Abraham, when he was tested, offered up Isaac, and he who had received the promises was in the act of offering up his only son, of whom it was said, "Through Isaac shall your offspring be named." He considered that God was able even to raise him from the dead, from which, figuratively speaking, he did receive him back.
Hebrews 11:17–19 (ESV)

Abraham's decision on how to respond to God's command was by no means as logical and unemotional as may be inferred from the account in Hebrews. For he was about to lose what was considered in his day to be the most important guarantor of a future—his son. And he would lose him for something that looked absolutely impossible and irresolvable, that is, a contradiction between the promise and the command of the LORD.

God had said that his promises to Abraham would be fulfilled through Isaac. But now he told Abraham to offer Isaac as a sacrifice. Abraham believed, however, that God could not compromise his faithfulness by turning against him. As before, when Abraham expected a child from his and Sarah's good-as-dead bodies, he hoped for more than it seemed possible to hope for. He told Isaac that God himself would provide the lamb. His faith was also his son's; Isaac, exemplifying the attitude that Jesus would have, cooperated completely in what God required.

Rather than looking to his own sensibilities and his own seed to ensure his future, Abraham looked to the God who had called, sealed, partnered, and blessed him. As Hebrews 11:10 puts it, "He was looking forward to the city with foundations, whose architect and builder is God." And God responded afterwards by renewing his covenant with Abraham.

It is only in retrospect that we can see that by this test, God was not merely discerning Abraham's faithfulness, but also refining, strengthening, and encouraging it.

February 10

The Seriousness of Sin

Genesis 22:9–18

Sin came into the world through one man, and death through sin, and so death spread to all men because all sinned... Therefore, as one trespass led to condemnation for all men, so one act of righteousness leads to justification and life for all men.
Romans 5:12, 18 (ESV)

The death of Isaac was the most difficult sacrifice Abraham could have been asked to make. This highlights the seriousness of human sin that makes such an ultimate sacrifice necessary.

The message, emphasized and repeated to generations of Abraham's descendants, was that there is no forgiveness of sin or peace with God without a suitable sacrifice to pay the price for sin. This same theme, continued in the pages of the New Testament, gives additional insight about both the awfulness of sin and the greatness of God's gift of Jesus Christ.

Scripture says that Abraham took Isaac to the region of Moriah to sacrifice him. There is some uncertainty about where this was, but some scholars believe that the spot is in Jerusalem at the temple mount, which is the former site of Solomon's Temple and the area where Jesus was crucified.

If that's correct, then on the mountain site God chose for Isaac's sacrifice and where God provided the substitute of a ram in Isaac's place, the Jewish people later offered sacrifices to God as a substitutionary way to receive the forgiveness of sins. Jesus made the ultimate sacrifice here too. Here he himself became the sacrificial lamb, paying the price for the sins of all humanity.

God didn't have to give up his one and only son. But he did it for our sakes, in spite of how ugly and deformed sin has made us. God was willing to experience the pain of the death of his beloved son so that his human creatures might have life. Oh that more people would take advantage of God's offer.

February 11

The Cost of Discipleship

Genesis 22:1–18

Whoever loves father or mother more than me is not worthy of me,
and whoever loves son or daughter more than me is not worthy of me.
And whoever does not take his cross and follow me is not worthy of me.
Whoever finds his life will lose it,
and whoever loses his life for my sake will find it.
Matthew 10:37-39 (ESV)

One more theme emphasized in this central story of the Old Covenant is the cost of discipleship. The choice Abraham faced is perfectly captured in the comments Jesus made to his disciples in Matthew 10:37-39. And the quality of Abraham's response is just what Jesus expects from each of his followers.

That is to say, Abraham took up his cross and followed the LORD. He gave up his impulse to save his own life and future to lose it for the sake of God. He put his entire world on the altar, and in doing so gained the world. And we must do as much if we wish to be faithful.

We may not judge the LORD. Nor may we wait to obey until we understand his reasons for what he requires of us. Obedience must sometimes come before understanding. When all avenues seem closed and no hope remains, the only thing left to do is leave the solution to God in order that he may open a way where we cannot yet see one.

God's testing, for us as it was for Abraham, is to make us fit to live with him—fit for heaven. It is to help us become increasingly submissive and obedient to Christ. As John Calvin once put it (paraphrased), "It is good for us that we reach the end of our wisdom so that we resign ourselves to be led according to God's will." Every time we lose our life by faithfully allowing God to refine, strengthen, and encourage us by testing, we become better able to see and more fit to inhabit what the Book of Revelation calls "the New Jerusalem."

February 12

Isaac and Rebekah

Genesis 24

Do not be anxious about anything, but in everything by prayer and supplication with thanksgiving let your requests be made known to God.
Philippians 4:6 (ESV)

As Abraham neared the end of his life, he took steps to help Isaac remain faithful to the covenant they had with God. Isaac was not Abraham's only son, but Abraham knew that it was through Isaac that the LORD's blessing would be fulfilled (Gen. 21:12).

Abraham's desires for his son were twofold: that Isaac would not select a wife from among the Canaanites, and that Isaac would not leave the land into which God had led them. A failure in either regard would have betrayed Abraham's commitment to the LORD and his willingness to trust that God would follow through on his promises.

To that end, Abraham commissioned his chief servant Eliezer to get a wife for Isaac from among Abraham's kinfolk in the homeland he had left so many years before. Both Abraham and his servant were confident that the God who had given Abraham such great promises would enable the success of this venture.

And so God did. In answer to the prayers of Abraham and his servant, the LORD revealed to Eliezer that Rebekah was the one chosen to be Isaac's wife. She, together with her father and brother, recognized the hand of the LORD in this encounter and gave their consent to the proposed marriage. It was a testimony of this family's willingness to cooperate with the LORD's plan to make a special people of Abraham and his descendants. The parting blessing of Rebekah's family echoes God's own blessing on Abraham.

The subsequent marriage and love between Isaac and Rebekah is a further indication of God's blessing on them and the continuation of the covenant promises.

February 13

Jacob and Esau

Genesis 25:21–34; 27:1–46

Though they were not yet born and had done nothing either good or bad—in order that God's purpose of election might continue, not because of works but because of him who calls—[Rebekah] was told, "The older will serve the younger." So then it depends not on human will or exertion, but on God, who has mercy.
Romans 9:11–12, 16 (ESV)

The births of Jacob and Esau signal both the blessing of the LORD and his continuing involvement in the fulfillment of his promises. Right from the start, God told Rebekah that it was the younger of her sons who would receive the rights and blessings usually awarded to the older. Even if she shared that news with her husband, it did not seem right to Isaac, who preferred the natural ruggedness and leadership abilities of Esau. But, as strong a man as Esau grew to be, he had little regard for the promises of God, showing that by his willingness to sell the inheritance that was his by right of birth.

Jacob, on the other hand, treasured what the birthright represented and sought to obtain what God had said would be his. Unfortunately, he and his mother felt they had to scheme to obtain the LORD's blessing.

Jacob managed to secure the blessing for himself. But he did not yet understand that his own actions had been entirely unnecessary and even unapproved by God. He paid a big price for his deceitfulness. As a result of taking matters into his own hands, Jacob was forced to flee the murderous anger of his brother.

By God's grace, Jacob would in time come to realize that the promises of the LORD cannot be purchased. He would also learn to trust in the LORD's timing. But that would only be after finding himself the victim of another's deceit—that of his future father-in-law, Laban—and after having to face the prospect of a reunion with the brother he had deceived.

February 14

Jacob's Ladder

Genesis 28:10–22

This poor man cried, and the LORD heard him and saved him out of all his troubles. The angel of the LORD encamps around those who fear him, and he delivers them. Oh, taste and see that the LORD is good! Blessed is the man who takes refuge in him!
Psalm 34:6–8 (ESV)

When Jacob fled to escape Esau's anger, he had to leave the place associated with the covenant promises. This was no small thing, for it actually called into question the fulfillment of those promises. The very requirement for Abraham and his descendants to remain in the place associated with God's promises was likely part of the reason that, years before, Isaac had remained behind while Eliezer traveled abroad to find a wife for him.

But Jacob had now been forced away from the Promised Land by his own impatient conniving. Despite God's announcement to his mother that he would receive God's covenant blessings, Jacob must have wondered whether the LORD would still bless him.

The answer came at Luz, where Jacob stopped on the first night to set up camp. In his sleep Jacob saw a stairway connecting heaven and earth with angels moving up and down upon it. God spoke to him, repeating the promises he had made to Abraham. With this, Jacob knew that one day God would graciously, through no merit of Jacob's own, give him both this land and descendants to inhabit it. He also knew that God would use those descendants to bring blessing to the whole world.

Jacob was so impressed that when he awoke he set up a monument to the LORD and dedicated the place to God. He renamed it Bethel—the house of God. Jacob also pledged to give the LORD a tithe of all his future possessions, understanding that there was no blessing he could receive that did not come by the grace of God. Jacob then continued his journey, considerably more at peace than when he'd arrived at his camp.

February 15

Covenant Blessings

Genesis 29:1–31:2

Remember his covenant forever, the word that he commanded, for a thousand generations, the covenant that he made with Abraham, his sworn promise to Isaac, which he confirmed to Jacob as a statute, to Israel as an everlasting covenant, saying, "To you I will give the land of Canaan as your portion for an inheritance."
1 Chronicles 16:15–18 (ESV)

Jacob traveled to the birthplace of his mother where he met and fell in love with Rachel. He agreed to serve Laban for seven years for the privilege of her hand in marriage. However, in a deception that was quite as remarkable as the one by which Jacob had stolen Esau's blessing, Laban substituted Leah for Rachel in the wedding. A week later, having agreed to another seven years of service, Jacob was allowed to marry Rachel as well. After fourteen years of service, he contracted for yet another period of service for a share of Laban's flocks and herds.

There are some peculiar ideas in these chapters about what people of this time thought about human and animal reproduction. However, neither these ideas nor the common practice of taking multiple wives and concubines are commanded or endorsed by Scripture. Indeed, the taking of multiple wives often, as it did with Jacob, led to conflict in the home.

What is clear in these chapters, however, is that God used these sinful people and their peculiar ways to continue to fulfill his covenant promises, even outside of the land associated with these promises. Jacob's family grew by eleven sons and a daughter during his time with Laban. And his flocks and herds became stronger and more productive than Laban's—so much so that Laban's clan became jealous of the ways that God was blessing Jacob's clan. The LORD was getting Jacob ready to go back home so that he could receive the next installment of God's covenant blessings.

February 16

Return to Canaan

Genesis 31:3–55

Therefore come go out from their midst, and be separate from them, says the LORD, and touch no unclean thing; then I will welcome you, and I will be a father to you, and you shall be sons and daughters to me.
2 Corinthians 6:17-18 (ESV)

Jacob's separation from Laban was precipitated by a message from the LORD whom he had met and pledged to serve at Beth-el. God told Jacob, "Leave this land at once and go back to your native land." But, apprehensive of how Laban would receive this news, Jacob waited to leave until Laban was some distance away and shearing his sheep.

Laban caught up with him ten days later. He was very unhappy and apparently even ready to do some violence to Jacob. Laban checked himself, however, after the LORD told him in a dream to be careful with his son-in-law. Laban's expressed concern was twofold: He had not had a chance to say good-bye to his daughters and grandchildren, and his household gods were missing.

The first concern is understandable; the second may be less so. We don't know the names of these gods, but they were certainly perceived to have value for protection and blessing, and were a common feature of Mesopotamian households, including the household of Laban. Remember that Laban was the grandson of Abraham's brother Nahor, who had remained in Haran after God had called Abraham out of idolatry to follow him to a new home and a new life in Canaan (Gen. 11 and Josh. 24:2).

Laban's family certainly respected the faith of Abraham, Isaac, and Jacob, but Laban and Rachel's attachment to their household gods indicates that idol worship continued to be common in Haran. So God now recalled Jacob to the land connected with God's promises. Only if he lived in wholehearted service to the one true God could all of the promises of the Abrahamic covenant be fulfilled.

February 17

How Jacob Prayed

Genesis 32

Will not God give justice to his elect, who cry to him day and night? Will he delay long over them? I tell you, he will give justice to them speedily.
Luke 18:7–8a (ESV)

When Jacob left Laban to continue on his way home he was met by angels of God. Despite the positive memories they evoked in him of his first encounter with God, Jacob still worried about seeing Esau again. He planned various strategies to placate his brother, and then took his concerns to God in prayer. Take note particularly of Jacob's attitude in prayer.

Jacob was desperate. He had done his share of strutting around. But now he was figuratively if not literally on his belly before God, desperate for help. And what went along with Jacob's sense of desperation was humility; he knew his proper place before God.

Such desperation and humility are fundamental to prayer. Desperation, or at least a deep sense of need, drives us to the only one who can meet that need. Humility is simply our recognition of the difference in status between us and the one who can answer our need.

Jacob's prayer was also marked by persistence. Often in prayer, we give up too soon. We may reason, "God already knows what I want, anyhow." And it's true that he does. But this very fact may be one of the most important reasons that we are to pray with persistence.

Jacob prayed as earnestly as Abraham had done many years before on behalf of Sodom and Gomorrah. He was insistent without losing his humility, and he persevered in his midnight wrestling match with an angel of the LORD until he received the blessing he so desperately wanted. In the process, God changed Jacob's name and character so that he would become ever more ready to do the work God had planned for this covenant partner.

February 18

What Jacob Prayed

Genesis 32

God is not man, that he should lie, or a son of man, that he should change his mind. Has he said and will he not do it? Or has he spoken, and will he not fulfill it?
Numbers 23:19 (ESV)

The content of prayer is fully as important as the manner of it. One of the most important principles with regard to the content of prayer is that prayer is more about putting us in touch with God's plans and purposes than about letting him know about ours. We may be most confident about what we pray when we remind God of his promises and ask him to fulfill them.

Jacob does that in verses 9 and 12 of Genesis 32, referring to God's original promise to his grandfather Abraham, which then came down to Isaac and finally to Jacob himself. Jacob asked God how those promises could possibly be fulfilled if God let Esau finally get his revenge on Jacob.

We need not worry that God is forgetful of his promises. He just wants our partnership in his work. By standing on his promises, our requests don't become frivolous but remain consistent with the coming of his righteous rule on earth. Such prayer is a way we can agree with God in his work. This assumes, of course, that before, during, and after our prayers, we are being as obedient as possible in doing what we think God calls us to do.

Sometimes, trusting God requires waiting instead of action. It is not always easy to understand which we should be doing—waiting or acting. But if, like Jacob, we take the time necessary for prevailing prayer, often God will be able to get through to us to suggest things we can do to help bring the answers. We work, not so that we might minimize the risk of trusting God so completely, but so that we may cooperate fully with him as the partners he has created us to be.

February 19

God Helps Jacob to Prosper

Genesis 33:1–35:15

Your name shall no longer be called Jacob, but Israel, for you have striven with God and with men, and have prevailed.
Genesis 32:28 (ESV)

There were two main threats to the ability of Jacob and his family to answer God's call to live in the land of his fathers. Most important in Jacob's mind was the hostility of the brother whose blessing he had stolen. However, God answered his prayers about this; Esau met him with a warm welcome and a pledge of friendship.

There was also an implicit threat posed by the native inhabitants of Canaan. Would they be willing to share the land? This question was settled by their sale of property to Jacob.

An even bigger threat in Jacob's mind was how he and his family could live next to Canaan's idol worshipers without compromising their calling to be God's covenant partners. This is the context for understanding the revenge that Jacob's sons took against the men of Shechem following the rape of their sister and the proposed intermarriage between her and the son of Shechem's ruler. While Scripture does not condone their actions, it is clear that what they did was a factor in keeping Jacob's household separate and protected for service to God.

As a sign of his family's consecration to God, Jacob ordered that they get rid of all idols and purify themselves. He took all the signs of his family's misplaced loyalty to God—no doubt, including the household gods that Rachel had stolen from her father's house—and buried them. It was shortly after this that the LORD reaffirmed the new name he had given Jacob following their encounter at Peniel. Jacob would be called Israel to commemorate his prevailing struggle with God. It was also the name that his family would assume in the future as a sign of God's continuing call and blessings.

February 20

Favorite Son

Genesis 37:1–11

I will make of you a great nation, and I will bless you and make your name great, so that you will be a blessing. I will bless those who bless you, and him who dishonors you I will curse, and in you all the families of the earth shall be blessed.
Genesis 12:2–3 (ESV)

The key person in the last part of the book of Genesis is Jacob's eleventh son, Joseph. His is the story of how Jacob's family transitioned from tribal life in Canaan to become the multitude in Egypt that Moses would later lead back toward the land that God had promised as a homeland to Abraham, Isaac, and Jacob.

Joseph was Jacob's favorite son, the firstborn of his favorite wife. That preference irritated Jacob's other sons so that they hated Joseph. What made it worse was a bad report Joseph had given their father about them and a dream he'd shared with them in which his brothers were in service to Joseph. Even Jacob thought the content of Joseph's dreams to be unseemly.

It is popular to read some negative things about Joseph into this story—that he was spoiled, a tattletale, and something of a braggart. However, the biblical writer says nothing critical of Joseph, either here or elsewhere. Joseph cannot be held responsible for any unwise action of Jacob, and what he told his father about his brothers was likely important information about a way they had betrayed Jacob's trust. Finally, there's no evidence that Joseph foolishly provoked his family in sharing his dreams; he was just as puzzled as everyone about them.

Scripture portrays Joseph as entirely blameless; there is probably no one else in Scripture, besides Jesus, who is depicted so uncritically. Through Joseph's life and activity Abraham's descendants are saved from certain death and grow into a nation—blessings that anticipate the much more complete salvation and blessing that Jesus would later bring Abraham's spiritual offspring.

February 21

Joseph Betrayed

Genesis 37:12–36

Even your brothers and the house of your father, even they have dealt treacherously with you; they are in full cry after you.
Jeremiah 12:6a (ESV)

Rivalry between siblings is not so unusual. But there is a big jump from sibling rivalry and anger at a brother to the premeditation of his murder. This was not only a significant moral failure, but also a complete disregard by the brothers for God's promise to Abraham, Isaac, and Jacob to make them a great nation. If any of the brothers had stopped to think about it at the time, their plan showed contempt for the very Word of God.

Reuben had a special responsibility as the oldest son. Since he was the one who would have to answer his father's questions on their return home, he was unwilling to have a hand in Joseph's murder. Judah also had some reservations, but apparently neither brother was willing to openly oppose the rest. Reuben hoped to solve the problem later with a secret rescue. But before he could do that, Judah proposed slavery as a substitute for murder.

Ironically, the slave traders were related to the sons of Jacob. They were descendants of Midian, half-brother of their grandfather Isaac (Gen. 25:1). So it was that these outside-of-the-covenant nomads now removed Joseph from the covenant circle God had drawn with Abraham and his descendants. With that, Joseph's brothers were certain that he was as much out of their lives as if he had, in fact, been killed by a wild animal—the very thing they now led their father to believe had happened.

Jacob was devastated—refusing to be comforted. If the brothers thought that by eliminating Joseph, their own relationship with their father would improve, they were disappointed. What's more, although they appeared for the moment to have gotten away with their sin, their lives would deteriorate and their past would eventually catch up with them.

February 22

Joseph's Testimony in Potiphar's House

Genesis 39:1–20

As each has received a gift, use it to serve one another, as good stewards of God's varied grace.
1 Peter 4:10 (ESV)

Until now, we've had little idea of how Joseph had been dealing with the chaos into which his brothers' betrayal had cast him. Here, however, we begin to see Joseph's character; he showed that he was determined to remain God's faithful servant.

The success Joseph had was surprising to Potiphar and his household. You see, this was a culture that believed that gods had territories. Yet, although Joseph was clearly outside the territory of the God of his fathers, it was apparent to Potiphar and everyone else that Joseph's God was with him and giving him success.

That success was severely threatened by the sexual advances of Potiphar's wife. Joseph knew that more than chastity was at stake; he recoiled at the idea of violating the trust his master had placed in him. In fact, this idea of kept or broken trust is important to help us understand the nature of sin as God sees it. Many people, if they think of sin at all, see it as a list of acts forbidden by God. That is how the Pharisees of Jesus's day saw it. But God labels as sin whatever people do to break trust with him. Every sin begins as a breach of trust with God and usually with people too. Of course, every breaking of trust with God then finds expression in what people do with sex or money or language or thoughts or whatever.

Potiphar's wife did not care to have her own sin exposed so she accused Joseph of attempted rape and had him removed from his position of trust and put into prison. For Joseph, this was like being sold into slavery again. All of his faithfulness appeared to have been for nothing. At least, that's how a person of lesser integrity might have seen it. But Joseph's following actions showed that he was still determined to remain faithful to God.

February 23

Joseph's Testimony in Prison

Genesis 39:20b–40:23

Bring me out of prison, that I may give thanks to your name! The righteous will surround me, for you will deal bountifully with me.
Psalm 142:7 (ESV)

If Joseph had been so inclined, he might have questioned why God had raised him up only to bring him down again. But we don't hear him asking these questions. Even if he did wonder if he'd ever see the outside of prison again, we see him being faithful; his behavior in prison was as it had been in Potiphar's house—above reproach. And as before, Joseph was a blessing to his masters. Just as Potiphar "did not concern himself with anything except the food he ate" (Gen. 39:6), so now the warden "paid no attention to anything under Joseph's care" (Gen. 39:23).

Joseph's exemplary character and amazing success did not mean that his time in prison and away from his family was not a hardship. But he accepted his hardship as from the hand of the LORD.

Even so, he could not have known the reason why his liberation would be so long delayed. Later on, Joseph may have recognized, as we now recognize with the benefit of hindsight, that Joseph's difficulties probably were necessary for his growth in maturity. Joseph's time in prison also served as an apprenticeship in which he honed the organizational skills he would later need for his position as administrator over all of Egypt.

Joseph's conduct gives us insight into the conduct of Jesus when he similarly found himself the victim of injustice. Jesus also was humiliated, entirely unjustly, but he entrusted himself to the Father and continued moment by moment in obedience to him. He did that not only to secure our salvation but also to show us with what attitudes and actions we are to meet the challenges and trials of our life. With Joseph and Jesus we can be sure that God means them for good.

February 24

Joseph's Promotion by Pharaoh

Genesis 41

When it goes well with the righteous, the city rejoices...
By the blessing of the upright a city is exalted.
Proverbs 11:10-11 (ESV)

Joseph knew that his ability to interpret dreams—first those of two of Pharaoh's chief stewards and later those of Pharaoh himself—was only by the power of God at work within him. It was something to which he freely testified at every opportunity. For his faithfulness, Joseph was promoted to be in charge of all the food collection and distribution for the upcoming famine.

Joseph's next few years were busy ones, first in collecting and storing food, and then in overseeing its distribution. Joseph's actions in famine relief made him in a real sense a savior of the world. His role was reflected in the Egyptian name he received: Zaphenath-Paneah, which means "redeemer of the world and preserver of life." But what happened in Egypt was secondary to a greater work to come, one that would involve saving Joseph's own people, and eventually through them, saving a world experiencing a famine of grace. This famine would be met by Jesus, whose name also means Savior.

Joseph's success as a savior did not make him proud or forgetful of his continuing dependence on God. We know this by the attitude he displayed later in the story. Another hint of his right priorities at this time was the names he gave to his sons.

- The first he called Manasseh, which means "causing to forget" explaining that it was because God had made him forget all his troubles. Already at this point Joseph may have anticipated that God would give him the opportunity to be a blessing to his father's household.
- Joseph called his second son Ephraim ("doublefruitfulness"). It was his way of saying that God had made him fruitful in the land in which he had been persecuted.

February 25

The Beginning of Restoration

Genesis 42

Repent therefore, and turn back, that your sins may be blotted out, that times of refreshing may come from the presence of the Lord.
Acts 3:19-20 (ESV)

When Joseph saw his brothers standing in front of him, he recognized what it was that God had been doing in his life all these years. Those dreams from his childhood had been God's way of letting Joseph know that God would use him to preserve his family in the great famine that the world now experienced.

Joseph knew that it wouldn't be long before he would be reunited with his father and the rest of his family. But he also knew that there was something hanging over the heads of his family that had to be corrected before there could be reconciliation. Forgiveness is not cheap; it is difficult and expensive. Those who receive it need to understand that and to admit their sin and their need for forgiveness. The brothers hadn't done that yet.

To start with, they underestimated the problems their conspiracy would cause. They expected that getting rid of Joseph would reduce their problems and make their lives better. But it didn't work that way. Jacob refused to be consoled. And the brothers did not expect the guilt that stuck with them like a leech. The cover-up, even though it fooled Jacob, took its toll on the brothers. They agreed, "Surely we are being punished because of our brother" (Gen. 42:21).

The brothers began to understand that their offense against Joseph had really been an offense against God, and they began to see that they were reaping the rewards of their sin. What an important step in the restoration of those who are guilty before God. Seeing the magnitude of sin and its consequences is the essential first step on the path to peace and reconciliation.

February 26

Lessons in the Wages of Sin

Genesis 43—44

For the wages of sin is death, but the free gift of God is eternal life in Christ Jesus our Lord.
Romans 6:23 (ESV)

The tension in these chapters grows as Joseph's brothers experience an escalation in the consequences of their prior disdain for the covenant that God had made with the patriarchs, and thereby with them all. They find out for themselves that sin results in death.

First Simeon must remain behind in Egypt as a hostage. He can be released only by Benjamin's arrival in Egypt. But Jacob will not consider such a thing. Reuben recognizes that the way out of this mess will come only by a sacrifice as big as the sin that brought the family to this point. So he offers his sons as pledge of his determination to make things right. But Jacob still won't hear of letting Benjamin go, not until the supply of food runs out and starvation again threatens the survival of Jacob's whole family. Only then does he allow Benjamin to accompany his other sons back to Egypt.

There, by Joseph's contrivance, Benjamin is accused of thievery and must remain in Egypt as Joseph's slave.

To the brothers, this is the worst possible thing that can happen. Judah is the spokesman for the group (Gen. 44:18-34). In his plea it becomes apparent that the brothers' attitude has completely changed. Previously they had nearly brought their father down to the grave in sorrow. Now, they cannot bear the thought of bringing him more sorrow, and, in fact, are themselves weighed down by his grief. Only now can they be forgiven and restored, since true repentance lives in their hearts.

Judah offers himself in sacrifice for Benjamin. It's the very sacrifice that his descendant Jesus would make one day, but to bigger effect: his life for the sins of the world.

February 27

God Sent Me Ahead

Genesis 45

If I ascend to heaven, you are there! If I make my bed in Sheol you are there...even there your hand shall lead me.
Psalm 139:8, 10b (ESV)

Throughout all of Joseph's difficulties, his faith that God was with him never wavered. He resisted the advances of Potiphar's wife, protesting his unwillingness to sin against God. He told Pharaoh's jailed servants, and later, Pharaoh himself, that he had no ability to interpret dreams but that God did and that he was God's servant. He gave his sons names that testified to God's help in overcoming his troubles and rendering fruitful service, even in a foreign land. And now Joseph not only told his brothers, but wholeheartedly believed: "God sent me ahead of you to preserve for you a remnant on earth and to save your lives by a great deliverance" (Gen. 45:7).

The brothers weren't sure whether to trust Joseph's testimony. Genesis 50:15 explains their recurring doubts after the death of Jacob; they feared that Joseph would now take his revenge on them. But what they found was true forgiveness and reconciliation in the face of great sin. What's more, they no longer had to worry about the killer famine that claimed so many lives in their world. Joseph brought Jacob and the whole clan from Canaan to live under his protection in Egypt, where they could prosper for a time, even if they would not live happily ever after in that place.

If only God's people today could have such confidence in God's presence and protection and his ability to totally transform human plans and make them correspond to his plan. God did it with Joseph; he did it in an even better way in Jesus. And until Jesus returns, God continues his loving and sovereign work for his people, calling them to believe that whatever their situation, it is God who has sent them ahead and who enables them to accomplish his purposes.

February 28

God's Plan Includes a Detour to Egypt

Genesis 46:1-7, 28-34; 47:1-12, 27-31

Be merciful to me, O God, be merciful to me, for in you my soul takes refuge; in the shadow of your wings I will take refuge, till the storms of destruction pass by.
Psalm 57:1 (ESV)

Jacob was overjoyed to hear that Joseph was still alive. Nevertheless, he had some concerns about immigrating to Egypt. Canaan was the homeland that God promised Abraham. What's more, God expressly forbade Jacob's father to go to Egypt during a previous famine. Jacob naturally wondered what such a move would mean for God's promise of a home in Canaan.

It was with this weighing on his mind that Jacob (also called Israel, the name of the nation he would become) stopped at Beersheba to worship God. There, God spoke to him in a vision, telling him not to fear going to Egypt, for God would go with him there and fulfill the promise to make him a nation. God also reassured Jacob that he would bring his descendants back to the land of the promise.

A related matter to which Joseph, and probably Jacob too, had given some thought was how to avoid religious assimilation in Egypt. Joseph's wise plan was to settle his family in Goshen, one of Egypt's most fertile spots and especially suitable for livestock. They could profit financially there, but would also be relatively secluded so that they could fulfill their destiny as a distinct and unique people for God's own purposes.

Jacob's sons did prosper and in the process became a blessing to Pharaoh and Egypt as well. Jacob was content to see this as evidence of God's providential plan. Even so, he knew that God had tied the future of his descendants to the promised land of Canaan. Therefore, he made Joseph promise not to bury him in Egypt, but to return his body to the Promised Land where he could be buried with Abraham and Isaac.

March 1

Blessings

Genesis 48—49

To all who did receive him, who believed in his name, he gave the right to become children of God, who were born, not of blood nor of the will of the flesh nor of the will of man, but of God.
John 1:12-13 (ESV)

Jacob blessed all of his sons before he died. I'll list two of the most significant of his blessings:

- Judah would rule God's chosen people (see Gen. 49:10). David was the first of these Judean rulers, and as the New Testament makes clear, Jesus was the one who ultimately fulfilled this.
- Joseph would receive a double inheritance in that his sons would both be blessed as Jacob's sons. Contrary to Joseph's expectation, however, his younger son received the blessing that belonged by natural right to his older son. It was another instance in which God's blessing went to one who could not claim it by right.

One of the main themes of Genesis is that it is only by the grace of God that life and blessing comes to those who don't deserve it.

- After Adam and Eve lost their place in Paradise, God gave them a family.
- When Cain murdered his brother, God gave Seth to Adam and Eve, and Seth and his line lived as God intended, calling on the name of the LORD.
- After the world again ran amok, God raised up Noah as a preacher of righteousness. Afterwards, in a world cleansed by the flood, Noah became like another Adam.
- God set Abraham apart for special service and blessing and promised to bless the world through him.
- Even though the recapture of paradise was proving to be very elusive, by the time the Genesis record ends, Israel was becoming a nation. God's promise of a permanent homeland had been repeated, and in the meantime, Israel was already beginning to become a blessing to the world.

March 2

Joseph Who?

Exodus 1

I saw all the oppressions that are done under the sun. And behold, the tears of the oppressed, and they had no one to comfort them! On the side of their oppressors there was power, and there was no one to comfort them.
Ecclesiastes 4:1 (ESV)

Jacob and his clan numbered seventy when they arrived in Egypt. Over the next few decades they multiplied greatly. Jacob's descendants were the envy of their Egyptian neighbors for their fertility and prosperity. In time, however, the culturally and religiously distinct Israelites came to be viewed with suspicion.

The matter came to a head with a change in Egypt's leadership. One dynasty with its succession of Pharaohs was overthrown and those associated with that royal family were killed or, at least, lost their power, wealth, and influence. In such cases, it was not uncommon for the victors to rewrite history as well. In any event, the new king either did not know about Joseph or did not care. From that time on, Jacob's descendants became progressively enslaved. Their forced labor was Pharaoh's answer both to concerns about the increasing numbers of these foreigners and to a need for cheap labor for his many building projects.

By God's grace, however, the cruelty and oppression did not slow down Israel's population growth. Even Pharaoh's order for what sounds very much like partial birth abortion did not work; those assigned the task feared God and so found ways to quietly disobey the king. And God blessed them for it.

Pharaoh next ordered the killing of all the male children whether or not they had been safely delivered. It was an order that severely challenged the continuing existence of Jacob's offspring. What would now come of the promises God had made so long before to Abraham?

March 3

Where Is God?

Exodus 2

"Because the poor are plundered, because the needy groan, I will now arise," says the LORD; "I will place him in the safety for which he longs."
Psalm 12:5 (ESV)

The compelling question that was always on the hearts of the oppressed Israelites was: "Where is God?" For all they knew, God had entirely forgotten them and all his promises and didn't even hear their cries for help. To be sure, the last verses of Exodus 2 say that God heard, remembered, and cared. But the Israelites did not know that at the time. All they could see ahead was more of the same mistreatment.

We who've heard the story know that help was on the way in the person of Moses. The whole first part of this chapter describes God's providential care for him.

- As an infant Moses was rescued from certain death.
- Pharaoh's daughter provided a protected environment in which Moses received the best Egypt had to offer.
- Moses escaped from the hands of those who sought to kill him for coming to the defense of a fellow Hebrew.
- Moses found a new home and life in Midian.

The prayers of those descendants of Jacob who remained faithful to God and persevered in crying out to him were heard, even though, to all appearances, the sufferers never got the hint of an answer. Indeed, what they learned more and more in the years ahead was that the God of their fathers never made a promise he couldn't keep.

It would be eighty years from the time of increased oppression under the new Pharaoh until the people began to see what they could now believe only through faith. God was certainly working more slowly and obscurely than they desired. Still, he was working. It's the very thing he continues to do today too, no matter what variety of oppression we must endure.

March 4

What Is God Like?

Exodus 2:23–3:5

In the year that King Uzziah died I saw the Lord sitting upon a throne, high and lifted up; and the train of his robe filled the temple... And I said: "Woe is me! For I am lost; for I am a man of unclean lips, and I dwell in the midst of a people of unclean lips, and my eyes have seen the King, the LORD of hosts!"
Isaiah 6:1, 5 (ESV)

I'm sure that Moses and his kinfolk circulated stories about their ancestors. But they didn't know much about the God who had made a great promise to Father Abraham—to make of him a great nation, to give that nation a land of their own, and to bless the whole world through them.

Was God forgetful? Had his promise to Abraham slipped his mind? Or was he an impotent God who sincerely wanted to follow through on his promise but didn't have the power to do so against the might of Egypt? Was God impassive, unmoved by the cries of people in distress? What was God like?

Moses was the first of his generation who began to get an answer to those questions. It happened while he was tending sheep near Mount Horeb (perhaps better known as Mount Sinai). Moses learned there that the God who appeared to him was the same God who had before revealed himself to the patriarchs; God had not forgotten his people after all.

Moses also learned about the holiness and purity of God, as symbolized by the fiery bush, the bare feet, and the holy mountain. This frightened Moses; he knew that he did not deserve to be in God's presence and was concerned that he himself might be consumed. His fear anticipates the fear Israel would later have just before God gave them his laws (see Ex. 19:16). However, Moses found that God, holy as he was, made it possible for him to stay there and talk to him. Furthermore, he found that God expected his service and would empower him for it.

March 5

What Is Your Name?

Exodus 3:6-15

The LORD is gracious and merciful, slow to anger and abounding in steadfast love…[The LORD is faithful in all his words and kind in all his works.] The LORD upholds all who are falling and raises up all who are bowed down.
Psalm 145:8, 13b-14 (ESV)

When Moses came to understand that God wanted him to confront Pharaoh and lead the Israelites out of Egypt, he wanted to know more about what God was like. So he asked him, "What is your name?" What he was really asking is, "Can you tell me more about what you're like?"

In response, God told him, "I am who I am." His response might also be translated, "I will be who I will be." What God meant was that he would be revealing more about himself in the process of liberating his people from Egypt. Moses and Israel would come to know what God was like over time, as they saw God come through on his promises to Abraham's descendants, including the promise to give them a land of their own.

It is at this time that Scripture begins to use another name for God, one that shows what he is willing to do for his people. Previous names emphasized God's sovereignty and power. But with YHWH (Yahweh/Jehovah, translated in Scripture as LORD), God shows himself to be personal—not just an Almighty God, but one who wants to be in relationship with people. He not only sees and hears; he sees and hears in the expanded sense of those terms. That is, he has a heart for what he sees and hears; he is merciful and compassionate. "I am concerned about their suffering," he says of Israel (Ex. 3:7).

This was the same God the patriarchs worshiped. However, he was more personal, merciful, and faithful than they had imagined, as Israel would come to know better in the days ahead by God's promise-keeping and faithful actions on their behalf.

March 6

Who, Me?

Exodus 3:10–4:17

Do not be ashamed of the testimony about our Lord...
but share in suffering for the gospel by the power of God,
who saved us and called us to a holy calling, not because
of our works but because of his own purpose and grace.
2 Timothy 1:8-9 (ESV)

God appeared to Moses in a spectacular way. He spoke of great things, of who he was, of what he had been doing, and of what he had planned for the future. That was all grand and exciting. But then God surprised Moses; he said, "So now go. I am sending you." I imagine that Moses swallowed hard. "Who, me? You must be kidding, God. I'm not some great general. Don't you know what kind of guy I am and how many foolish and sinful things I've done and how many times I've failed? And my age! I'm not the eager young man I once was. For goodness sakes, I'm eighty years old. Who am I that I should go and bring the Israelites out of Egypt?"

Moses was timid when it came to getting in front of people. He knew his own faults. In fact, they loomed so large in his mind that he could not see his gifts and how God had prepared him for his task. Moses did not really doubt God's ability to do what he promised; he doubted only that God could use him to do it.

What Moses did not know was that the knowledge of one's own weakness and sinfulness is one of the best preparations for God's work. So long as those whom God calls do not get lost in contemplating their inadequacy, they rely all the more on God to help them, and that is their salvation. Those who decide to obey God in a difficult situation, if they are wise, do so, not out of confidence in their natural abilities but, because they have confidence that God knows what he is doing and will help them do what he calls them to do. Indeed, if you burn with fire for the Lord, he will give you everything else you need to answer his call.

March 7

Signs of God's Presence and Calling

Exodus 3:11–4:17

Show me a sign of your favor, that those who hate me may see and be put to shame because you, LORD, have helped me and comforted me.
Psalm 86:17 (ESV)

God was gracious in responding to Moses's requests for signs of his presence and calling. The first signs were given right away, to convince both Moses and his skeptics; the other signs, Moses had to trust, would be given at the appropriate time.

- Moses's staff became a snake and then was turned into a staff again; this would be a sign for Israel of the legitimacy of Moses's call to leadership.
- Moses saw his hand change from healthy to leprous white and then back to healthy again; this was a sign both of God's authority and the cleansing for the unclean that God intended for his enslaved people.
- Moses would not see the third sign until he appeared before Egypt's leaders. Then, water taken from the Nile—honored as one of Egypt's gods—would change to blood when it was poured out on the ground. It would be a sign to both Egypt and Israel of Yahweh's authority over Egypt's gods.
- Moses would have to wait even longer to see the final and culminating sign—another meeting with God at Sinai after he had led the people out of Egypt. At the time, Moses was probably not overly impressed with this sign; he preferred something more immediate. But he would need this sign of God's presence and power more then than now. In looking back he would see faith justified and would have the strength to meet his continuing challenges as the leader of God's people.

Sometimes you and I may get one of those more exciting and visible signs from God. But isn't it true that God's signs for us are often like the final one he offered Moses? "Walk down the road of obedience, and after a while you'll know that I've been with you all along."

March 8

Declaration of another Dependence

Exodus 5:1–6:12

Live as people who are free, not using your freedom as a cover-up for evil, but living as servants of God.
1 Peter 2:16 (ESV)

Pharaoh, the master of Egypt, had laid claim to the service of the people of Israel. He wanted their allegiance and service, but at the same time was afraid of their growing strength; their God-blessed multiplication threatened his mastery over Egypt. When Moses showed up demanding permission for Israel to worship their god, he impatiently dismissed him. He already knew something of the truth of a statement Jesus would make famous two thousand years later, "No one can serve two masters" (Matt. 6:24). Pharaoh knew that if he wanted to keep Israel in service to Egypt, he could not allow their god to demand such all-encompassing service to himself.

Pharaoh correctly perceived the initiatives of God through Moses to be a sort of declaration of independence from Pharaoh. However, God's desire for Israel's freedom was not so that they could have the right of self-determination, but so the Israelites could declare their dependence on another ruler—Yahweh. As strange as it may sound to modern ears, there is no freedom apart from dependence upon the Creator and Redeemer of the world.

God made very clear to Moses that what he was doing here directly followed from the response Abraham had made to God's call to be in relationship with him. In saying, "I will take you as my own people, and I will be your God" the LORD repeated the promise he had made to Abraham and reaffirmed that it was for Abraham's descendants too. What God was after, with both Abraham and his descendants, recalled an even earlier time: the original servant partnership for which God had created humankind. The struggle over who had the rights to Israel's allegiance would be a costly one to both Israel and Egypt.

March 9

God Shows His Power over Pharaoh

Exodus 7—11

The LORD has established his throne in the heavens,
and his kingdom rules over all.
Psalm 103:19 (ESV)

Step by step, God demonstrated to Moses and Israel, as well as to Pharaoh and Egypt, that he was the rightful king of Israel and powerful enough to claim their service. At Yahweh's command, Moses came first with a sign of what was to come. Aaron's rod became a snake that swallowed up all of the snakes the magicians of Pharaoh could throw at it. For one who had eyes to see, it was clear that Pharaoh would be overcome by Israel's God in the conflict over Israel's service.

But Pharaoh's heart was hard, and he would not listen to God's servants. So God began with the plagues which, in the biblical account if not in Pharaoh's mind, came in waves of three, each group more disastrous than the preceding. In the end, Pharaoh's heart remained hard. At times it appeared that he would break—he changed his mind briefly. But when the plagues disappeared, so did his repentance. At the end of nine plagues, Pharaoh's heart was still hard, and he would not let the people go. His stubborn resistance to God's claim was overcome only with the tenth and final plague, and then again only temporarily.

The plagues progressively destroyed life in Egypt. What God had spoken into existence, he now spoke out of existence. The water was affected, the land lost its ability to produce, the animals and plants were destroyed. The windows of heaven rained hail upon the earth, and the light bearing bodies that God had placed in the heavens were extinguished. The mighty Creator, who had so long before brought order out of chaos, now reversed that gracious work by bringing chaos out of order. In the end, God once again proved his ultimate authority and the legitimacy of his claim to the service of his people.

March 10

Changing Attitudes

Exodus 7—11

The Lord is not slow to fulfill his promise as some count slowness, but is patient toward you, not wishing that any should perish, but that all should reach repentance.
2 Peter 3:9 (ESV)

As you read through the story of God's deliverance of Israel, you can see the gradually changing attitudes of all the participants in this conflict. As for Moses, at first he was quite unsure of himself. However, with God's reassurances, he soon made the transition from faltering lips to faith, strength, and confidence.

The Israelites made that same transition. At the beginning they shut their ears and hearts to Moses's announcements of God's purpose, but by the end they were ready to do just what the LORD had commanded (see Gen. 12:50). Their faith grew, their depression was lifted, and their hope was rekindled as they saw the power that Yahweh demonstrated over Egypt.

The attitudes of Egypt's people were changing too. The Egyptians had been quite satisfied with Israel's forced service. But they soon began to see that they were no match for Israel's God. At first the magicians and sorcerers were able to simulate the plagues, but they failed in the third plague, unable to duplicate what Moses had done by the word of Yahweh. Nor did they have the power to reverse any of the plagues. They saw the power of Israel's God in everything that was happening.

Pharaoh's own officials begged him, "Let the people go. Do you not yet realize that Egypt is ruined?" (Ex. 10:7). In fact, all of Egypt came to regard Moses and his people so highly that, when Pharaoh finally gave them permission to leave, they showered the Israelites with gifts of silver, gold, and clothing (Ex. 12:35–36). Some of the Egyptians even joined Israel in their exodus, their joining being a testimony, not only of changed political allegiance but, of a change in who they worshiped.

March 11

Hard-Heartedness

Exodus 7:3–5, 14; 8:19, 30–32;
9:7, 12, 33–35; 10:16–20, 27–29; 11:9–10

Today, if you hear his voice, do not harden your hearts.
Hebrews 4:7b (ESV)

The story of the battle between the LORD and Pharaoh over the right to the allegiance of Israel contains several references to the hardness of Pharaoh's heart.

On the one hand, the Bible makes clear that Pharaoh hardened his own heart. No matter what chances he got, he remained unrepentant. He thought better of his stance at times. In the hailstorm, he attested to the superiority of Yahweh, confessing, "This time I have sinned" (Ex. 9:27). But, right after the hail stopped, he reverted to rebellion. His repentance was temporary and superficial.

On the other hand, the Bible says that God hardened Pharaoh's heart. However, neither in Exodus nor in any other instances of hardheartedness can it be said that God is to blame for a person's unwillingness to come to repentance.

So then, who must bear the responsibility for hardheartedness? The biblical answer is that it is the hard-hearted person. At the same time the Scriptures repeatedly affirm that God is sovereign over all, and that nothing is beyond his control.

Another point to make about hard-heartedness is this: For those who keep saying no to God there comes a point from which it seems there is no return. The more Pharaoh chose against God, the more he separated himself from God and bound himself into the straitjacket of hard-hearted rebellion. It is the same for people today as it was for Pharaoh: The more they resist stopping their rebellion in favor of dependence on God, the less free they become, and the more enslaved by the mastery of sin and Satan.

March 12

What the Tenth Plague Meant to Egypt

Exodus 11:1–10; 12:29–32

All the firstborn are mine. On the day that I struck down all the firstborn in the land of Egypt, I consecrated for my own all the firstborn in Israel, both of man and of beast. They shall be mine: I am the LORD.
Numbers 3:13 (ESV)

For Egypt, as for Israel, the firstborn of families and flocks had special significance. They were the proof of blessing and the promise of a future, regarded by all as the best a family or nation had to offer. It was for that reason that the sacrifice of firstborn animals was held to be the best possible gift that could be made to appease a god.

In this milieu, it was a significant honor for God to refer to Israel as his firstborn (Ex. 4:22). This also makes clear what a terrible thing Pharaoh was doing. He had stolen the one selected to inherit God's wealth and blessings. So God told Moses to say: "I told you, 'Let my son go, so he may worship me.' But you refused to let him go; so I will kill your firstborn son" (Ex. 4:23).

The honor of being God's firstborn was not without danger to Moses. Right after God told him what to say to Pharaoh, God showed great displeasure with Moses, who had failed his covenant obligation to circumcise his sons; it was a neglect that fell to his wife Zipporah to speedily rectify (see Ex. 4:24–26).

When the firstborn of Egypt died, everyone in Israel and in Egypt knew that Yahweh was the Lord and Master of both Israel and Egypt. Pharaoh had no choice but to let the Israelites go. Nor was Israel surprised to find out that when Yahweh brought them out of Egypt, they now owed him their firstborn (Ex. 13:2). The firstborn were to be used in the practices and support of God's worship—to be set apart and made holy so that they could serve as ties to bind God to his people. For, as it was, there was a great gulf between them, a gulf that could be bridged only by God's continuing grace.

March 13

Protected by the Blood of the Lamb

Exodus 12:1–13:16

Without the shedding of blood there is no forgiveness of sins.
Hebrews 9:22b (ESV)
You were ransomed…with the precious blood of Christ,
like that of a lamb without blemish or spot.
1 Peter 1:18–19 (ESV)

The people of Israel were not immune from God's judgment on the firstborn of Egypt unless they carefully followed his instructions and applied the blood of the Passover lambs to the doorposts and lintels of their dwellings. Then their firstborn were spared from death and became part of the victory parade that left Egypt. As a reminder of the deliverance that God had brought about, he decreed an annual celebration of the Passover, and the dedication to him of the first offspring of every womb. However, God said that lambs could substitute on the altar for firstborn donkeys. And he said that every firstborn son of Israel was to be similarly redeemed.

That pattern of substitutionary sacrifice had already been established in Abraham's time when God provided a ram as a substitute for Isaac. Later the Levites were set aside for service to God as substitutes for Israel's firstborn sons, and their livestock as substitutes for the firstborn of the rest of Israel's livestock (Num. 3). By rights, the lives of all Israelites were forfeit to God as the one who had redeemed them. But what God wanted was that firstborn sons, as representatives of Israel's strength, be set apart for his service in their life rather than by their death. Israel's main duty was to live for God, not to die for him.

Since then, Jesus Christ has taken the place of all the firstborn who were set apart for God's service. By his one sacrifice he has rendered blood sacrifice obsolete, for he has fully satisfied God's requirement for holiness in himself. What's more, the door is open to every person, through true faith in Christ, to a better inheritance than Israel's firstborn ever dreamed of.

March 14

Can God Finish What He Starts?

Exodus 13:17–14:14

My eyes are weary with looking upward.
O Lord, I am oppressed; be my pledge of safety!
Isaiah 38:14b (ESV)

Israel was elated to leave Egypt but, as they followed the pillar of smoke and fire, they must have wondered if God really knew what he was doing. They wondered more when the first reports of the pursuing army came. The Israelites were trapped between the water and the army and armed only with primitive weapons against the steel and chariots of Egypt's finest. With sinking hearts they knew they were doomed. And they blamed Moses for it. They had been happy enough to escape slavery but, the way they remembered it now, Egypt hadn't been so bad after all, and they had told Moses to leave well enough alone.

To answer Israel's terror, Moses gave the answer that people of faith must always give in the face of despair, "Do not be afraid. Stand firm and you will see the deliverance the LORD will bring you today...The LORD will fight for you; you need only to be still" (Ex. 14:13-14). What a statement for Moses to make. You'd almost think he knew ahead of time what God was going to do. But he didn't. He was not only ignorant about **how** God would deliver Israel. He didn't even know **that** God would deliver Israel. He had God's promise; and he had faith, but that's the only guarantee he had. So even though he may have said it confidently, Moses was all the while praying his heart out—that God would not make him out to be a liar but would do what Moses said he would do.

Today, too, we hardly ever know ahead of time **how** God will show us his saving grace. Nor do we know **that** he will, except by faith in his promises. Still he calls us to exercise that faith, both for ourselves and in order to build faith in others around us; he calls us to declare his saving word.

March 15

Yes, He Can!

Exodus 14:14-31

Oh sing to the LORD a new song, for he has done marvelous things! His right hand and his holy arm have worked salvation for him.
Psalm 98:1 (ESV)

In the midst of Moses's desperate prayer, the LORD surprised him by questioning him about why he was crying out to him. It was not a criticism for praying, but one for prayer without appropriate action. No, Moses didn't have the benefit of knowing in advance what God would do, but he was called to keep moving in the direction that God was leading, even though he could see ahead only as far as the fire of God's presence.

With that, God moved between Israel and Egypt to keep them separate while Israel passed through the sea to safety. God's salvation became more and more evident as the day progressed and the foes that pursued Israel got no closer. The actions of God, which meant favor for his people, threw the enemy into confusion, and the soldiers recognized the hand of Yahweh in it.

It was the same pillar of fire and cloud that stood between Israel and Egypt, and the same God who looked down on both. But what meant life for the one meant disaster for the other. What an apt picture of Judgment Day when we all will stand before the same God and what is joy and peace for some will be terror for others.

Egypt's army realized too late what was happening. And so this mighty power that had challenged Yahweh's right to the service of his people was overthrown and its army drowned in the sea. The victory was complete, finally and firmly establishing God's right to Israel's service. Yahweh's power and faithfulness as well as his character as a kind, merciful, and powerful God—in question until now—was finally proved beyond doubt. For the first time Scripture says, "The people feared the LORD and put their trust in him and in Moses his servant" (Ex. 14:31).

March 16

Keep the Memory Alive

Exodus 15:1-21

Take care, and keep your soul diligently, lest you forget the things that your eyes have seen, and lest they depart from your heart all the days of your life. Make them known to your children and your children's children.
Deuteronomy 4:9 (ESV)

Moses and the Israelites rightly celebrated their great deliverance from the power of Pharaoh and his army. They recounted the story of what God had done and how he had done it. They did that with God's approval; in fact, God told them repeatedly over their forty years in the desert not to forget what he had done for them.

One who did not know better might think that the people should not need to be told not to forget. It seems impossible that anyone could forget such a miracle of deliverance as they had just experienced. And yet they would, and very soon. Not that the memory of it would actually disappear from their minds, but it would fade into insignificance in the light of other troubles.

If forgetfulness is so prevalent among those with personal experience of God's saving mercy, how much more understandable it is for the next generations who hear the story secondhand. Those escaping slaves needed to keep celebrating and remembering, both to help them honor God, and to help the next generation to do the same.

There are too many Christians in our own day who do not regularly celebrate and remember what God has done for them. We can and should do this with regard to events in our own personal history. But we should also do this with regard to the shared history we have as God's people. The salvation that the Israelites celebrated is also part of the story of every one who benefits from the grace of Jesus Christ. We who, by God's grace, have received Christ's help to escape the slavery of sin, need to celebrate and keep the memory alive.

March 17

Hardship Continues

Exodus 15:22–16:3; 17:1–7

The LORD your God has led you these forty years in the wilderness, that he might humble you, testing you to know what was in your heart, whether you would keep his commandments or not.
Deuteronomy 8:2 (ESV)

The Israelites left the scene of their deliverance singing, thinking that the worst was behind them. But then they headed into the desert, traveling for three days without finding water. That was enough to crush any optimism. Finally they found water, but their elation was short-lived; the water was not fit to drink. They complained at Marah, finding bitter water and bitter disappointment.

The next hardship was a lack of food. They complained again, exaggerating the benefits of their former existence in light of the present food shortage. They continued in this manner with the next water shortage, blaming Moses for taking them away from Egypt, where at least there was water to drink.

It was clear by this time that their hardship was not over. What wasn't so clear, however, was whether the people would learn to respond with faithfulness in the face of unexpected hardship. In fact, that was the point of these tests of Israel by the LORD. The Israelites were free from the power of Egypt but they needed to understand that the point of their freedom was that they live in a covenant relationship with their Creator and Redeemer, obeying and trusting him in good times and bad.

Even as God tested Israel, he provided signs of grace to encourage their trust. He made the bitter water of Marah sweet; he provided an oasis, Elim in the desert; he brought life-sustaining water out of dry rocks. He also provided food where none was available: quail in abundance, and then forty years' worth of bread for forty years in the desert, one day at a time. Although they were not yet finished with hardship, it wasn't all hardship.

March 18

Lessons in the Manna

Exodus 16:4–36

He humbled you and let you hunger and fed you with manna,
which you did not know, nor did your fathers know,
that he might make you know that man does not live by bread alone,
but man lives by every word that comes from the mouth of the LORD.
Deuteronomy 8:3 (ESV)

God promised that if the people followed his instructions regarding the manna, each person would have enough. He also told them not to worry about tomorrow; God would give them enough then as well. Some of the people of Israel didn't quite believe that so they tried to store up manna for the future. Then they wouldn't have to worry about tomorrow wondering if God would come through. But, it didn't work. The manna spoiled and got stinky; it became food for maggots. The people learned eventually that they had to trust God for tomorrow, just as they had to trust him for today. There was no insurance that they could substitute for trust in Yahweh.

The purpose of the manna for Israel was not only to provide for the need of the people, but to test whether they would follow God's instructions. Today, in God's provision for us, he also tests us in the same way. Will we live in daily dependence on him, or will we try to provide some sort of insurance for ourselves to minimize that need for constant trust?

Good stewards save and invest, and even buy insurance. But they never try to make themselves less dependent on God. Every day we need to take advantage of the grace and gifts God offers. What we get will be enough. And it will be the same tomorrow—what he provides will again be just right. As we keep doing this we will come to know and trust God more and more. And we will come to know ourselves as continually and totally dependent on God, daily seeking more of his refreshing word and presence to nourish us and keep us going.

March 19

Prelude to a Constitution

Exodus 19:1–6

But you are a chosen race, a royal priesthood, a holy nation, a people for his own possession, that you may proclaim the excellencies of him who called you out of darkness into his marvelous light.
1 Peter 2:9 (ESV)

Moses and Israel were led by God to Mount Sinai, the place of the burning bush, where God gave them the constitution of his kingdom. God began with a statement of his authority to do this: His liberation of Israel imposed on them the duty to obey him and keep his covenant. Clearly, God was setting up not a democracy—rule by the people, but a theocracy—rule by God.

It is important to note the order in God's speech, which is the same as the order of the events in Israel's life. First came God's deliverance; then came God's rules to live by. Obedience was not a precondition for Israel's deliverance, but a consequence. It is the same for our salvation. There are no innate virtues that people must possess before God sets them free in Jesus Christ; salvation is a gift of grace. But, like God's gift to Israel, salvation has consequences; grateful obedience is required of those who by grace have become God's treasured possession.

Grateful obedience both honors God and becomes part of the means by which the world comes to know him. God informed Moses of the plans he had for his people; he wanted them to be "a kingdom of priests and a holy nation" (Ex. 19:6).

In other words, just as Moses had been called by God to be a mediator between him and Israel, so Israel was to be a mediator between God and the world—both the beginning of God's reclamation of his world, and a living testimony to the benefits of life under God's rule. Israel's commission was thus a preview of the so-called Great Commission in which Jesus would instruct his disciples to go out and make more disciples (Matt. 28:18–20).

March 20

Preparation for the Constitution

Exodus 19:7–25

Since we have these promises, beloved, let us cleanse ourselves from every defilement of body and spirit, bringing holiness to completion in the fear of God.
2 Corinthians 7:1 (ESV)

What the LORD did next was tell the people how to get ready to receive his constitution for the nation. That constitution would set the boundaries within which God's people could live and prosper. To transgress those boundaries would mean disaster. By these serious preparations, God let his people know how holy he was in comparison to them and how highly he wanted his law to be regarded.

In effect God said, "You must make yourself clean and stay on the other side of the boundary. If you cannot obey this, you'll never be able to live by my constitution either, because cleanliness and boundaries are essential to it. My law reflects my holiness, and if you violate that, you invite death."

When the people had finished consecrating themselves, they stood at the foot of Mount Sinai and saw a dense cloud of smoke cover the mountain. God was in the cloud and spoke to Moses so that the people could hear. We are not sure what they understood, but they knew, at the least, that it was the voice of God. Up until that time they had heard only second-hand about God's communications with Moses; now, in the hours before God actually gave his word for Israel, they heard for themselves. By this, God let the people know that whoever refused to listen to Moses's words was refusing to listen to God himself.

When the people saw this display of God's might they were properly impressed. The mountain trembled violently, and so did the people. It was a solemn preparation for receiving the constitution that God was about to give the people.

March 21

God's Law in Today's World—Part 1

Psalm 1; Deuteronomy 27:1–9

The law has but a shadow of the good things to come instead of the true form of these realities.
Hebrews 10:1a (ESV)

The passages for today extol the virtues of living by the law of the LORD and the disastrous results of ignoring or rebelling against it. Those who do the later, Psalm 1 calls wicked. It says that they will not be able to stand in the judgment. But one might wonder which of the LORD's laws the Psalmist is speaking about and how the laws given to Israel are relevant in today's world. In answer, it will help to distinguish three types of law given to Israel, the first two of which we will consider today.

Civil Law: Israel was set up as a theocracy—a nation governed directly by God and subject to his laws. The teaching of the New Testament is that God's kingdom now is not identified with a particular nation living by certain laws, but with a spiritual kingdom, ruled by Christ. Citizenship in this kingdom is open to all people, regardless of nationality, who have been forgiven by Christ and who live for his honor and glory. We conclude, therefore, that although there may be wisdom in some of ancient Israel's civil laws, they were given only for those times.

Ceremonial Law: Many of God's laws for Israel had to do with diet and proper and improper sacrifice. Although some people today still abide by the same dietary restrictions (for example, Jews and Muslims), most Christians no longer feel bound by Old Testament ceremonial laws. This is because of the New Testament testimony that the sacrifices and ceremonies of Old Testament times were meant only to foreshadow the coming work of Christ. The book of Hebrews is especially clear in proclaiming the truth that Jesus was the one sacrifice that ended all sacrifices and the temple of God who made the old temple irrelevant.

March 22

God's Law in Today's World—Part 2

Psalm 1; Exodus 20:1–2

Blessed are those whose way is blameless,
who walk in the law of the LORD.
Psalm 119:1 (ESV)

Moral Law: Laws in this category are not merely for certain historical situations, but obligatory for every time and place.

- An example is found in Leviticus 19:15: "Do not pervert justice; do not show partiality to the poor or favoritism to the great, but judge your neighbor fairly."
- Another example is the Ten Commandments, which were summarized already in Moses's day as, "Love the LORD your God and...walk always in obedience to him" (Deut. 19:9), and "Love your neighbor as yourself" (Lev. 19:18). This is the same summary Jesus gave of the moral law of God, concluding this way: "All the Law and the Prophets hang on these two commandments." (Matt. 22:40)

The moral law of God says that there is right and there is wrong. And every person is created with a sense of how to distinguish the two. But it also helps us immensely to study the Ten Commandments that God gave his people Israel, and the commentary on them given by Jesus and the New Testament writers.

What made the Ten Commandments compelling for Israel was what their great God had done for them. He had rescued them from a life of slavery and delivered them into the freedom of his good care. That's also what Christ did even more completely for all who have come to him in repentance and faith. But we still need direction on how to walk in the life to which God calls us. As Moses told Israel just before they crossed into the Promised Land: "[The words of this law] are not just idle words for you—they are your life. By them you will live long in the land you are crossing the Jordan to possess" (Deut. 32:47). It's not that God's moral law gives life and freedom; God alone does that. But his moral law helps people walk in the freedom of obedience to him.

March 23

How the Moral Law of God Helps Us

Psalm 19:7–14; 119:9–16

Do not think that I have come to abolish the Law or the Prophets; I have not come to abolish them but to fulfill them.
Matthew 5:17 (ESV)

Before we take a look at the individual commandments, let us consider what John Calvin, one of the theologians of the Reformation, identified as three uses for God's moral law.

- Civil Use: God's moral law helps restrain evil in the world. Imagine how much more theft there would be if there were no laws against it and no penalties for stealing what belongs to someone else. The moral law of God is a deterrent in the civil sphere of life, with law enforcement to back up the threat.
- Theological Use: God's moral law is a mirror reflecting both our sinfulness and his righteousness. Galatians 3:24 refers to the law as a tutor or teacher leading us to faith in Christ. In other words, the law shows us how hopelessly we fall short of the righteousness God requires. Just when we think we are not quite as bad as our neighbors, the law puts us on trial and compares us—not to those whose sin is most on display, but—to God. God does not do this to drive us to despair or to leave us there but so that we may seek our shelter from his anger over our sin in Christ's righteousness alone. The law cannot save us, but it can drive us into the arms of Christ.
- Moral Use: God's moral law is a guideline for conduct. Since sin entered the world we are incapable of perfectly obeying God's rules. Even if we have not engaged in the most egregious violations of God's Law and cannot be convicted in a court of law, we are nevertheless all guilty of such things as idolatry, bearing false witness, adultery, murder, and so on. We have failed in so many ways to meet God's standards of loving him above all and our neighbors as ourselves. The moral law in its words and spirit, while it cannot save us, holds before us the standard of how God wants us to live, both then and now.

March 24

No Other Gods

Exodus 20:1–3

The God who made the world and everything in it, being Lord of heaven and earth, does not live in temples made by man…
Yet he is actually not far from each one of us, for
"In him we live and move and have our being."
Acts 17:24-28 (ESV)

God went to a lot of trouble to rescue his people from Egypt so that he could rule over them unopposed and they could serve him unhindered. Along the way he proved himself to be a gracious and merciful master. However, even gracious and merciful masters must have rules, and God does as well. So, while still leading his people to the Promised Land, God had them stop at the holy mountain where forty years prior he had appeared to Moses and called him to leadership. Here God made clear through Moses the sort of service he wanted.

The first of the commandments is the most important and the basis for all the rest. "You shall have no other gods before me" is not simply a prohibition against the worship of other gods, but a statement that there really is no one else who can be God. Since God alone has existed from eternity, everything else is part of his creation and therefore illegitimate as an object of service and worship. If Israel did not know this they could never hope to have the kind of relationship with God that he had saved them for. Nor can we if we do not know it.

Not even the best of God's gifts are worthy of worship; they are all meant to help raise our hearts in thanksgiving to the one who gives them. All proper service to God begins with obeying this commandment, not reluctantly but, eagerly and with love that imitates God's love for us. God is the only legitimate anchor of faith; there is no other life than what he provides by grace through faith in Christ. Each of us must start where God wanted Israel to start, by knowing that God is the only one who gets the credit for everything that we are and everything that we have.

March 25

No Images of God

Exodus 20:4–6

[Christ] is the image of the invisible God, the firstborn of all creation.
Colossians 1:15 (ESV)

It is possible to worship the right God, but to do so incorrectly—the focus of the second commandment. Israel violated this commandment already at Sinai. After Moses had been on the mountain so long that the people despaired of his return they got Aaron to make them golden calves to precede the people in their travels. Aaron had reservations, but did so anyway. The next day "he built an altar in front of the calf and announced, 'Tomorrow there will be a festival to the LORD'" (Ex. 32:5).

It seems that the people saw those golden calves not as alternate gods, but as aids in worshiping the one true God of Israel. But, even though the surrounding nations represented their gods by images, God outlawed this for his people.

The use of images in worship is forbidden because Christ is the only image of the invisible God (Col 1:15). This means that any representation of God other than Christ is not only false, but an insult to his exclusive claims: "Anyone who has seen me has seen the Father" (John 14:9). And also, "I and the Father are one" (John 10:30).

The jealousy of God that this commandment speaks about refers to God's unwillingness to let the people he created live in a way that can't help but end in their destruction. Sin has consequences, not only for sinners, but also for their children and grandchildren. Whoever hates or even ignores God sees spiritual consequences for generations to come.

Thank God that righteousness has even greater benefits. For those who are faithful and serve him according to his desires, he shows love to a thousand generations of those who love him and keep his commandments.

March 26

Don't Misuse God

Exodus 20:7

Let us continually offer up a sacrifice of praise to God, that is, the fruit of lips that acknowledge his name.
Hebrews 13:15 (ESV)

To take God's name seriously is to take God himself seriously. By contrast, to misuse the name of God is to misuse God himself—to fail to show him the honor and respect he deserves. This might show up in any of a number of ways:

- Blasphemy: This might be expressed in cursing, or alternately, in false claims to be God.
- The claiming of God's authority for non-biblical ideas or actions: Slavery in this country and apartheid in South Africa both existed because people falsely claimed God's authority for it. Some of the secular reaction against Christians today is deserved in that Christians have sometimes used the Bible inappropriately to support their own political or social agenda. Scripture itself never defends slavery.
- Hypocrisy—the pretense of godliness: Paul speaks of such people in Titus 1:16, "They claim to know God, but by their actions they deny him." All such hypocrites take God's name in vain.
- False doctrine—a twisting of what the Bible teaches: That God's word is sometimes "hard to understand" doesn't have to result in heresy or distortion of Scripture.
- Casual or irreverent use of God's name: "Oh my God" is a very appropriate way to begin a prayer, but not as a substitute for "You've got to be kidding."

God takes his name seriously because his name is directly related to his character. Again, to misuse God's name misuses God himself. To discredit the name of God pours contempt on the very one we worship. It dishonors the only one is whom we may find life, both physical and spiritual, and both temporal and eternal.

March 27

Sabbath Rest

Exodus 20:8–11

Let us consider how to stir up one another to love and good works, not neglecting to meet together, as is the habit of some, but encouraging one another, and all the more as you see the Day drawing near.
Hebrews 10:24-25 (ESV)

The emphasis of this commandment is on regaining communion with God. The Bible is clear that both the "rest" that Abraham's descendants experienced in the Promised Land, and proper Sabbath observance, would help God's people keep their eyes on God, the only source of true rest.

However, neither the Promised Land nor the keeping of the Sabbath Day were the final rest that God had in mind; this would be found only in Jesus Christ, who provided a permanent answer for the sin that separates people from God. That explains Jesus's invitation to the weary: "Come to me… and I will give you rest" (Matt. 11:28). And also the confirming statement of Hebrews 4:3: "Now we who have believed enter that rest."

That means that everyone in union with Christ is already living in the seventh day, the eternal Sabbath, the eternal Rest of God. Since Christ has come, the command for Sabbath observance that God gave through Moses is now fulfilled when people are born again and live as followers of Jesus Christ. Therefore, to break the Sabbath today, as Jesus himself made clear, is less about avoiding physical work on one day than about breaking covenant with Christ, who is the fulfillment of the Sabbath.

That said, until Christ's work in and with us is fully accomplished, there are still strong and sufficient reasons to keep the tradition of setting aside one day each week for special meditation, prayer, fellowship, and attention to the Word and sacraments. That will help us make every day a day in which we never try to work alone, but always let the Lord work in us through his Spirit.

March 28

Honor Your Parents

Exodus 20:12

Children, obey your parents in the Lord, for this is right. "Honor your father and mother" (this is the first commandment with a promise), "that it may go well with you and that you may live long in the land."
Ephesians 6:1–3 (ESV)

Here in the second table of the Law, the focus changes to how we relate to other people. Jesus summarized our duty by saying that we need to love our neighbors as we love ourselves. All neighbors need our love, but first in priority are our closest neighbors—our parents; we are told to submit ourselves to those whom God has placed over us in the home. This involves our obedience to them while we are young, and our continuing respect and care for them as they age.

Behind this command that children honor their parents, of course, is also the assumption that parents must care for their children in the same way God cares for all his children. It's an assumption that Scripture expands upon in many places, but here the focus is upon the duties of children to their parents.

This command to honor parents is complicated by our parents' sinfulness. Think of the difficulty that godly children of Moses's day had in watching their parents, just a short while after they had received this commandment, sacrificing to the golden calves Aaron had made with their jewelry (Ex. 32).

Some parents today are physically, emotionally, or spiritually immature and even abusive and do not provide their children the whole-hearted love and good leadership they need. As a result, such children may find it difficult to understand or relate to a heavenly father who always loves them and has their best interests at heart. Even so, children are called to honor their parents, with the understanding that obedience to this command must be subordinate to and consistent with obedience to the first and greatest commandment, to love God above all.

March 29

Not Murder, But Love

Exodus 20:13

You have heard that it was said, "You shall love your neighbor and hate your enemy." But I say to you, Love your enemies and pray for those who persecute you, so that you may be sons of your Father who is in heaven.
Matthew 5:43–45 (ESV)

This commandment, as with the ones that follow, is put negatively: "You shall not murder!" But this is much more than a prohibition; it is an encouragement to be pro-life—and not just in the restricted sense of how to treat an unborn infant. As Jesus later makes very clear in condemning murder and the root from which murder springs—hatred—God tells us to love our neighbors as ourselves, to be patient, peace-loving, gentle, merciful, and friendly to them, to protect them from harm as much as we can, and to do good even to our enemies.

Therefore, as the Heidelberg Catechism asserts, this commandment reaches beyond hate and murder to also forbid insulting or belittling our neighbors by thoughts, words, looks, or gestures. This turns what might have appeared to be the easiest commandment to obey into one of the most difficult.

Every time we engage in some hidden form of murder, whether it is insult, gossip, belittling, or something else, we attribute a fault or weakness to others that we do not think about in ourselves. That is a failure to take our own sin seriously enough. Christ's goal in speaking of the root of murder is not to condemn or destroy us, but to restore us to full fellowship with God. So too, we are called to be praying and hoping for that very same thing in others.

Loving our neighbors according to the radical demands of the sixth commandment is meant in our day, as it was when it was originally given, not only for the benefit of God's people, but to be an astonishing testimony that may lead those who see it in action to be drawn to the source of our freedom.

March 30

Marital Faithfulness

Exodus 20:14

You have heard that it was said, "You shall not commit adultery." But I say to you that everyone who looks at a woman with lustful intent has already committed adultery with her in his heart.
Matthew 5:27–28 (ESV)

The single most important covenant described in the Bible is the covenant that God makes with people—and which he continually restores after people mess up on their end. In this covenant, God makes unconditional promises to love and care for his people, and based on his resolve and commitment to that covenantal relationship, his people are to submit themselves to him in love and obedient service.

God calls people to enter into similar relationships or covenants with other human beings, the foundational among them being marriage. In other words, the covenant of marriage is based on, and an imitation of, God's covenant with people. And those who decide to enter into marriage must regard it as highly as God does.

The promises of a marriage covenant are sealed with sexual intercourse, which is why sexual intercourse is not to happen outside of the covenant bonds of marriage. Sexual activity outside of this institution and with someone other than one's marriage partner is an attempt to enjoy the pleasure of this covenant without the responsibility of it. As many promiscuous people have found out, however, the gift itself becomes an empty thing apart from the covenant it is meant to seal.

Adultery is more than an act, too; it is unfaithfulness of the heart and mind. Adultery never enhances marriage, even if it happens consensually. Nor is marriage ever served when the partners in it are most concerned about the satisfaction of their own desires. Each marriage partner should ask, "What more can I do with God's help to build our relationship and enhance our marriage?"

March 31

Not Theft, But Work

Exodus 20:15

Let the thief no longer steal, but rather let him labor, doing honest work with his own hands, so that he may have something to share with anyone in need.
Ephesians 4:28 (ESV)

Scripture makes very clear that God, as the Creator, has the right of ownership over everything he has made. Still, this truth does not contradict the idea of individual property rights that is implicit in this commandment. It says that whatever we own—land, houses, toys—is really a gift of God for which he has made us responsible. And no one should steal what someone else has been given to control. No one has the right to take or invade another person's property.

Nor, in keeping with the spirit of the command, does anyone have the right to defraud their neighbor by such means as inaccurate measurements, excessive interest, counterfeit currency, or fraudulent merchandising.

There are also less obvious ways in which people steal what is not theirs. How many people, for example, assume credit card debt or other obligations that are beyond their ability to repay? And how many live beyond their means with the result that they must default on loans or even declare bankruptcy?

Governments, too, can steal if they misuse funds given for certain purposes, or if they do a poor job with the resources they have, or if they live beyond their means in such a way as to place intolerable burdens on future generations.

The Bible has no interest in helping people walk as closely as possible to the line of stealing. It informs us of the honesty and quality we owe our neighbors who buy from us, and also says that work is a gift of God to help us provide for our own needs as well as provide assistance to those who cannot adequately provide for themselves.

April 1

Tell the Truth in Love

Exodus 20:16

Speak the truth to one another; render…judgments that are true and make for peace; do not devise evil in your hearts against one another, and love no false oath, for all these things I hate, declares the LORD.
Zechariah 8:16–17 (ESV)

Throughout the ages, the main place this command has been applied is within the legal system. In ancient Israel, one protection against false testimony was the two-witness requirement for conviction on a charge. Similar safeguards are in place in today's courts. And today libel, slander, and especially perjury, merit very serious consequences.

But the ninth commandment also applies to situations outside of the legal system. In keeping with the spirit of the law, which is to help us love our neighbors as we love ourselves, God's concern is that people may know the truth and have the truth spoken about them.

This means more than just the avoidance of making incorrect statements. It's possible, after all, to lie without speaking, by means of gestures or facial expressions. Also, such communications as gossip and rumormongering, even if technically accurate, and even if given under the pretense of being helpful and having regard for the truth, are inconsistent with the biblical ideal of loving our neighbors as God desires.

Humans are able to communicate in extraordinary ways, but we must never use this ability to tear down and destroy. God expects us to use our ability as he uses his: He keeps his promises and is reliable in all of his communications. God expects us to imitate him in these things. The Bible urges us to cling to the truth and defend it the best we can—by lifestyle as well as by words. In other words, if you want to keep the ninth commandment, do your best to understand and live by the spirit of this command of God.

April 2

Contentment Rather than Coveting

Exodus 20:17

Godliness with contentment is great gain, for we brought nothing into the world, and we cannot take anything out of the world. But if we have food and clothing, with these we will be content.
1 Timothy 6:6–8 (ESV)

Someone has said that living beyond our means—or even wanting to do so—is a good definition of coveting, and I believe it. Both rich and poor are tempted to confuse material and spiritual blessings and to be discontented with the resources God has given them. It is not wrong to try to gain wealth or improve one's material condition, for it is not money itself but the love of it that is the root of all evil. In fact, contentment is largely unrelated to material well-being. The lack of contentment is a spiritual issue.

Israel provides a historical example of the challenge to see God as a provider even in the absence of what we regard as essential. Even though God performed miracles for his people, beginning with the Exodus from Egypt, they continued to sin against him, rebelling in the desert against the Most High (see Ps. 78:17). The one thing they did more consistently than anything else was grumble; they coveted what they did not have instead of being thankful for what they did have.

This commandment is related closely to the eighth. Both require a level of contentment with the resources that God has entrusted to us. The more we can remember that we're created first of all for God and not for ourselves, the more the discontentment of covetousness can be replaced by contentment.

How do you see prosperity? Mainly as a way of increasing your ability to get and consume? Or mainly as a blessing of God that provides increased opportunities for giving and serving? The latter is what God wants for us, not merely for our own peace of mind, but because he wants us to use our resources to make a real difference in the lives of the people and the world he cares about.

April 3

Confirmation of the Constitution

Exodus 24

Your word is a lamp to my feet and a light to my path. I have sworn an oath and confirmed it, to keep your righteous rules... I incline my heart to perform your statutes forever, to the end.
Psalm 119:105–106, 112 (ESV)

After God's people received the Ten Commandments and other laws, both civil and ceremonial, Moses and Israel's elders made preparations to testify to Israel's commitment to obey them. The people gave their verbal assent, but this was to be followed by a confirmation ceremony involving sacrifice.

At the LORD's command, Moses built an altar at the foot of the mountain. Its twelve pillars represented the tribes of Israel. The sacrifices that the people made to God on this altar were a blood oath that they would abide by the terms of their covenant with God.

Some of the blood from the sacrificed animals was sprinkled on the altar as an offering of life to the LORD; this symbolized God's forgiveness of the people and his acceptance of their offerings. And some of the blood was sprinkled on the people; this symbolized their willingness to be struck dead by God—the animal blood becoming their own blood—if they did not live by the terms of this covenant.

With that, Moses and other leaders of Israel ascended the mountain again, where they saw the God of Israel. It was an astonishing thing to them. Except for Moses, they had previously been warned to worship at a distance. Now, however, God invited all the leaders of Israel into his presence where they saw the glory of God and ate and drank; the blood of the sacrifice had sanctified them. This covenant meal was a foreshadowing of the new covenant meal, the Lord's Supper, which has been made possible by Christ's sacrifice on the cross, and which celebrates the eternal bond between him and those he died to save.

April 4

The Tabernacle

Exodus 25—27

He will hide me in his shelter in the day of trouble; he will conceal me under the cover of his tent; he will lift me high upon a rock.
Psalm 27:5 (ESV)

God's instructions for the construction and use of the tabernacle (sacred tent) are very importance in the Exodus story. That's because the tabernacle represented the point of contact between God and his people. God's blueprint for this symbol of God's presence with them was precise.

The outer court of the tabernacle had a basin for water to be used for ceremonial cleansing and a bronze altar for sacrificing burnt offerings to God.

The Holy Place within the tabernacle was furnished with:

- A table that held bread to show that God always provided for his people.
- A golden lampstand to remind the people that with God's help they were called to be a light to the world.
- An altar where incense was burned to represent the prayers of God's people.

In the part of the tabernacle called the Most Holy Place were the Ark of the Covenant holding Aaron's staff, a jar of manna, and the Ten Commandments (see Heb. 9:4). This was God's throne room, and only the high priest could enter it once a year to sprinkle lamb's blood on the cover of the ark, blood that God would accept as a substitute for the people's own. There, in this most sacred place, God would meet with Moses and give him his commands for the Israelites (see Ex. 25:22).

God was equally particular about the priests' clothing and the exact procedures they were to follow in using and transporting the tabernacle. Each instruction of God and each part of the tabernacle and its furnishings was a message to Israel about the holiness of God and his conditions for remaining in their midst.

April 5

Worship

Exodus 31:12–17

Worship the LORD in the splendor of holiness;
tremble before him, all the earth!
Psalm 96:9 (ESV)

The LORD had bound himself in love to Israel even though they didn't deserve such grace. He wanted to stay at the center of Israel's life. His presence was to be shown not only by the tabernacle, with its furnishings, ceremonies, and servants, but by the designation of one day each week as holy to the LORD. Israel also had to honor the LORD in their other activities and on the other days of the week, but the tabernacle and the Sabbath were the clearest reminders for Israel that God wanted them to love him with all their heart and soul and strength (see Deut. 6:5).

Abraham Heschel calls the Sabbath "a sanctuary—a cathedral in time," a day on which we are called to turn from the world of creation to the creation of the world. This continues to be a need and obligation for all of God's people today. That is, our attention and desires need regularly and systematically to be turned from the gifts and opportunities God has given us, to the God in whom we live, move, and have our being.

Worship does several things in and for us:

- It cultivates the sense of God's presence and helps give us an eternal perspective in our temporal lives.
- It helps prevent the disorientation that comes from overvaluing the activities and possessions of our lives.
- It makes us available in a special way for the power of God to renew our minds and make them conform more closely to his purposes.

More clearly than anyone, Jesus honored God's intentions for the Sabbath. Everything Jesus did and taught came out of proper worship. Worship is equally indispensable for helping us live the balanced and fruitful life God wants for us.

April 6

Rebellion against the Constitution

Exodus 32:1–14

My eyes shed streams of tears, because people do not keep your law.
Psalm 119:136 (ESV)

While Moses was receiving God's law on Mount Sinai, the impatient people down below went to Aaron asking him to make physical images to strengthen their flagging faith and enhance their worship. Aaron succumbed to the pressure and manufactured an idol and an altar for it. Afterwards the people celebrated this idol and sacrificed to it. This was nothing less than rebellion against the constitution God had given the people.

God was so angered by Israel's rebellion on this occasion that he threatened to destroy them and transfer his promises to Moses alone. God was certainly within his rights to do so, but Moses asked God to remember the covenant he had made with Abraham. Rather than justice, Moses prayed for mercy for the sake of the fame and reputation of God himself. We will do well to learn both from Israel's inconsistency in their loyalty to God, and from Moses's prayer on their behalf.

First, the commitment the people made to serve the LORD, although sincere, was too easily derailed by fear and impatience. "What if something has happened to Moses and we are actually alone in this world?" "Why is God taking so long; has he forgotten us?" Such questions plague God's people today, too. When trouble comes, we also turn too easily to old and familiar idols for comfort. If we'd think it through, we'd know that these idols can't help and that the only way to live is by faith—faith that we've got to build in the good times so that it becomes second nature when times get tough.

As to Moses's prayer, how much God's faithful people today need to ask God for mercy and delay of judgment as we see rebellion both in Christ's body and in the world. Such prayer reflects God's own long-suffering heart.

April 7

The Effects of Sin and the Price of Mercy

Exodus 32:15–35

We have been sanctified through the offering of the body of Jesus Christ once for all.
Hebrews 10:10 (ESV)

By their rebellious actions the people were actually saying that they preferred Egypt and its gods to waiting for the LORD and being ruled by him. Their sin had big effects.

- Those who persisted in rebellion, ignoring Moses's call to get on God's side, lasted no longer than Pharaoh and his army in the Red Sea—they were put to death. Death should not have been a surprise; it was the very penalty the Israelites had agreed to earlier in the constitution ratification ceremony.
- Those who repented received God's forgiveness. But God's mercy did not totally erase all of sin's effects for them. In fact, sin often continues to bear evil fruit even after it has been forgiven. In this case those whose lives were spared experienced a punishment much the same as Egypt's people had earlier received in the plagues on their country.

Let's also consider the price of God's forgiveness. Although it is mercifully free for those who repent, it is never cheap. Moses, faithful servant and mediator that he was, put his own life on the line. He didn't argue Israel's guilt; that was plain. But he did offer to give up his own life and future if God would be merciful to Israel (see Ex. 32:32). After Moses prayed, Yahweh relented and was gracious, despite the unrighteousness of the people.

Moses was a forerunner and imperfect pattern for a perfect mediator who would come two thousand years later. Jesus also stuck his body between God and the people, between God and us, to absorb God's righteous anger and to save us from death. He saved us even before we knew the extent of our trouble. What's more, with Jesus's sacrificial life and death, God expanded beyond measure the salvation that Israel experienced.

April 8

How Can We Continue Without God?

Exodus 33:1–17

Restore us, O God of hosts; let your face shine, that we may be saved... Give us life, and we will call upon your name!
Psalm 80:7, 18 (ESV)

Even with God's forgiveness and his purging of persistent rebels from the camp, Israel faced an immense crisis. Although God promised an angel to help his people occupy the Promised Land, he himself declined to go farther with them. It had been God's intention to travel with Israel in the tabernacle he had ordered to be constructed. But now the people were commanded to leave Sinai without first building the tabernacle. Sin did for Israel precisely what it always does for us—separated them from God.

Moses and all of Israel were devastated by the news. They understood that God's presence was essential for their life and well-being. So Moses went to God in prayer. He said that he didn't want to leave if God was not going with them. He asked, "How will anyone know that you are pleased with me and with your people unless you go with us? What else will distinguish me and your people from all the other people on the face of the earth?" (Ex. 33:16).

Here again, Moses was doing what Jesus would do in a much bigger way many centuries later, and also what Christians today are called to do for their communities and nations. He prayed for the continuing presence of God with his people. Religious institutions and ceremonies are not sufficient; all people have such things. It's only the actual presence of God in and among his people that distinguishes them from the world and also provides them both protection and power for service.

The LORD answered Moses in the way he'll always answer the prayer of every true servant for his presence: "I will do the very thing you have asked, because I am pleased with you and I know you by name" (Ex. 33:17).

April 9

The Glorious Presence of God

Exodus 33:18–23; 34:29–35; 40:34–38

I will consecrate the tent of meeting and the altar. Aaron also and his sons I will consecrate to serve me as priests...And [the people of Israel] shall know that I am the LORD their God, who brought them out of the land of Egypt that I might dwell among them.
Exodus 29:44–46 (ESV)

The point of Israel's exodus from Egypt was that they might know and cherish God's glorious presence with them. Moses had previews of this in the burning bush and when he brought the people back to Sinai to receive God's laws. One time, God protected Moses in a rock cleft so that he might not die from exposure to God's overwhelming glory (Ex. 33). The people knew when Moses had been speaking with God by his radiant face.

The climax of Exodus is found in the last verses of the book. The tabernacle had been completed according to God's instructions, and then God, in all his glory, made himself at home with Israel. He was right where everyone could see the evidence of his presence and live in constant touch with him, close enough to lead and direct the people, yet separate enough so that their imperfect lives were not consumed in the holiness of his presence.

The Israelites had begun this journey not knowing much at all about God but, through the events of the exodus, they came to know the one who said his name was Yahweh as:

- Deliverer from slavery.
- King and Governor.
- Gracious and Forgiving God.
- The God who graciously consented to live among them.

It was the very thing for which God had created Adam and Eve and the whole human race. Israel was by no means as sinless as the first couple had been in the beginning, and their desert home was by no means as glorious. However, the glorious presence of God in their midst was nothing less than a taste of paradise.

April 10

How to Live with God

Leviticus 19:1–2

As he who called you is holy, you also be holy in all your conduct, since it is written, "You shall be holy, for I am holy."
1 Peter 1:15–16 (ESV)

It was wonderful for Israel when God came to dwell in their midst. But not all danger was past once the tabernacle was built and God came to live there. Nor was it Israel's external enemies that posed the biggest challenge. To be sure, the people had learned that they served a covenanting God who was faithful beyond measure to his promises. But they had also found him to be a holy God, perfect in every way and therefore unable to tolerate their all too frequent sin.

The book of Leviticus addresses the problem of how an unholy people can live with the holy God. It gives God's rules concerning the legitimate candidates and conduct for Israel's priesthood. It also outlines the rules by which holiness could be preserved and unholiness remedied. To make a person or thing unholy was to profane it; to restore holiness was to sanctify it.

Not everything connected to Israel had to be holy. Some things, such as eating utensils and clothes, were ordinary and not set apart for service to God. But everything and everyone connected to Israel did have to be clean. Israel was forbidden contact with that which was permanently unclean (such as the dead) and certain animals (such as carnivorous birds, shellfish, and pigs). Furthermore, if one came into contact with something unclean, that pollution would have to be addressed by cleansing practices.

It is noteworthy that God did not give his laws and procedures for holiness as a way for the people to **get** right with him, but as a way for them to **stay** right with him. The people had been rescued and made right with God before he gave laws to help them continue in the freedom to which God called them—living with God and enjoying his company.

April 11

Holiness in Space and Time

Leviticus 25

No longer will there be anything accursed, but the throne of God and of the Lamb will be in [the New Jerusalem], and his servants will worship him. They will see his face, and his name will be on their foreheads.
Revelation 22:3–4 (ESV)

God's concern for holiness is reflected in the organization of Israel's camp.

- Outside of the camp were Gentiles and unclean or infected Israelites, and also the unclean food—off-limits to Israel.
- Inside the camp, surrounding the tabernacle, were the Israelites with their edible and clean animals and clean utensils.
- In the center of the camp was the tabernacle with its outer court (for blind or lame priests and imperfect sacrificial animals), the inner court (for unblemished priests and sacrificial animals), and the Most Holy Place, the dwelling place of God, into which only the high priest was allowed access annually.

God's concern for holiness is also reflected in the laws regarding Sabbath observance.

- The Sabbath was to be observed once a week.
- A Sabbath year was to be observed one year in seven. During this year both the people and the land would rest, depending completely on God's provision.
- A Sabbath of Sabbaths or Year of Jubilee was to be celebrated after seven Sabbath years. At this time, all slaves were to be set free. Also, if a family had lost its portion of inheritance in the Promised Land, the land was to be returned to them.

The organization of Israel's camp and the commands regarding Sabbaths, Sabbath years, and Years of Jubilee were to remind God's people of the allegiance they owed to their Creator and Redeemer and of their absolute dependence on his provision. The people had a special taste in space and time of what paradise had been like and what it would be like again when God had finished redeeming his creation.

April 12

Authorized and Unauthorized Fire

Leviticus 9:1–10:5

You will prosper if you are careful to observe the statutes and the rules that the LORD commanded Moses for Israel. Be strong and courageous. Fear not; do not be dismayed.
1 Chronicles 22:13 (ESV)

At God's command, Moses gave detailed instructions on the proper procedures for priests to follow in offering their sacrifices to God on behalf of Israel. Upon hearing these, Leviticus 8:36 tells us, "Aaron and his sons did everything the LORD commanded through Moses." The result was a marvel to the priests and the people. The glory of the LORD appeared to them, and fire from the LORD ignited the sacrifices on God's altar. It was an occasion for great joy mixed with some apprehension, which the people showed by falling facedown.

However, something terrible happened some time later. Aaron's sons Nadab and Abihu offered the LORD what Scripture calls "unauthorized fire." Although we don't know exactly what they did wrong, it was not a simple mistake, but rather a knowing transgression against the instructions they had received and, therefore, against God's holiness. Nadab and Abihu paid for their sin with their lives. It was a terrible object lesson for Israel and its priests that no one can take God's instructions casually.

Indeed, no one can live in the presence of the LORD who does not come to him on his terms. That's what Moses had learned years before at the burning bush. There Moses had feared for his life but dared to come near only after he obeyed God's command to show reverence by removing his sandals (see Ex. 3:5-6).

If God's judgment on Nadab and Abihu seems harsh, then we must realize how severe their crime was. After all, God is perfectly righteous and just; with him the punishment always fits the crime. Their disobedience earned them the reward ultimately due all who rebel against God—death.

April 13

Passing on the Blessing

Numbers 6:22–27

Christ redeemed us from the curse of the law by becoming a curse for us…so that in Christ Jesus the blessing of Abraham might come to the Gentiles, so that we might receive the promised Spirit through faith.
Galatians 3:13-14 (ESV)

One thing you can't help but notice, if you study religious and family life in the Old Testament, is the importance of blessing and passing on the blessing. The tangible blessing of life in the Promised Land with the God of the promise was ceremonially reinforced in this blessing with which God told Aaron and the priests to bless the people.

A couple of the blessings that the people treasured the most were their freedom of worship and the land that God had promised to give them. The first of these came through Moses. The second was still to come through the efforts of Joshua and the army of Israel. On this and other occasions the people learned that God loved to bless his people. They learned as well that he usually passed on his blessings through the words and actions of his priests, and later through kings and prophets. All of them—priests, kings, and prophets—were set apart for service to God.

However, Israel as a whole was also set apart for service to God, and therefore called to pass on blessings by loving actions toward God and each other as instructed by the law of God.

- Parents were to bless their children by instructing them in the ways of the LORD (Deut. 6:7).
- God's people were to bless each other by heartfelt obedience to the commandments in the second table of the Law, and also by special provisions for the disadvantaged of their world—widows, orphans, and even foreigners residing within Israel.
- Nor could Israel forget that God intended to use the whole community of Israel to bring blessing to the rest of the world. They were blessed so they could be a blessing.

April 14

Complaints or Trust?

Numbers 10:33–12:16

Trust in him at all times, O people; pour out your heart before him; God is a refuge for us.
Psalm 62:8 (ESV)

After staying at Sinai for eleven months, the Israelites were led into the Desert of Paran where, in very short order, they began to complain. An initial complaint about their hardships brought God's discipline in the form of a consuming fire from the LORD. Moses intervened in prayer until the fire died down.

Next, the people complained about the boring diet of manna by which God was sustaining them. They selectively remembered the advantages of life in Egypt, especially the variety of food they had there. In answer, the LORD gave them meat, but also struck them with a plague that killed many of them.

After a few more days and miles even Miriam and Aaron began to grumble, complaining about Moses. They both had positions of responsibility: Miriam was a prophetess and Aaron, the high priest. Yet, they resented the superior leadership position of their brother. In response, God told them that their complaints against Moses were nothing less than complaints against God himself. God struck Miriam with leprosy and she endured seven days of uncleanness outside the camp. She was healed only after Moses prayed for her.

It was the third complaint and the LORD's third judgment in the relatively brief time since Israel had left the region of Sinai. It was not a good start for the people who had been so blessed by God and were on their way to even greater blessings in the land that God was going to give them. Even if you didn't know the next part of the story, you might get the idea that the book of Numbers is turning out to be a record of how the people of Israel did their best to mess up God's plans to bring them into in the Promised Land.

April 15

Obedience or Rebellion?

Numbers 13:1–14:10a

If you say in your heart, "These nations are greater than I. How can I dispossess them?" you shall not be afraid of them but you shall remember what the LORD *your God did to Pharaoh and to all Egypt.*
Deuteronomy 7:17–18 (ESV)

The spies from Israel's twelve tribes were astonished by seeing firsthand the riches of the land that God promised them. However, they also saw the powerful cities and mighty warriors of Canaan. For most of the spies, their fears were weightier than their happy amazement; they were pessimistic about God's ability to give them this land.

Caleb and Joshua presented a more optimistic report. They were confident that the LORD could lead Israel into the land and give it to them. Moses and Aaron supported the good report as well, even making clear that the bad report constituted rebellion.

Nevertheless, many people aligned themselves with the faithless spies. They became so agitated that they threatened their leaders with death by stoning. Having come to the borders of the Promised Land they decided that rather than risk their lives under the leadership of God and Moses, they wanted a leader who would take them back to Egypt to serve another master and other gods.

That desire was not only a rejection of Moses and the others whom God had appointed for his people, it was also a rejection of God's law and even Yahweh himself as Israel's God. All of God's work and planning on their behalf was as nothing to the ten spies and the rebellious people who supported them. All of God's promises to Abraham, Isaac, Jacob, and their descendants—to install his people in a land of their own and dwell with them—were as nothing to them. In their confidence that they, better than God, knew the next steps they should take, they repeated the original sin of Adam and Eve.

April 16

The Consequences of Rebellion

Numbers 14

Today, if you hear his voice, do not harden your hearts, as at Meribah... when your fathers put me to the test...though they had seen my work... Therefore I swore in my wrath, "They shall not enter my rest."
Psalm 95:7b-9, 11 (ESV)

God may sometimes delay punishment for rebellion, but he never tolerates rebellion; he did not in this case either. Moses, Aaron, Joshua, and Caleb, realizing the danger Israel was in, tore their clothes and fell on their faces before the LORD. Moses pled with God not to change his mind or go back on his promises. He asked that God would bring Israel into the land so that God's strength might be displayed and his character confirmed—both his love and mercy and his concern for justice.

God heard Moses's prayer, but said he would delay leading the people to their inheritance until all the disobedient adults of that generation had died. God's judgment was hard but gracious, too, for God did not go back on his covenant. Yes, the people who sinned had to be punished; God let them see the consequences of their choice for independence from him. The first to die in the desert—by a plague—were the ten unfaithful spies. But God did not reject his promise. He merely postponed its fulfillment to the following generation.

As so often happens in the aftermath of judgment, the people recognized how foolish they'd been. Not content, however, to accept the dismal reward of their rebellion, they tried to gain the inheritance on their own. But they failed miserably without God's presence and leading.

This story speaks clearly to God's people today, for we all must repeatedly decide whether to believe and follow God or try to go our own way. And we all must repeatedly decide whether or not to honor his timing, waiting patiently when God requires it, and moving ahead despite fear when he directs active response.

April 17

Sin's Effects in Successive Generations

Numbers 14:18

The wickedness of the wicked shall be upon himself.
Ezekiel 18:20b (ESV)
Our fathers sinned, and are no more; and we bear their iniquities.
Lamentations 5:6 (ESV)

Although God holds no person responsible for the sin of another, sin does have natural consequences that echo in families for generations. Our children are affected not only by what we might call gross sins. All sin bears evil fruit, and part of that fruit is in the impact it has upon the lives and character of our children.

This is not to make us despair, but to give parents yet another motivation for keeping short accounts with God. God expects all of his people to be open to his correction, and even to invite his revelation of sin in our lives. When we become aware of sin we must confess it and repent as soon as possible. We do this, not only for our own benefit, but also for the benefit of our children. They will have fewer consequences of our sin to deal with. And they will hopefully learn to imitate our readiness to confess sin.

Just as in families, so also one culture can be relatively better or worse than another. One culture may send on to its heirs relatively more blessings or evil rewards. Every one of us is affected for the good by the righteousness in our culture, and for the bad by the sin in our culture.

Satan is after your children. But so is God, in whose image they are created, and to whom they belong. The legacy that we leave in both our families and our culture will be determined by how well we practice and teach ongoing and active and positive response to God and his word. Pray therefore, for the Holy Spirit to work in us today so that successive generations may not have to reap the bitter fruit of the sin of their ancestors, but may have a better chance to celebrate personally the gracious and loving character of the Lord.

April 18

More Ingratitude and Rebellion

Numbers 16:1–40

When men in the camp were jealous of Moses and Aaron, the holy one of the LORD, the earth opened and swallowed up Dathan, and covered the company of Abiram. Fire also broke out in their company; the flame burned up the wicked.
Psalm 106:16–18 (ESV)

Korah, Dathan, and Abiram had a grievance that was similar to an earlier protest lodged by Miriam and Aaron (see Num. 12:2). They resented the authority of Moses, arguing that the whole community of Israel had been set apart as holy to the LORD. That much was true. But they erred in supposing that this truth erased all distinctions in responsibility or authority among Israel's leaders. After all, Moses had not assumed leadership on his own initiative, but at the command of the LORD. Moses announced a test for the following day that would prove who was right.

The rebels had their say prior to the test. In their insolent complaint they referred to Egypt in the very way that God had described the Promised Land, as "a land flowing with milk and honey." Many in Israel were swayed by the criticism of the prominent men. How soon they had forgotten both their slavery and the rebellion that had condemned them to stay in the desert for years.

Moses was deeply dismayed by the charge that he had usurped power. Even so, he said that the judgment to follow would be shown to be the LORD's rather than his. He pled that God would not destroy the whole assembly for the rebellion of a few. In that, Moses again proved to be a leader after God's own heart. For the LORD is never eager to destroy the work of his hands. He judges in order to ensure the accomplishment of his saving plan. God's judgment here meant that he would not leave his people to a false vision of the milk-and-honey land, but would graciously take them to the real place where they could find the freedom for which God had delivered them from Egypt.

April 19

The Authority of God's High Priest

Numbers 16:41–17:13

The former priests were many in number, because they were prevented by death from continuing in office, but [Jesus] holds his priesthood permanently, because he continues forever. Consequently, he is able to save to the uttermost those who draw near to God through him, since he always lives to make intercession for them.
Hebrews 7:23–25 (ESV)

The people apparently learned little from the judgment on Korah, Dathan, and Abiram; they continued to complain against God's anointed leaders. Is it any wonder that this generation of Israelites was often referred to in Scripture as a hardhearted and rebellious generation? Not that they were so much worse than their descendants, or any non-Jewish people for that matter. It is too often the case that even those most blessed by God are forgetful of his blessings and prone to complain against him when something doesn't go their way.

The plague that God sent on these complainers was stopped only by the atonement made by Aaron as Israel's high priest. Aaron's position was further verified by a test involving the staffs belonging to Aaron and the other leaders of Israel. The staffs were only dry sticks of wood, but they served as signs of leadership authority. These were placed overnight into the Tabernacle, where they remained unchanged except for the staff of Aaron, which had miraculously budded, blossomed, and produced almonds.

This obviously confirmed Aaron as God's chosen high priest, the first of those certified as priests—mediators between God and Israel. Many other high priests would succeed Aaron; some of them would be faithful to their calling and others would be unfaithful. But not until Jesus would there be a high priest whose atonement would be perfectly complete and permanent. Thank God that rebels such as we can find life and access to God through Christ.

April 20

The Waters of Quarreling

Numbers 20:1–13, 22–29

They angered [the LORD] at the waters of Meribah,
and it went ill with Moses on their account.
Psalm 106:32 (ESV)

Moses and Aaron stood as faithful mediators between the LORD and Israel. However, they had moments in which it became clear that not even the best of sinful humanity is equal to the challenge of being the mediator that we need. Moses and Aaron both failed at Kadesh. Short of water and tired of dealing with the grumbling Israelites, they prayed to God for relief. But afterwards, instead of speaking to the rock as instructed by the LORD, Moses struck the rock in anger. Water gushed out and the place became known as the Waters of Meribah—the name means quarreling.

Scripture makes clear that the Israelites angered the LORD here with their grumbling. But so did Moses and Aaron on this occasion. God labeled what they did here as rebellion and accused them of not trusting him enough and thereby undermining Israel's respect for the holiness of God.

Both Aaron and Moses paid a big price for this failure to honor the LORD; they were forbidden entry into the Promised Land. Aaron's death is recounted at the end of this chapter, and that of Moses in Deuteronomy 34:1–5.

Their disqualification from entering the land should not, however, be taken as a final statement of the LORD's displeasure. Enough Scripture speaks approvingly of the service of both Aaron and Moses. And the book of Hebrews leaves no doubt that both should be counted among the ancient people who lived by faith, seeking that better country that would come only in Christ. Yet, it should also be clear that grumbling against the LORD is never profitable. This is sometimes difficult in the frustrations of ministry, but all who follow Christ must always seek to trust him and honor him as holy.

April 21

The Bronze Serpent

Numbers 21:4–9

As Moses lifted up the serpent in the wilderness, so must the Son of Man be lifted up, that whoever believes in him may have eternal life.
John 3:14–15 (ESV)

We who read of ancient Israel's constant frustration and impatience with God and with their leaders may wonder about their exceptionally short memories of the many times God answered their prayers and provided for them.

We should remember, however, that Scripture gives us snapshots of their forty years in the desert. This is not to excuse their rebellions, but to help us realize that what may appear to be exceptional ingratitude for God's blessings may not be too different from our own. We quickly grow frustrated with the trials of life and usually see only in hindsight how much smaller yesterday's struggles seem in the light of those we face today. That old hymn is very scriptural when it advises us to *Count Your Blessings.*

For this sin of Israel God sent venomous snakes among the people. They saw the snakes as a judgment of God and therefore a reason for repentance. But they still had to deal with the poison aftermath of their sin. In answer to their prayers, the LORD told Moses to cast a bronze snake and put it up on a pole where everyone could see it. Those who looked on it in faith were healed. Of course there was no healing power in the figure; it was only a sign of God's grace. However, many years later an image of the snake had become an object of false worship (see 2 Kings. 18:4).

With the help of the New Testament, we see in that bronze serpent a preview of one without sin who would be lifted up on a pole so that everyone who looks to him in faith might have eternal life. "God made him who had no sin to be sin for us, so that in him we might become the righteousness of God" (2 Cor. 5:21).

April 22

Moab's Fear of Israel

Numbers 22:1–7

We have heard how the LORD dried up the water of the Red Sea before you when you came out of Egypt, and what you did to the two kings of the Amorites...to Sihon and Og, whom you devoted to destruction.
Joshua 2:10 (ESV)

The Israelites had been dodging hostile forces for about forty years when they set up camp on the plains of Moab just east of the Jordan River across from Jericho. This was a big horde to be in Moabite territory, and Moab was filled with dread, no doubt partly because they were afraid of payback for their earlier refusal to help Israel in their escape from Egypt (see Judg. 11:17).

Moab and King Balak had heard what Israel had done to the Amorites—how they had defeated them and taken over their cities, a mere ten miles away (Num. 21:21–35). Of course, everybody had gods, but it seemed that the God of Israel was somewhat stronger than the others.

The Israelites were quite likely fearful themselves at being so close to hostile forces, even with those recent victories over the Amorites. They wondered when God would say that it was time to enter the Promised Land. But this generation had learned something about waiting on the LORD. So they did that while, unknown to them, Balak planned his next move.

Balak wanted an edge, something more than superior weapons or manpower; it was apparent that ordinary means would not be strong enough to preserve his peoples' land, life, and possessions. Balak sought supernatural help. Armed with a large fee for such a large task, he sent messengers to the sorcerer Balaam to solicit a powerful curse against Israel.

At the same time, however, God was constantly at work to guard and protect Israel and carry out his purposes. Not only would he frustrate Balak's plan to curse Israel, he would use Balaam to pronounce blessings on them.

April 23

Balaam's Greedy Heart

Numbers 22:8–39

Balaam…loved gain from wrongdoing, but was rebuked for his own transgression; a speechless donkey spoke with human voice and restrained the prophet's madness.
2 Peter 2:15–16 (ESV)

On the surface it seems that nothing in Balaam's conduct was worthy of criticism. He made clear to Balak that he could do nothing against the LORD. Yet, Balaam was intrigued and tempted by Balak's offer; he coveted the rewards Balak offered and sought permission to earn them. In his heart Balaam was willful and preferred money to serving God. He was a man who loved the wages of wickedness, as both Peter and Jude put it in their New Testament writings. As a result, Balaam's decision to go made God very angry.

As a sorcerer, Balaam was used to finding out things about the supernatural world from unusual occurrences in the natural one. He should have been able to see from the extremely unusual behavior of his donkey that something unprecedented was happening here. But he was strangely blind; his donkey was able to see more clearly than he. Balaam seems to have been unusually dense as well; the only thing more strange than the donkey speaking to him is that Balaam speaks in turn to the donkey.

Finally God opened Balaam's eyes to see the LORD himself blocking the way. Then Balaam fell on his face in terror. He had thought that he could play around with sorcery and curses against the chosen people of the Almighty LORD of heaven and earth. How foolish it is to give oneself to causes that are not God's own.

Now, at least temporarily, Balaam thought better of it and offered to go back home. However, God had other plans. He would use both Balak's initiative against the Israelites and Balaam's greedy heart to proclaim the blessings in store for Israel.

April 24

Blessings Instead of Curses

Numbers 23–24

The LORD your God would not listen to Balaam; instead the LORD your God turned the curse into a blessing for you, because the LORD your God loved you.
Deuteronomy 23:5 (ESV)

After much feasting and many sacrifices, to the chagrin and astonishment of Balak if not also to the surprise of Balaam, the sorcerer spoke out blessings instead of curses on Israel. The Spirit of God gave Balaam four oracles of blessing for Israel. In short, here is what he said about God's chosen people:

- Israel would be separate from the other nations, blessed with descendants as uncountable as dust, and could look forward to a wonderful future.
- Israel had been rescued by God from Egypt, and now enjoyed the presence of God with them, and was becoming more and more strong and victorious.
- Israel was destined to live in a paradise, following a great king, with the assurance of blessings to continue and curses against them to be ineffective.
- Israel would give rise to a coming ruler who would lead God's people to ultimate and permanent victory.

This was much more than a local squabble with temporary significance. It was a revelation of what God had been doing and was planning for the future. God's promises to Abraham were coming true. God had won the battle with Pharaoh over the right to govern his people and enjoy their worship, and he was now getting ready to settle them in the land he had promised. He would never stop working until all opposition had disappeared.

The security and blessing prophesied for ancient Israel is even surer for God's people today. All who have inherited these blessings and more in Christ may know that, in a world full of spiritual conflict, God is always with us. He will continue growing his kingdom until all his purposes have been accomplished.

April 25

God Doesn't Tolerate Double-Loving

Numbers 25

You have some there who hold the teaching of Balaam, who taught Balak to put a stumbling block before the sons of Israel, so that they might eat food sacrificed to idols and practice sexual immorality.
Revelation 2:14 (ESV)

God's wonderful word through Balaam was followed by great sin in Israel. It was sin in which Balaam had a hand; he may have been the one to suggest that Moab's women could bring the harm to Israel that God had prevented him from accomplishing. Israel was a threat only insofar as it remained the special people of God. Moab was not opposed to intermarrying or to allowing Israel to add their own favorite god to the gods Moab worshiped. If the Israelites joined in the religious and cultural practices of Moab, they would no longer be a threat.

However it started, some of Israel's men began to join in the worship of Moab's fertility gods. Even though this happened outside of Israel's camp, it violated God's law against unfaithfulness in marriage. Even worse, Israel's immorality constituted spiritual adultery and was a direct affront to God who claimed the exclusive worship of his people and the credit for the fertility of their flocks and people. God punished Israel with a plague.

Zimri, in demonstration of even greater contempt for the covenant, brought a Midianite girl inside Israel's camp and even into his tent. Phinehas, priest and grandson of Aaron, killed them both, acting with the righteous anger of God to root out this terrible, nation-destroying sin. Only by this, and the execution of the other offenders, did the plague come to an end.

We no longer have the warrant to punish physical and spiritual adultery in this way. Yet all Christians are called to vigilance and self-discipline in order to prevent unholy compromise in their own lives. God may delay punishment for double-loving, but whoever does it must give account in the Judgment.

April 26

An Inheritance for All God's People

Numbers 27:1–11

Has not God chosen those who are poor in the world to be rich in faith and heirs of the kingdom, which he has promised to those who love him?
James 2:5 (ESV)

The inheritors of God's promises to Abraham included those who were normally given little regard by the cultures of that day: foreigners, women, and children. It was standard practice in the ancient world, including Israel, for the inheritance to be passed on through the sons of the family. All the others in a household would be enfranchised by virtue of their connection to a son.

That system worked to a degree. But it offered little in the way of protection against exceptional circumstances. Foreigners, widows, and orphans particularly were at risk after the death of the man through whom they had a share in the inheritance. However, God made a point to protect and provide for them. One provision was that they could live off the tithes of produce brought by the landholders of Israel (Deut. 14:28–29).

The daughters of Zelophehad, however, asked for further consideration. These were five sisters whose father had died without siring a son to receive his family's share in the Promised Land and ensure protection and provision for his sisters. As a result, their father's land was destined to pass out of the family.

So the elders of Israel made an exception for these women, ruling that their family might keep its share of the inheritance. They required only that Zelophehad's daughters marry men of their father's tribal clan so that the original allotments of land to all the tribes could be maintained (see Num. 36:8).

The decision was perfectly in line with the concerns demonstrated later by Israel's prophets and by Jesus himself—the condemnation of favoritism to the powerful, and the encouragement of mercy shown to the powerless.

April 27

United Obedience

Numbers 32:1–32

The hand of God was also on Judah to give them one heart to do what the king and the princes commanded by the word of the LORD.
2 Chronicles 30:12 (ESV)

When the time came to go into the Promised Land and fight to make it their own, the tribes of Gad and Reuben asked Moses if they might be allotted the territory east of the Jordan River.

Moses responded in anger; he interpreted the request as an attempt by these tribes to avoid God's command to enter into and take the Promised Land. Moses thought these tribes were unwilling to trust God—the same sort of rebellion than had kept the previous generation of Israel wandering in the desert for forty years. So he was harsh with them, calling them a "brood of sinners" and saying that if they persisted, the LORD would again leave the whole of Israel to wander homeless in the desert.

The leaders of Gad and Reuben quickly assured Moses that they did not intend rebellion. They had learned from the negative actions of their ancestors and fully intended to obey the LORD. They only wanted permission to build homes for their families in the land they were to inherit. Then, they promised, their men would gladly help the other tribes to secure their inheritance across the Jordan.

With that explanation, Moses was satisfied of Israel's united commitment to follow where God led. Israel still did not know the particulars of the challenges that lay ahead of them, but the tribes were united in their commitment to enter the land.

The same commitment to follow where God leads is required of God's people today. There is no shortcut or good alternative to this. Without unified and faithful obedience, we're doomed to live a barren and fruitless life. But with obedience Christ's people secure the fullness of what we've received by grace.

April 28

God's Unfailing Love and Grace

Deuteronomy 4:32–39; 7:7–11

Neither death nor life, nor angels nor rulers, nor things present nor things to come, nor powers, nor height nor depth, nor anything else in all creation, will be able to separate us from the love of God in Christ Jesus our Lord.
Romans 8:38–39 (ESV)

Deuteronomy is a book of sermons in which Moses reminds the people what God has been doing for them and confirms what God will continue to do for them in the new challenges ahead. The people Moses addressed were a different generation than the one that left Egypt. Most of them knew little else than life in the desert. But now they were on the brink of entering the land that God promised Abraham so long ago. It would be a different life for them. They would no longer be nomads living in tents, but settlers with permanent dwellings. Their diet would change as well; the provision of manna would stop, and they would eat the produce of the fertile land of Canaan.

Moses made clear that the fulfillment of God's promises required a fresh commitment of the people to their covenant with God. But he also emphasized God's commitment to them. The repeated emphasis of Deuteronomy is that God's gracious actions are motivated by his undying love for his people (see Deut. 4:37, 10:15, 23:5). God's love is not fickle like so much of human love; it is as unchanging as God's own eternal character. Jesus also emphasized this very thing and quoted often from Deuteronomy.

Israel was cautioned, however, never to think of the love of God as something they merited. "God did not choose you," Moses said, "because you had already prospered and become great" (Deut. 7:7–8). He said further, "Do not say to yourself, 'The LORD has brought me here to take possession of this land because of my righteousness'" (Deut. 9:4). It was an important caution; people too often attribute their success more to their own merits than they do to the gracious help of God.

April 29

Tell Your Children

Deuteronomy 6

Fathers, do not provoke your children to anger, but bring them up in the discipline and instruction of the Lord.
Ephesians 6:4 (ESV)

It has been said that God has no grandchildren. This is not to minimize God's faithfulness to the succeeding generations of those who love him, but merely to affirm that everyone must make their own commitment to God. That's why God emphasized the constant retelling of the story of his love and faithfulness to the next generations. Then as now, any society or family that shuns or neglects the story of how God came through in the past and leads in the present, and what he has in mind for the future, is fighting a losing battle with their children.

The telling of this story must be accompanied by a life of spiritual integrity. In fact, the single greatest thing parents can do to promote the spiritual health of their children is to make sure that they themselves are walking closely with God. Parents must root out and destroy the idols of their own hearts, and as much as is appropriate, model this for their children.

Moses specifically concentrated on one of these idols—materialism. Prosperity can make you forget that everything you have is a gift of God. It can also make you careless so that you turn from worshiping the LORD to worshiping his gifts. So Moses was clear that when God blessed his people by giving them a home they were not to forget the LORD who freed them from slavery in Egypt and gave them that home.

There are probably many more influences on children today than were found in Israel, where most of the education was up to parents. Notable among these are the schools our children attend and the media they consume. This complicates the task given today's parents and Christian community. Nevertheless, our task is the same; we must impress God's commands on our children.

April 30

Blessed to Bless

Deuteronomy 8:10–20

The love of money is a root of all kinds of evils.
It is through this craving that some have wandered away
from the faith and pierced themselves with many pangs.
1 Timothy 6:10 (ESV)

Moses did not give many specifics on how to manage wealth. But the basic principle is as clear for us as it was for Israel. We are called to remember that everything we have—possessions, as well as the ability to increase them—is a gift from the LORD our God. If we remember this single thing, which is the thrust of many other Scripture passages as well, then we have a chance at pleasing God with how we handle the resources he's given us. But if we forget the source of our blessings—including the wealth that we have—then we are certain to stumble and fall.

Israel became a case in point. In later years the hearts of Israel's kings and people became proud and they forgot how much they owed God for their land and their lives. As a result, God eventually allowed the nation to be overthrown by its enemies and the people to be sent into exile. We must never become so proud and forgetful. So we must cultivate a biblical understanding of the various idols that undermine the worship of God, especially the fiction that we may do as we please with the wealth we possess. Do not underestimate your own vulnerability to the love of money and things.

The proper question for Christians is not: "How much do I have to give to keep God off my back?" but "Where can I find additional resources to use in God's service; how can I contribute more to his work?" If we are not rich toward God from the heart, we are idolaters and must repent and turn from that, being faithful in little things as well as in great things. We cannot be mastered by both the Lord and love for money. Unfaithfulness in managing wealth is unrighteousness, and that affects our eternal destiny.

May 1

Alternative Consequences

Deuteronomy 28

Blessings are on the head of the righteous,
but the mouth of the wicked conceals violence.
The memory of the righteous is a blessing,
but the name of the wicked will rot.
Proverbs 10:6–7 (ESV)

The book of Deuteronomy deals extensively with the blessings that follow obedience and the curses that follow disobedience to God's commands. Blessings for obedience include health and well-being for children, livestock, and crops, as well as prosperity, success in life, and protection from enemies. Blessings abound for those who are faithful to the covenant with God.

The curses are just the opposite; they spell disaster for children, livestock, and crops, and result in exposure to enemies, poverty, failure, disease, slavery, sorrow, pain, scorn, etc. The curses that result from disobedience to God's covenant commands leave people terrorized and despairing.

We can see the truth of this in Israel's history. When the people were faithful, they were richly blessed, but ultimately they were unfaithful and, as a result, suffered the curses associated with covenant unfaithfulness, including exile from the Promised Land.

Many blessings and curses that came upon Israel and that come upon people today are simply natural consequences of obedience or disobedience. Not every hardship is evidence of God's judgment; even the most faithful of God's people endure hardship. Nor is every blessing an evidence of godly living. But it is always better to live in a way that honors the one who gave us life and without whose constant care we have neither life nor hope. We can be confident as we do, that "In all things God works for the good of those who love him, who have been called according to his purpose" (Rom. 8:28)

May 2

Moses's Parting Challenge

Deuteronomy 30:11–31:8

As for that [seed] in the good soil, they are those who, hearing the word, hold it fast in an honest and good heart, and bear fruit with patience.
Luke 8:15 (ESV)

As Moses neared the end of his life, he considered again the long history of the gracious and loving actions God had taken to save his people and bring them into covenant with himself. He also reviewed the promised blessings that would follow obedience, and the curses that were sure to follow disobedience.

Israel had already received many blessings from the LORD. Still, living in covenant with God had proved to be difficult. Israel had failed on multiple occasions to trust and love God above all and so had experienced his curses along with his blessings. And now that Moses would no longer be Israel's leader, the people were afraid that they would find it even harder to please God.

Nevertheless, Moses reassured Israel that what God commanded was not beyond their ability to obey. Moses would no longer be around. Nor would God lead as he had done for forty years in the desert—by a pillar of cloud and fire. Even so, Moses reassured both Israel and his successor, Joshua, that the LORD would go with them and never leave nor forsake them. Therefore, they didn't have to be afraid.

The key to their success would be their attention to God's word. The main problem would not be that they would not know what to do or which way to go; it would be the will to obey what God had put in their hearts and mouths. Behind Israel lay the wilderness and Egypt with all that they implied about separation from God and being under foreign domination. In front of them was the Promised Land—a new paradise—where Israel could live without fear, directed and sustained by the word and presence of God while continuing in wholehearted service to him.

May 3

Prologue to Paradise

Joshua 1

The LORD loves justice; he will not forsake his saints...
The righteous shall inherit the land and dwell upon it forever.
Psalm 37:28–29 (ESV)

Joshua is not the primary character of the book named for him. That is, the title does not so much proclaim the man as it does the message of his name: "The LORD saves." The book begins by showing where Joshua got his instructions and who should get the credit for the imminent fulfillment of God's promise of a homeland for Abraham's descendants.

The promised land of Canaan (Palestine) was much more than a piece of real estate; it carried with it many spiritual implications. This was the place chosen by God to be a new paradise with a new Adam and Eve—Israel. It was not perfect like the original paradise, but Israel was to be both the beginning and a model of the redeemed creation. Unlike the original paradise, however, Israel's promised inheritance was not purely a gift. Yes, the LORD was giving the land to his people, but they had more to do than sit and watch God do all the work. The inheritance was theirs, but now Israel had to secure it by displacing those who were occupying what God had claimed for his own.

The LORD's expectation came as no surprise to Joshua or Israel; they had known for a long time that they would have to establish their right to the land by conquering the other nations who lived there. They knew that it would be difficult, which was why a previous generation had agreed with the ten spies and decided to disobey God rather than enter the land of the promise.

The apparent difficulty of gaining the inheritance, however, was lessened by the LORD's assurance to Joshua that he would be with him every bit as faithfully and constantly as he had been with Moses. That promise was to be Joshua's lifeline and the source of his courage.

May 4

A Rehearsal of God's Conditions

Joshua 1:7–8

If you obey the commandments of the LORD your God...
by loving the LORD your God, by walking in his ways, and
by keeping his commandments and his statutes and his rules,
then you shall live and multiply, and the LORD your God will
bless you in the land that you are entering to take possession of it.
Deuteronomy 30:16 (ESV)

The conditions under which Joshua and the people would be successful had to do with keeping God's law: "Meditate on it day and night, so that you may be careful to do everything written in it" (Josh. 1:8). What the LORD told Joshua to tell the people is just what Moses repeatedly emphasized to Israel; God and his servant-leaders never tire of making clear the conditions for life.

The law that God wanted Israel to meditate on and obey was more than the Ten Commandments; it included everything God had taught them—the entire law, including these three things:

- God's people must be moral.
- God's people must obey the detailed provisions of his leadership on specific duties.
- God's people must always keep their mission in view—to live in the land under God's rule.

Forty years before, when the call had come to enter the land, Israel had balked, and all that generation had died in the desert. But now, this new generation of Israel was ready when they got God's message. They agreed to treat Joshua as God's appointed mediator and to respect him as they had Moses. They agreed to put their lives on the line as God's partners. They agreed to all the conditions that God had laid down in his comprehensive law: to good moral conduct, to obedience of specific commands, and to their mission. They even called down death upon any of their number who failed to do as they had promised. And they echoed the refrain that the LORD had drilled into Joshua's head, "Be strong and courageous."

May 5

Rahab's Decision

Joshua 2

Arise, shine, for your light has come, and the glory of the LORD has risen upon you...Nations shall come to your light, and kings to the brightness of your rising.
Isaiah 60:1, 3 (ESV)

The Canaanites were spiritual descendants of Cain; they had rejected the true God to prostitute themselves to false gods. You could scarcely find a better person than a prostitute to represent what the Canaanites meant to Israel and Israel's God. By contrast, the spies were representatives of the God of Israel. So this first encounter between Israel and Canaan had an immense, even cosmic, significance.

Rahab told the spies about the fear that Israel's presence had generated in the hearts of her people. The territory of Sihon and Og, already conquered by Israel, was almost as large as the whole territory west of the Jordan. Furthermore, Jericho had not been built to withstand the attacks of armies capable of defeating such people as the Amorites with their vast resources and territories.

But, in the minds of the Canaanites, the miracle at the Red Sea was even more frightening. In Canaanite religious mythology, Baal ruled the land because he had overcome the powerful god of the sea. But when the God of Israel overcame the sea, making a path through it to save his people, he proved himself the king of all gods, more powerful even than Baal of the Canaanites.

Most of Canaan was still determined to resist, but Rahab was willing to change her cherished beliefs and serve the true God of land and sea. Her actions to save the spies of Israel gave evidence of her faith that the LORD would be victorious. It was on the basis of her demonstrated faith, then, that Rahab asked for similar help in the coming invasion. Her decision, which resulted in her salvation, stands as a model for the commitment required of everyone who hears the claims of the gospel.

May 6

Faith and Courage Strengthened

Joshua 2:8–11; 23–24

Fear not, for I am with you; be not dismayed, for I am your God. I will strengthen you, I will help you, I will uphold you with my righteous right hand.
Isaiah 41:10 (ESV)

The two spies had been sent to Jericho to gather evidence of God's ability to deliver on his promise. This would help Israel to be courageous enough to do what God called them to do. The report of the spies focused on the overwhelming fear of the Canaanites, who clearly believed in the Lord's power. Except for Rahab, however, the city was still determined to oppose God and his people; belief is not the same as willingness to trust.

Among the people of Israel, the major effect of the spies' report was to confirm and strengthen their faith in the LORD. This is also the effect that hearing the story has had on every generation of God's people since then. We can see that the advance of God's kingdom is irresistible. We can also take heart in the knowledge that nothing can stand in God's way or frustrate his purposes. He will make sure that his people will gain the ultimate victory. That is a great assurance for those on God's side, and for those who are not, a great incentive to get on his side.

Either way, the advance of God's kingdom inevitably divides people. In Jericho the division was between the one who had decided for Israel and Israel's God, and the one who was determined to destroy them—between Rahab and Jericho's king. Today the division is between the true followers of Jesus Christ and those who reject his salvation and his control over their lives.

Who will inherit the earth? The testimony of Rahab and Israel was "God's people." And the life, resurrection, and ascension of the second Joshua, Jesus, echoes that—"God's people." No true believers will either fail to follow faithfully or stop looking for those, like Rahab, who are willing to join them on God's side.

May 7

Another Barrier Demolished

Joshua 3:1–17; 5:1

Count it all joy, my brothers, when you meet trials of various kinds, for you know that the testing of your faith produces steadfastness.
James 1:2–3 (ESV)

The ark of the covenant had been with Israel in the desert as the symbol of God's powerful presence and his ability to fulfill his promises. Now, by God's direction, the ark would precede Israel across the final barrier between them and the Promised Land. Before that, the people had to purify themselves; their external cleansing was a symbol of the cleansing of their hearts that was necessary for them to remain in communion with God. Without clean hearts they would not be able to meet God, who would appear in their midst as the LORD. Receiving deliverance from was not enough. In that deliverance, Israel had to know the LORD and worship him.

When the priests with the ark stepped into the flooding Jordan, it dried up. And then, with the ark and the priests in the middle of that dried-up river, all the people crossed over. Afterwards, when the feet of the priests carrying the ark touched the far bank, the floodwaters returned. The crossing was a miraculous confirmation of God's power.

As the enemies of God and Israel got confirmation of what they were up against, the terror of which Rahab had spoken to the spies of Israel continued to mount hour by hour: "Their hearts melted in fear and they no longer had courage to face the Israelites" (Josh. 5:1). Another effect was that that Joshua's leadership was solidified: "That day the LORD exalted Joshua in the sight of all Israel; and they stood in awe of him all the days of his life, just as they had stood in awe of Moses" (Josh. 4:14). Of course, faith in God was strengthened as well, just as it has been and will continue to be with every other "Jordan of difficulty" that God's people successfully cross.

May 8

Memorial of the Crossing

Joshua 4

We will...tell to the coming generation the glorious deeds of the LORD, and his might, and the wonders that he has done.
Psalm 78:4 (ESV)

Before Israel had fought a single battle, the entire land was theirs for the taking. Such a miracle deserved a memorial, which is just what God commanded to be built. Like all memorials, this one was meant to help keep the story alive. Although the eyewitnesses would not soon forget what God had done, it would be a different matter for future generations unless the story of God's miracle was told and retold. So, in later years, the older people might take their children and grandchildren down to Gilgal to see the memorial and tell them the story: "This is the place where we came into our inheritance. And you must always follow God if you want to keep your inheritance."

These later generations of Israelites could also apply the message to their own day. They could reason, "If God gave his people the land once, he can do it again." And they would also realize, if the story was told correctly, that God's help would not come without expectations: obedience to his commands and the sanctifying (setting apart) of themselves for service to God.

If Israel ever forgot how they got into the Promised Land, or why they were there, it would cease to be the land of promise, for the LORD would no longer be with them. It was also important that the nations remember this story, for as Joshua 4:24 informs us: "[God] did this so that all the peoples of the earth might know that the hand of the LORD is powerful."

For God's people today too, a sure knowledge of what God has done serves to prevent human pride and to promote true worship and service to the LORD. And for the nations, including those of today, knowing what God has done can serve as a testimony to the futility of opposing him and the wisdom of joining him.

May 9

Covenant Renewal

Joshua 5:2–12

The LORD your God will circumcise your heart and the heart of your offspring, so that you will love the LORD your God with all your heart and with all your soul, that you may live.
Deuteronomy 30:6 (ESV)

The wilderness experience had been a low point in Israel's covenant history. To be sure, God had led his people by the pillar of cloud and fire and he had fed them with manna. But Israel had not celebrated the Passover since the night of their departure from Egypt. Nor had they carried out circumcision, the sign of Israel's covenant with Yahweh. Things had to be different now in this place of full and intimate fellowship between the LORD and his people. This was to be the new Eden, a paradise "flowing with milk and honey." Here, in this land above all places, the laws of God had to be properly observed.

So Joshua and the people obeyed God's command to circumcise Israel's men as a sign of their covenant with God. They named the place *Gilgal,* meaning *to roll away.* This marked the end of the shame of being the LORD's people in a land of slavery. Now they were God's people in their own land—a land of freedom and life in which they could properly honor the LORD their God.

By God's design, the day of Israel's crossing of the Jordan was also the anniversary of the day that Israel started getting ready to leave Egypt by setting aside a Passover lamb. Now again, they killed and ate the Passover lambs to commemorate their deliverance by the hand of God. And on the first day of the feast that followed they began to eat the produce of this land, which was every bit as rich as God had promised it would be.

Israel had doubted God many times, and it would also falter many times in the future. But now in this new land, as the people ate and drank in celebration in the shadow of Jericho's walls, they had boundless faith that God would deliver on all his promises.

May 10

Instructions for Success at Jericho

Joshua 5:13–6:5, 17–19

Do not fear or panic or be in dread of them, for the LORD your God… goes with you to fight for you against your enemies to give you the victory.
Deuteronomy 20:3b–4 (ESV)

Joshua knew that Jericho's citizens were terribly afraid, but he also knew that they had no intention of giving up. The city had walls thick enough to house people and plenty of food and water. So Joshua needed a battle plan. But what he got was doubtless different than what he had imagined. On a scouting expedition to Jericho he met an unusual soldier; the way he identified himself told Joshua that God had more than human soldiers at his disposal. Joshua responded by falling on the ground in reverence. Then he asked for God's message. What was he to do?

What Joshua got first was an instruction to take off his shoes for he was on holy ground and in the presence not just of God's messenger, but of someone as holy as the holy God himself. By this, Joshua would have recognized the similarity between what Moses had experienced at the burning bush and what he was now experiencing.

What Joshua then learned was that the first battle was to be the model for all of Israel's battles. It was not a model for battle techniques, but a model for showing that it was the LORD God who was in charge of every single venture. God himself would make Jericho's walls collapse, making very clear here again that it was God who delivered every victory to his people.

Joshua also got clear instructions on what would happen after this. The city and everything in it would be put under the ban—under God's judgment. Except for certain items for the LORD's treasury, and for Rahab and her family, who were saved because of the covenant the spies had made with her, everything would be destroyed. It would be a sign for Canaan and for Israel of God's ultimate victory and his intolerance for the unholy.

May 11

Judgment and Mercy at Jericho

Joshua 6:6–27

The LORD knows the way of the righteous,
but the way of the wicked will perish.
Psalm 1:6 (ESV)

The walls of Jericho fell according to God's plan. The Israelites cooperated in God's judgment by destroying everything but that which had been exempted by God. It was a harsh judgment, but not undeserved. For many years, instead of giving God the allegiance he demanded, the Canaanites had flaunted their worship of false gods. Now was the day of judgment in which they would reap the reward for their steadfast opposition to God.

With the benefit of hindsight, we can see that what happened in Jericho was a preview of God's final judgment. Everyone who persists in their rebellion against the one true God is subject to eternal destruction. Ultimately there is no way that life can continue except by the permissions and limitations that the Creator originally set down for human existence. The very ruins of Jericho were supposed to serve as a permanent reminder of this truth. The penalty for rebuilding the city was severe, fitting the crime—the death of the builder's sons and his consequent disinheritance from the community of God's people.

But, here as always, God's judgment was given for positive reasons too; the ruins of Jericho were to be a permanent reminder that Israel's people and land belonged to God. Judgment for Jericho actually meant grace for Israel and security for those in covenant with God. And even those under sentence of judgment, such as Rahab and her family, could receive grace if only they joined God's people in submitting to his rule.

God was not content with a corner of creation surrounded by the opposition. His installation of Israel into this land was only the first stage of God's world conquest. In his plan, it was Jericho, Canaan, the world.

May 12

Back to Basics

Joshua 7:1–23

[I ask] that they may become perfectly one, so that the world may know that you sent me and loved them even as you loved me.
John 17:23 (ESV)

Both Joshua's fame and the fear of the Canaanites had been growing. But there was trouble within Israel, trouble that was not perceived until the terrible failure at Ai. Before Ai, the hearts of the Canaanites had been melting; now the melting hearts belonged to Israel.

Joshua, as God's representative and advocate for the people, took his concerns to God in prayer.

- He knew that Israel's failure was a sign of God's disapproval.
- He knew that unless something changed, Israel's enemies would be quick to eliminate their opposition.
- He realized, most importantly, that God's honor was tied to Israel and that Israel's failure would make God a laughingstock among the nations.

God gave Joshua the answer he needed. God was angry because his people had violated their covenant with him by failing to destroy all that he had said to destroy. God did not owe Israel an explanation for this command; even so, he gave them one (see Josh. 6:18). They had to destroy Jericho or else Jericho would destroy them by enticing God's people to worship other gods. This would effectively be a return to the bondage of Egypt from which God delivered his people.

Achan's sin was the sin of only one man or, at most, of one family. However, it had already caused the death of thirty-six soldiers in the battle of Ai, and it further threatened all that God was doing with and for Israel in this new land. The sin of one affected the whole covenant community. It still does, which helps explain the New Testament emphasis on the need for unity in faith and obedience within the body of Christ.

May 13

Punishment and Restoration

Joshua 7:24–8:35

The one who sows to his own flesh will from the flesh reap corruption, but the one who sows to the Spirit will from the Spirit reap eternal life.
Galatians 6:8 (ESV)

In giving in to his covetous impulses, Achan committed the unthinkable sin of stealing directly from the LORD himself. He disobeyed a direct command of God and stole from the first fruits that were to be devoted entirely to God. However, in unswerving determination to rescue his people, and through them his world—and for the sake of the coming Messiah—God gave Israel yet another in a long series of second chances.

When Israel purged the sin from their midst God helped them carry out their previously appointed task, this time giving them an overwhelming victory. Israel learned its lesson yet again; there is no victory without close attention to what the LORD wants. Besides that, God gave Israel the spoils of battle, the very thing that Achan had tried to steal from the LORD. Afterwards the community had a worship service: Joshua built an altar to the LORD and the people brought sacrifices. Then Joshua read for Israel all the words of God's Law.

Achan's sin should not surprise us; it is too much like our own. There's something in us all that tries and sometimes succeeds in shutting down the warnings of the Spirit in our hearts. The New Testament calls it the sinful nature. It's that same nature that tempts us to judge the Lord for the consistent way he deals with every threat against his plan to complete the redemption of his fallen creation.

It's only by God's grace that not all of us end up like Achan. Thank God for that amazing grace by which he provides what we could never achieve on our own. God put our punishment on his own son so that all who believe in and live for him might have blessings and not curses—life and not death.

May 14

The Assimilation of Gibeon

Joshua 9

[The inheritance] depends on faith, in order that the promise may rest on grace and be guaranteed to all [Abraham's] offspring—not only to the adherent of the law but also to the one who shares the faith of Abraham, who is the father of us all.
Romans 4:16 (ESV)

Normally the kings of Canaan were suspicious of each other and always trying to extend their own territories at each other's expense. However, after the defeat of Jericho and Ai they joined together to fight Israel. Only Gibeon did not join the coalition. Instead they sent a delegation to Israel, disguised to make it seem that they did not live close enough to pose a threat, and asked for a covenant agreement between their peoples. Israel's leaders agreed to Gibeon's request without consulting the LORD.

But this agreement was potentially a major problem. For the sake of Israel's purity, God had prohibited any treaty of friendship with those who served other gods. God's concern was not racial purity; since the people had left Egypt they had been a "mixed multitude." However, God wanted no compromise of Israel's spiritual purity. What Israel's leaders eventually proposed as a solution was making their treaty with Gibeon one of submission rather than friendship. This meant that the Gibeonites were permitted to be among the people of God, not as friends who retained their own worship practices but, only if they renounced their idolatry and pledged to serve the LORD.

Rahab and her family were the most recent additions to Israel; she had proved her loyalty by risking her life for the sake of Israel's spies. Now the Gibeonites also made the decision to leave their neighbors and join Abraham's descendants in the worship of the LORD. It wasn't an easy decision and it would have consequences, but Gibeon would find out what Rahab had discovered—that you never lose by deciding to serve the LORD.

May 15

Victory Complete

Joshua 10–11

Come to me, all who labor and are heavy laden, and I will give you rest. Take my yoke upon you and learn from me, for I am gentle and lowly in heart, and you will find rest for your souls.
Matthew 11:28–29 (ESV)

The strength of the alliance between Israel and Gibeon was tested when Gibeon was attacked by the Amorites. Israel quickly responded to the challenge, saving the Gibeonites. Afterwards the armies and cities of the Amorite coalition suffered the same fate as Jericho: "All these kings and their lands Joshua conquered in one campaign, because the LORD, the God of Israel, fought for Israel" (Josh. 10:42).

This also applies to Israel's success with the armies of Hazor and its allies in the north of Canaan. The mopping-up operations took a long time (see Joshua 11:18) but, as God ordered, the cities of the north were destroyed.

There is one more group of Canaanites whose downfall was especially significant—the descendants of Anak who, years before, had made the ten unfaithful spies of Israel feel like grasshoppers in the presence of giants. These giants had not gotten smaller, but they were not too big or powerful for the LORD's army. Only a few survived, among them the ancestor of Goliath in Gath.

The conclusion of the entire series of battles to take the land is given in the final verse of Joshua 11: "Then the land had rest from war." It was the fulfillment of God's promise to Moses in Exodus 33:14, "My presence will go with you and I will give you rest." Joshua also reminded the people of this promise at the beginning of Israel's entry into Canaan: "The LORD your God will give you rest by giving you this land" (Josh. 1:13).

It was an early installment of an even more complete rest and greater inheritance to come.

May 16

Distribution of the Inheritance—Part 1

Joshua 14:1–15:1; 16:1–4; 17:14–18

The scepter shall not depart from Judah, nor the ruler's staff from between his feet, until tribute comes to him; and to him shall be the obedience of the peoples.
Genesis 49:10 (ESV)

Israel occupied the land, but there was still much work to be done, for they were surrounded by many who would continue to oppose the people of God. Nevertheless, it was time to allocate the inheritance. In keeping with the blessing that Jacob had pronounced on his sons, Judah had priority among the tribes of Israel, and so received the first tribal allotment. Judah inherited a large territory, but one with enemies on every side: Moab to the east, Edom (Esau's descendants) to the south, the Amalekites to the southwest, the Philistines to the west, and to the north, in the territory of Benjamin, the Jebusites. The Philistines especially would give Judah problems for hundreds of years.

One of Judah's leaders, Caleb, was given a special territory of his own. Caleb was actually related by blood to the Edomites, who would later be cursed for their opposition to the LORD and Israel. However, Caleb had become part of Judah and had proved his loyalty to Yahweh and Israel as one of the faithful spies sent out by Moses (see Num. 14). Caleb's inheritance was in the territory of the fearsome Anakites. He still had some work to do to secure that land, but fully expected and received the LORD's blessing in doing it.

The tribes of Joseph, Ephraim and Manasseh also received their inheritance. They complained about the size of their allotments but Joshua told them that they had received enough if only they would apply themselves to driving out the Canaanites who lived there (Josh. 17:17–18). Instead, Ephraim subjected them to forced labor. In later years, the Canaanites would grow stronger and make them pay for not following the LORD's commands.

May 17

Distribution of the Inheritance—Part 2

Joshua 18:1–10

[We desire] that you may not be sluggish, but imitators of those who through faith and patience inherit the promises.
Hebrews 6:12 (ESV)

The inheritance for the remaining tribes of Israel was doled out by lot. But even before this happened, Joshua assembled Israel at Shiloh where the tabernacle was set up. There, he reproved them for failing to take possession of the land that God had given them. Even though the LORD had given Israel the land, the people still had a duty to work and to take hold of what God gave them to inherit. They needed more than a degree of control as well; they needed to make this a place in which there was no idolatrous competition for wholehearted service to God.

Joshua's question, "How long will you wait before you begin to take possession of the land that the LORD, the God of your fathers, has given you?" is as good a question for us today as it was for Israel. When we settle for less than what God wants, when we get lazy or tired and start dragging our spiritual feet, then, if we have ears to hear it, we can hear God asking: "How long will you wait to take me at my word, and obey me, and displace the enemy from the territory that belongs to you?"

This is not a call to reinstate the theocracy of Joshua's day; it is simply a call to persist against other enemies. "For our struggle is not against flesh and blood, but against the rulers, against the authorities, against the powers of this dark world and against the spiritual forces of evil in the heavenly realms" (Eph. 6:12).

This admonition from James neatly captures what Jesus did and wants every disciple to do: "Submit yourselves, then, to God. Resist the devil, and he will flee from you. Come near to God and he will come near to you" (James 4:7–8). As with ancient Israel, we have a rightful claim to a God-given inheritance and must not fail to pursue it.

May 18

Distribution of the Inheritance—Part 3

Joshua 20:1–21:3

He remembered his holy promise, and Abraham, his servant. So he brought his people out with joy, his chosen ones with singing. And he gave them the lands of the nations, and they took possession of the fruit of the peoples' toil, that they might keep his statutes and observe his laws.
Psalm 105:42–45 (ESV)

The Levites, who were dedicated to the special service of the LORD, received no land. They were to consider the LORD alone as their inheritance. However, they did get food by way of offerings from the other tribes and forty-eight cities scattered throughout Israel to live in. This both provided for the Levites and constantly reminded the rest of Israel of the service they owed God.

Six of the Levite cities were designated as Cities of Refuge. Anyone who accidentally caused the death of another person could flee to one of these and ask for protection. If the city elders determined that the death truly was accidental, the perpetrator could stay there, safe from the revenge of the victim's family.

The Levite allotments and the cities of refuge completed the distribution of Israel's inheritance. Even though the tribes would have to continue to fight to solidify their hold on their property, the inheritance was theirs. Every tribe had its place, and every family within the tribe. And if the Year of Jubilee provisions were observed (see Lev. 25, 27), each family would continue to have a place in the Promised Land. The only condition was that they all be loyal to the LORD and observe his commands.

Joshua 21:44–45 concludes the account of the distribution of Israel's inheritance this way: "The LORD gave them rest on every side, just as he had sworn to their ancestors. Not one of their enemies withstood them; the LORD gave all their enemies into their hands. Not one of all the LORD's good promises to Israel failed; every one was fulfilled."

May 19

Israel's Unity Threatened

Joshua 22

All who believed were together…
Acts 2:44 (ESV)

Now that the inheritance was secure, Joshua called together the fighting men from Reuben, Gad, and the half-tribe of Manasseh to send them back to their families and settlements on the east side of the Jordan. First, however, he gave them a sermon on loyalty: "But be very careful to keep the commandment and the law that Moses the servant of the LORD gave you: to love the LORD your God, to walk in obedience to him, to keep his commands, to hold fast to him and to serve him with all your heart and with all your soul" (Josh. 22:5).

Thus, the rest of Israel became horrified when the men of these tribes stopped to build an altar by the Jordan. That's because the LORD's altar was in Shiloh, and they assumed that any other altar would be for promoting the worship of Canaanite gods. These tribes might have said, "Let those rebels go their own way. If they want to serve other gods, that's their problem, not ours." But Israel was the community of God's people; they had to stand together, or they would fall together. They were accountable to each other for their loyalty to the LORD. If one failed, they all would suffer, and they did not want the LORD's anger to burn again as it had with the sins of Peor and Achan.

That's why all of Israel was very relieved to hear that the altar at the Jordan had been built as a witness to future generations of the trans-Jordan tribes' continuing loyalty to the LORD; the name they gave the altar testified to its purpose: "A Witness Between Us—that the LORD is God.

It is still true that all who pledge loyalty to the LORD are accountable to each other. With mutual and loving discipline, we too may present to the world a united and powerful testimony of the inheritance we have in Christ.

May 20

Israel's Real but Incomplete Rest

Joshua 23

Whoever has entered God's rest has also rested from his works as God did from his. Let us therefore strive to enter that rest, so that no one may fall by the same sort of disobedience.
Hebrews 4:10–11 (ESV)

So far the book of Joshua has given us an account of Israel's first taste of life in the Promised Land. The final chapters highlight the conclusion of Joshua's ministry and life. Here, as a prelude to reinforce to the leaders of Israel the responsibilities of their offices, Joshua asserts: "Not one of all the good promises the LORD your God gave you has failed. Every promise has been fulfilled" (Josh. 23:14). It's an extraordinary claim, and one that repeats the assertion of verse 1: "The LORD had given Israel rest from all their enemies around them."

At the same time, this chapter makes clear that the fulfilled promises and rest from enemies that Israel enjoys does not mean that life in the Promised Land is yet all that God intends it to be. There are still enemies in the land, enemies to be "pushed back and driven out" (verse 5). And until that happens completely, there should be no mixing of Israel with the various Canaanite tribes, and especially so in the practices of worship (verse 7).

The situation is here as it has been all along; the gracious gifts of God do not relieve his people of the responsibility to claim what the LORD gave them. The certainty of what God did for Israel is indicated by use of the past tense; the obligation for them to pursue the fullness of this reality is indicated by use of the imperative.

Hebrews and the rest of the New Testament repeats this emphasis for every child of God. We cannot enter into God's rest without his initiative and power. Thank God for providing these! But those who receive God's gifts must make every effort to stay true to him and so reach the complete rest that he wants for us.

May 21

A Future for God's People

Joshua 24

Blessed is the nation whose God is the LORD, the people whom he has chosen as his heritage...Let your steadfast love, O LORD, be upon us, even as we hope in you.
Psalm 33:12, 22 (ESV)

Joshua wanted Israel's future to be as good as their present. Before he died he assembled the leaders of Israel at Shechem for a final warning and testimony. Shechem was the site of the first altar that Abraham had erected to the LORD, and it was also the first land purchased by Jacob upon his return to Canaan from Laban's home in Mesopotamia.

At the assembly Joshua rehearsed the history of God's care for them and the standards by which Moses and he had led Israel. He warned that for Israel to continue in their inheritance, they must not associate with the idol worshipers left in the land or swerve from the worship of the one true God. Nor was it enough for Israel merely to control the land and coexist with their ungodly neighbors. If God's people did not drive them out, Israel would inevitably come under the influence of the false gods and misplaced loyalties of the Canaanites. In this way Israel would destroy the paradise into which God had led them.

Joshua told them further that serving the LORD would not be easy, and he counseled against too hasty a choice. Even so, the tribes followed his lead and renewed their binding covenant with God. Although events in the years ahead would bear out the truth of Joshua's warnings, Israel seemed to believe that there was really no good alternative to what Joshua advocated.

Indeed, there is not. There can be no paradise, temporal or eternal, apart from a living relationship with the LORD. What testifies to the grace of Christ in which God's people stand is a life of unswerving loyalty to him, a life guided by his word and empowered by his Spirit.

May 22

Vicious Cycles

Judges 2:6–22

Blessed is the man who remains steadfast under trial,
for when he has stood the test he will receive the crown of life,
which God has promised to those who love him.
James 1:12 (ESV)

This chapter affirms the choice that Israel made in response to Joshua's challenge. However, Israel's obedience was an inconsistent one. The last half of Judges 1 tells of the attempts of Israel's tribes to make their inheritance secure. But in each case they were unable to complete the task of driving the Canaanites from the territories God had assigned his people. While the first generation of Israel's life in the Promised Land was marked by a relative faithfulness to the LORD, succeeding generations forgot most of the mighty acts of God by which they had been led into their inheritance. They made more and more compromises with their idolatrous neighbors, compromises involving not only treaties but also intermarriage and false worship.

The LORD was understandably provoked by Israel's faithlessness and he gave their enemies power over them. God's purpose in this was not merely to punish, but also to correct. When, in their afflictions, the people would repent and turn again to the LORD, God would send judges to rescue them and lead them again in proper service.

Unfortunately, Israel's ensuing faithfulness would not long endure; they soon resumed their godless ways and again were subjected to the LORD's correction. The book of Judges tells the story of several such vicious cycles occurring over a period of several centuries. Each response of the LORD to the cries of the people and each judge raised up by him to deliver them and call them again to true devotion, was a test to see whether they would "keep the way of the LORD and walk in it as their ancestors did" (Judg. 2:22). And every mercy of God today, too, is a similar test. May each of us prove to be faithful.

May 23

God Gives Gideon a Mission

Judges 6

Fear not, little flock, for it is your Father's good pleasure to give you the kingdom.
Luke 12:32 (ESV)

This chapter takes us to a time following successive cycles of Israel's on-again, off-again relationship to God. This time, Israel's faithlessness resulted in seven years of severe oppression by the Midianites. Finally, Israel remembered to cry out to the LORD for help. In response he sent his angel to enlist faithful, but insecure, Gideon to rescue his people from Midian.

Gideon became convinced that his messenger was actually from the LORD only after supernatural fire consumed his offering. In the strength of that revelation he did what the angel told him to do: he demolished the altar of Baal and erected on its remains a proper altar upon which he made a sacrifice to the LORD.

The people of Gideon's town responded with hostility, sure that the Midianites would now exact a fearful revenge for this desecration. However, enough of Israel's men saw that the Spirit of the LORD was clearly with Gideon and they answered his call to take up arms and join him in the coming fight against Midian. Gideon was tentative and prudent enough to ask the LORD for confirmation that he truly would save Israel. And then, just to make doubly sure, he asked for and received a second miraculous confirmation.

Although Gideon felt himself to be an unqualified leader, he showed his character in the events that followed. God used him for forty years to free Israel from the oppression of the Midianites. It may well be that Gideon had strengths of leadership that needed to be drawn out. The main thing that ensured his success, however, was his attentiveness to the LORD's directions and his confidence that his mission was really the LORD's mission and empowered by God's presence and strength (see v. 14).

May 24

God Gives Gideon Victory

Judges 7:1–8:21

I am the vine; you are the branches. Whoever abides in me and I in him, he it is that bears much fruit, for apart from me you can do nothing.
John 15:5 (ESV)

Gideon prepared for battle with the army of Midian with thirty-two thousand men from Israel. But these were not all eager warriors; two thirds of them took advantage of Gideon's God-ordered permission that anyone who desired could return to their homes and avoid the coming battle. Then, following additional directions from the LORD, the remaining troops were further reduced to a force of three hundred. God made his purposes clear in this; it was so it would be very obvious to Israel that any victory had come not by their might but by the power of God.

And that's just what should have become very obvious in the events that followed. The army of Midian also included the Amalekites and other eastern peoples; they outnumbered Gideon's reduced force three or four hundred to one. Nevertheless, at Gideon's nighttime attack, the soldiers of this vast army panicked and turned their swords on each other as they fled for their lives.

Yet, some of the Israelites seemed to be unclear about who was responsible for this great victory.

- Some Ephraimites criticized Gideon for leaving them out of the fight, apparently unaware that he had simply been following the LORD's commands.
- The towns of Succoth and Peniel seemed to be more afraid of Midian's remaining soldiers than of Gideon's forces, for they refused to help with provisions for them. It was an affront not merely to Gideon, but to the LORD, who had showed himself to be so mighty in rescuing Israel from its oppressors.

Even in victory, it was difficult for Israel to recognize and support the LORD's hand in the events of their time. Let us take care that we today do not repeat Israel's mistakes.

May 25

Gideon's Tarnished Legacy

Judges 8:22–9:57

Seek the LORD and his strength; seek his presence continually! Remember the wondrous works that he has done, his miracles, and the judgments he uttered.
Psalm 105:4–5 (ESV)

The request of the Israelites that Gideon establish a dynasty to rule over them is a further indication of their failure to give God all the credit for their deliverance from Midianite oppressors. But Gideon didn't fall for the flattery; he knew that he couldn't have done what he did without God. He also remembered what God had said earlier—that he himself would rule over his people without a go-between or mediator-king. So Gideon refused the offer and reaffirmed that Israel would continue to be subject to the direct rule of the LORD.

Gideon was a good leader in that sense. However, he did make a foolish request of his petitioners. His intention was probably good; he wanted to make an ephod—a holy robe—from the Midianite gold taken in the battle. This was something that the priests might wear in their sacrificial service to God. The trouble was, it didn't help Israel worship the one true LORD. Instead Gideon and his family and all of Israel began to worship the ephod rather than the LORD for whose service it had been made. Things got worse after Gideon died. Then Israel's faulty worship transitioned to the worship of idol gods.

Gideon's legacy was also tarnished by the failure of the citizens of Shechem and Gideon's son Abimelech to honor Gideon's refusal to establish a dynasty in Israel. Another of Gideon's sons, Jotham, exemplified the spirit of his father, but he had no voice in Israel, and in fact, his life was in danger there. Between Israel's faulty worship and their desire to secure their own future through a ruler who had no regard for serving the LORD as Gideon had done, Israel was headed right back toward the low point of the vicious cycle.

May 26

God Raises another Deliverer

Judges 13

O LORD, you hear the desire of the afflicted; you will strengthen their heart; you will incline your ear.
Psalm 10:17 (ESV)

The oppressors of Israel in the time of the judges varied by region and time, but the results were much the same. Apart from isolated victories, the life of God's people in the Promised Land was neither happy nor peaceful. In the days of Manoah, it was mainly the Philistines who oppressed Israel. At least some of that suffering was because of Israel's unfaithfulness to the LORD and was used by the LORD to bring them to a consciousness of sin and repentance. For God did not let his people go, but provided continuing evidence of his intention to see them living as his people in his land.

This time, the LORD revealed a bit of what he was planning to a childless couple from the tribe of Dan. Manoah's wife was sterile but, as had happened with Abraham's wife Sarah so many years before, she was promised a miracle child; this child was chosen for service to God in the matter of Israel's deliverance from the Philistines.

It was not an easy thing for Manoah and his wife, unholy as they knew they were, to meet with and hear from the holy God. But they believed the LORD's promise, reassured by their survival of the encounter and by God's acceptance of their offerings. When their son was born they taught him about the LORD's plan to keep him pure and to use him in service. And afterwards the family saw the way the LORD was blessing him.

As it happened, a childless couple from Ephraim had just received a similar gift from God. That is another story (see 1 Sam. 1) but both sons, chosen for service before birth, were to be used to deliver Israel. Their lives testify to the truth that the LORD's love and choosing always precede any useful service for him.

May 27

Samson's Flawed Leadership

Judges 14–15

[A Nazirite] shall eat nothing that is produced by the grapevine...
He shall let the locks of hair of his head grow long...
He shall not go near a dead body...He is holy to the LORD.
Numbers 6:4–8 (excerpts) (ESV)

Samson and his family saw evidences of the LORD's blessing upon him during his formative years. God's blessings continued in Samson's adult life, albeit mitigated by Samson's lack of wisdom in maintaining the purity of his devotion to the ways of the LORD. You see, Samson liked to walk very close to the line that separates devotion to God from attachment to worldly attractions. He had a heart for the LORD and wanted to serve him, but he also had a tendency to make himself susceptible to compromise with what was forbidden by God.

- Samson made plans to take a Philistine wife, flouting God's specific rules about intermarriage with idol worshipers, rules that had often been emphasized by Moses and Joshua (see for example, Deut. 7:1–6, Josh. 23:12–13).
- In Samson's willingness to eat honey from the corpse of the lion he had previously killed, he disregarded the Nazirite rule about contact with the unclean.

Scripture does not overtly criticize Samson for the first of these violations, perhaps because it is more concerned to tell us that the LORD had a purpose in Samson's proposed marriage to a Philistine. Nor does it spell out God's reaction to Samson's violation of his Nazirite vows. But, neither omission signals that the LORD had changed his mind about such things. At issue is the fact that God would follow through on his intention to use Samson to confront the Philistines about their unlawful domination of his people. God would even turn Samson's inadequacy and faulty obedience into something good for Israel over the next twenty years. However, God's people would have to wait considerably longer for the perfect service that only Jesus could supply.

May 28

Samson's Downfall and Final Victory

Judges 16

Time would fail me to tell of...Samson [and others] who through faith conquered kingdoms, enforced justice, obtained promises, stopped the mouths of lions...were made strong out of weakness, became mighty in war, put foreign armies to flight.
Hebrews 11:32–34 (ESV)

Samson's downfall came because of a final compromise of his Nazirite vows in the stress of a situation he should not have been in. He'd been given special strength from God to stir up Israel's faith in God and help deliver them from the Philistines. Now he could no longer be God's blessing for Israel, betraying both them and the LORD, who had called him to this service before birth.

The enemies of God had a great victory celebration over Samson's humiliation because they understood that this also meant humiliation for his people and his God. They praised an idol while they blasphemed the name of the LORD over the defeat of his handpicked mediator.

By the grace of God, however, this is not the end of the story. For Samson's hair began to grow again, and with it his devotion to the LORD and his desire to act as the mediator God had appointed him to be. Samson's later actions show that he repented of his weakness and rededicated himself to serve the LORD and his people. His revenge was not born in human weakness, but was reflective of the judgment of God's justice and righteousness on evil. You might say that Samson's eyes of faith became strong after his physical eyes were put out. That's when he gained the vision necessary to complete his mission against those who sought to tear down the rule of the sovereign God.

Samson's final victory is just a little taste of the ultimate victory over sin and death in store for all who put themselves under the leadership of Jesus Christ, the only mediator and judge who can perfectly deliver us from evil and lead us into life everlasting.

May 29

Micah's Idols

Judges 17–18

They served their idols, which became a snare to them.
Psalm 106:36 (ESV)

These chapters tell of Micah, a man from Ephraim, who cast idols of silver and made a shrine for worship in his home. Micah's concern for worship was proper but, in his use of idols as well as in his choice of his son to be his priest, there was little to distinguish his household from those of the Canaanites whom the LORD had warned his people to have nothing to do with.

Micah did, however, remember enough of his religious heritage so that he took advantage of the opportunity to secure a legitimate priest, one from the tribe of Levi—the only tribe authorized by God for this purpose. But neither Micah nor his priest took account of the law that clearly forbade the use of idols in worship.

Micah's contentment with his provision for worship did not endure very long. The army of the tribe of Dan, on its way to new territory in the north, stole Micah's idols and convinced his Levite to be their priest. Micah was beside himself with dismay, throwing aside caution to go after the much larger force. He was dissuaded from foolishly attacking them, but revealed his distress with the words, "What else do I have?" That cry was an indication of how far short he and his generation had fallen of meeting the expectations of the LORD who had delivered them from Egypt so that they might give him their exclusive service.

Four times in the last five chapters of the book of Judges we find this phrase, "In those days Israel had no king." And in one other place beside the last verse of the book this phrase is followed by an indictment: "In those days Israel had no king; everyone did as they saw fit" (Judg. 21:25). Chaos and disunity prevailed among Abraham's descendants in the land into which the LORD had brought them.

May 30

Sodom Revisited

Judges 19–21

As Isaiah predicted, "If the Lord of hosts had not left us offspring, we would have been like Sodom, and become like Gomorrah."
Romans 9:29 (ESV)

The legendary wickedness of Sodom is revisited in this less familiar story about life in Israel in the time of the judges. A town of the tribe of Benjamin—Gibeah—refused hospitality to a traveling Levite. Even worse, they tolerated wicked men who, when denied the opportunity to rape the visitor, so abused his concubine that she died.

After returning home, the Levite issued an unmistakable call to the rest of Israel to avenge this atrocity. To their credit, there was at this time enough consciousness about the life to which God had called his people that "the men rose up together as one" to remove the evil from among Israel. However, the tribe of Benjamin would not give up the wicked men for judgment, assembling instead to go to war against the rest of Israel.

The LORD's position on the issue became clear in the severe losses suffered by Benjamin; after the battle only six hundred of their men were left and few, if any, of their towns. But, rather than celebrating, the rest of Israel grieved because the tribe of Benjamin was destined for extinction, the people having taken an oath to let none of their daughters marry into this tribe.

The Israelites wondered what would now become of God's promise to Abraham. They were ingenious, however, in finding a way to keep the tribe of Benjamin from dying off. They took seriously the need to punish this egregious violation of God's law, but they were equally serious about preserving intact the whole family of Abraham's offspring through Isaac. In a time when Israel had no king and everyone did as they saw fit, here was a small sign of hope and a sign that perhaps Israel could still be the treasured possession that God had called them to be.

May 31

Naomi's Trouble

Ruth 1

With God are wisdom and might; he has counsel and understanding... Though he slay me, I will hope in him.
Job 12:13; 13:15a (ESV)

The book of Ruth dates from the time of the judges, likely about a century before David's reign. It gives insight into some of the trials of living in Israel during this time. It also shows that God worked behind the scenes to ensure the survival of his people.

It must have been difficult for Elimelech and his family to immigrate to Moab. Even if there were some good reasons for it, and even if the language and customs there weren't that different from what they were used to, it still wasn't easy to leave the chosen people of God and the land where God had given them an inheritance.

Although Elimelech's family found relief from the famine, the next few years took an unexpected toll on them; all of the men died, leaving Naomi alone and destitute in a foreign country. Her prospects were dismal since the security of women in her day lay in being under the care and protection of a father, husband, or son. Naomi had none of these; nor was she of an age to remarry.

There was the possibility of remarriage for Naomi's daughters-in-law, but their best chance for that lay in Moab. As outsiders to the covenant community in Israel, they were not eligible to depend upon a kinsman of their dead husbands to marry them and give them sons to carry on Elimelech's family name and inheritance. As a result, Naomi encouraged them to stay in Moab. She herself, however, made plans to return home.

Naomi, who now asked to be called Mara as a sign of her emptiness, felt that her life was ruined and was certain that God was behind her misfortunes. But she didn't blame God for what had happened; like the biblical Job, she found it impossible to give up her trust in the LORD.

June 1

Ruth's Decision

Ruth 1

Trust in the LORD forever, for the LORD God is an everlasting rock.
Isaiah 26:4 (ESV)

Orpah saw the logic of Naomi's argument and remained in Moab. It was more than logic that compelled her; now she wouldn't have to leave her home and gods. But Ruth wouldn't leave in spite of Naomi's repeated urging.

Don't make the mistake of thinking that this is a story about human loyalty, one daughter-in-law deserting her mother-in-law while another remains faithful to her. Loyalty is a minor theme, but this is mostly a story about faith—an idol-worshiping Moabite woman making a choice to serve Yahweh, the God of Israel, in spite of the lack of any tangible incentive to do so.

- Will there be acceptance in Israel? Ruth doesn't know.
- Will there be a way for Ruth to provide for herself and Naomi? She doesn't know.
- Will there be the possibility that Ruth can find another husband and have children? Probably not.

Ruth goes because of her faith and her determination to serve the LORD. Even though she does not see any possible rewards, Ruth casts her lot with Yahweh, trusting him for the future that she cannot see and sealing her commitment with an oath that was standard in her day. Not flippantly, but in all seriousness, Ruth says something like "May God damn me if I ever leave you." She realizes that it is hell to live outside of the place where God dwells and the people to whom he shows his mercy.

So two women return, old Naomi with hope almost gone but clinging to a bit of faith, and the convert Ruth who puts her life on the line for her faith. Part one of the story concludes with their arrival at the start of the barley harvest. There's just a hint of hope in this; it's certainly better than the famine that prompted their departure.

June 2

Righteous Boaz

Ruth 2

There is no one who has left house or brothers or sisters or mother or father or children or lands, for my sake and for the gospel, who will not receive a hundredfold now in this time... with persecutions, and in the age to come eternal life.
Mark 10:29–30 (ESV)

There was a law in Israel that what the harvesters left behind, the poor could take for themselves (see Deut. 24:19). However, gleaning did not always work out so well in practice. Over the years, more than one of God's commands had been conveniently forgotten by those who had the most to lose by being generous. The success of Ruth and other poor gleaners depended on finding farmers who actually lived by God's law and encouraged, rather than harassed, the poor people in their fields.

Boaz was such a man; he went beyond obedience to the letter of God's law to honor the spirit of it, going out of his way to provide a safe and fruitful environment for a hungry foreigner. He instructed his hired help not to harass Ruth and also told Ruth to help herself to the water provided for his workers and to stay in his fields rather than go elsewhere, where she might not be safe.

Reflecting the perspective of God himself, Boaz was impressed with the willingness of Ruth to leave her own father, mother, and homeland for the service of Yahweh. It was just the sort of action that Jesus would praise many years later.

In a time when "everyone did as they saw fit" Boaz was more concerned with what God wanted done in every situation. He believed that God's grace was for all, even former enemies of God, who entrust themselves to him. Boaz believed that his own position and wealth were gifts of God to be used in God's service. His actions are a testimony to God's kindness and mercy and a model for the relationships that can exist in the covenant community between rich and poor, and men and women.

June 3

Signs of Hope

Ruth 2

But when the fullness of time had come, God sent forth his Son, born of woman, born under the law, to redeem those who were under the law, so that we might receive adoption as sons.
Galatians 4:4–5 (ESV)

Ruth was amazed at the way Boaz treated her. Naomi was equally impressed, even if she was not quite ready to quit calling herself Mara. Naomi understood that it was by God's grace that Boaz showed kindness to the living (her and Ruth) and to the dead (Elimelech and her sons). How Boaz was showing God's kindness to the living is clear enough: the women of Elimilech's family now had food to eat. But just a hint of a way that Boaz would show God's kindness to the dead is seen in Naomi's reference to Boaz as a kinsman-redeemer. Naomi saw the possibility that the inheritance lost through the deaths of her husband and sons could be restored through Boaz.

How this might be done becomes clearer as the story progresses, but already we may be sure that this is more than a simple story about a pair of poor widows in Israel who benefit at the hands of a rich and generous landowner. The kinsman-redeemer Boaz foreshadows another redeemer—a much greater one—Jesus Christ, who would give to many what Boaz gave to Ruth: undeserved mercy and protection in the difficulties of life. The journey of Naomi from emptiness to fullness foreshadows the journey of every Christian who has come to fullness from the emptiness of life apart from Christ.

What Boaz did for Naomi and Ruth, Christ Jesus has done for billions of people since their day; he has brought them from emptiness to fullness—a much greater fullness than Naomi ever imagined. If you have ever doubted God's goodness and provision, notice it here. Believe that in Christ we are promised a joy and fullness of life that no earthly sorrow can destroy.

June 4

A Risky Proposition

Ruth 3:1–15

King David's prayer against one who stands
in opposition to a faithful servant of the LORD:
May his posterity be cut off; may his name be blotted out in the second generation...the memory of them from the earth!
Psalm 109:13, 15 (ESV)

Boaz was not the closest living relative of Elimelech. Yet his kindness toward Ruth suggested to Naomi that he might go beyond strict duty to fulfill her distant hope of a home, family, and security in Israel. So she devised a plan by which Ruth might approach Boaz and ask him to take her as his wife (symbolically represented by spreading the corner of his cloak over her).

There was danger in what Naomi suggested. Would Boaz, who had so far appeared to be a righteous man, prove to be so in his ongoing conduct? Would the way Boaz responded to Ruth's overture destroy her reputation or would it secure her future?

The answer became clear by Boaz's immediate response. Seeing that Ruth had not acted selfishly by seeking marriage with a man her own age, he called what Ruth was doing a kindness to Naomi. Ruth understood that marriage to anyone other than a kinsman-redeemer of Elimelech might secure her own future, but it wouldn't ensure the preservation of Elimelech's family line.

The dying out of a family line and the consequent loss of an inheritance in the Promised Land was regarded as a punishment suitable only for the wicked (see Ps. 109:13, 15). However, if God's provisions for orphans and widows were followed, neither death nor poverty could separate a faithful Israelite family from their rightful place in the land and with the chosen people, serving the one true God, Yahweh. With that in mind, Boaz assured Ruth of his intention to pursue the matter. Then, taking care to preserve both her safety and her reputation, he sent Ruth back to Naomi with a gift of food.

June 5

Hope Restored

Ruth 3:16–4:12

The one who looks into the perfect law, the law of liberty, and perseveres, being no hearer who forgets but a doer who acts, he will be blessed in his doing.
James 1:25 (ESV)

Naomi was happy to hear about Boaz's response to Ruth's symbolic proposal of marriage. True to his word, Boaz went to meet the elders of Bethlehem where he negotiated with a closer relative of Elimelech for the right to purchase Elimelech's land.

This man was interested obtaining Elimelech's land. But his interest waned when he found out that with the land came the obligation to marry Ruth. He was willing to go a little way down the road of responsibility, as God's law had outlined but, like Ruth's sister-in-law Orpah, he could not go far enough. So he authorized Boaz to redeem the land and exercise the rights and obligations that came with being the kinsman-redeemer.

It should be clear that Ruth and Boaz did not pursue the possibility of marriage primarily as an outlet for passion or romantic feelings. Rather, they treated it as a kind of business proposition, and in a way it was. Ruth could perhaps have married someone else, but only if she married Boaz or another kinsman-redeemer would the line of her dead father-in-law, Elimelech, be preserved—the first son of the marriage would be treated as if he were the blood son of Elimelech and Naomi.

The words of blessing of the elders to Boaz, therefore, are appropriate for one who so unselfishly pledged to preserve the inheritance of his dead relative by marrying and fathering a son who would be classified as the son of Elimelech. This was a matter of some risk for Boaz since such a son wouldn't contribute to the continuation of his own family line. Yet, in completing the contract Boaz, like Ruth, made a commitment that fully satisfied the spirit of God's laws for his people.

June 6

More Blessed Than They Knew

Ruth 4:13–22

Blessed are the people...who walk, O LORD,
in the light of your face, who exult in your name
all the day and in your righteousness are exalted.
Psalm 89:15-16 (ESV)

The businesslike marriage contract between Boaz and Ruth was not unusual for their day. But it did not mean that they were committing to a loveless marriage; they knew that with marriage came the duty before God to love and serve each other. They also knew something that many people of our day too easily forget—love is more than a feeling; it is the word and action expression of a deep and lasting commitment to another.

God blessed their union with a son whom the women of the town saw as Naomi's own, given by God to a now barren widow woman to ensure the security of her place among God's people. And so, she who had returned to Israel bitter and empty was now contented and complete.

Yahweh had provided for widows and strangers in his law but it took truly devoted people such as Boaz and Ruth to make those blessings real. Together, this man to whom God's law was important and this outside-of-the-covenant immigrant woman modeled for God's people what it meant to live by God's law.

Their son, Obed, would become an even bigger blessing than anyone living in that time could have known. As the grandfather of David, the greatest and most beloved king of Israel, and the ancestor of David's most famous descendant, Jesus, Obed became a link in the chain of God's provision for all of Israel and for the Gentiles too. Indeed, it is a beautiful coincidence that a descendant of the Gentile Ruth—Jesus—is the one who provides free access for all Gentiles into the very presence of God. Who could have guessed that the implications of the faithfulness of Naomi, Ruth, and Boaz would be so far-reaching?

June 7

Epilogue to Ruth

Ruth 1–4

Do you not know that you are God's temple and that God's Spirit dwells in you?
1 Corinthians 3:16 (ESV)

God's people today receive much worldly advice—things like: "Look out for number 1," and "If you don't do it someone else will." We hear, directly and indirectly, of the importance of prosperity and of freedom to pursue our own interests and create our own reality without regard for God's interests and his reality.

But we also have Ruth and the other main characters of this story as models. We have a childless foreign widow without prospects making a decision for a new land, a new people and a new God—and Naomi and Boaz, never forgetting God's promises but determining to live in expectation that God would bless their obedience. *Ruth* shows us that God's activity is ongoing and is tied to the specific covenant-keeping actions of ordinary people. There is a real and intimate connection between divine and human activity. It's not that a young widow today ought to do exactly the same things Ruth did; we live in a different time and culture. But everyone ought to have the same attitude that she and Boaz had and translate that attitude and that devotion to God into actions that are appropriate for our time and setting. That's how ordinary Christians become the instruments God uses to accomplish his extraordinary salvation.

We may live to see some, but not nearly all, of the results of our obedience. However, all of them are important. God guides and directs, motivates, and refines every bit of obedience for use in his great plan to redeem a hurting world and bring people into his eternal kingdom. It honors our Lord and brings meaning and purpose to our own lives when we act as mediators of God's grace so that those around us, like Naomi, are brought from the emptiness of spiritual poverty to fullness of life.

June 8

Hannah's Miracle Child Released to God

1 Samuel 1

You shall teach [my commandments] diligently to your children, and shall talk of them when you sit in your house, and when you walk by the way, and when you lie down, and when you rise.
Deuteronomy 6:7 (ESV)

We feel sorry for couples who earnestly desire children but are not able to have them. Even though their physical well-being and status in society probably does not depend on having children, we feel sorry for them. But it seems that the dilemma of childless people, and especially women, in Old Testament times was even more a reason for compassion, for those who remained childless were often looked down upon. That was certainly the case with Hannah, at least as far as Elkanah's other wife was concerned. Hannah was sick about it; she wanted a child more than anything, even promising the LORD that she would dedicate her child to his service.

It is not unusual for people to make such conditional promises to God; what is more unusual is for them to keep those promises as Hannah did when God answered her prayers. She gave up little Samuel when he was perhaps three years old. It was an act with greater consequences than she knew, for Samuel would have an important task to fulfill in Israel's history.

The ways that God used Samuel may have been greater than the ways he will use our own children; only God knows what he has for each person to do. However, what every Christian parent can know is how important it is to have Hannah's perspective and follow her example. Although we wouldn't give up our children in quite the same way she did, we can and must dedicate and release them to God. As much as we love them, they don't really belong to us; they are on loan to us as gifts from the LORD. Parents are called to prepare their children for service to God by teaching them to love him and by a lifestyle that is consistent with biblical faith and values.

June 9

The Secure Future of God's Servants

1 Samuel 2:1–10

The LORD is God in heaven above and on the earth beneath; there is no other. Therefore you shall keep his statutes and his commandments... that it may go well with you and with your children after you.
Deuteronomy 4:39–40 (ESV)

This is Hannah's personal song of praise and thanks to God. Her boast is not an improper "Ha! Ha!" to Peninnah, but joyful amazement at the change in her position that God has brought about. Hannah's focus is on God and his salvation. The theme of her prayer and life is this: "God gets the credit for all that is good in my life."

Hannah's prayer also fleshes out why she thinks God is so great, and why he's the center of her life. It's because of who he is, what he does, and where those who belong to him will end up.

- Who is God? He is holy, strong, wise, and fair, beyond measure and without equal.
- What does God do? He exercises control over all on earth because he put it all together. He alone has the power over life and death, over riches and poverty, and over honor and disgrace. He brings down those who are full of themselves and exalts those who are full of him.
- What will the future bring? A righteous kingdom that will prevail against all opposition. It began with the creation of the world. It grew, albeit invisibly to many eyes, during Hannah's life. And it would become more visible and stronger when God's anointed king came to power. The proximal fulfillment of this would be with David, but its ultimate fulfillment would be in Christ.

Pray that you, like Hannah, will build your life around the unchangeable truth of God's character and providence and the sure future that is coming. Pray as well that both your children and others may come to love the Lord and grow in the ways of biblical servanthood.

June 10

A Scarcity of Insight in Israel

Proverbs 29:18

We do not see our signs; there is no longer any prophet,
and there is none among us who knows how long.
Psalm 74:9 (ESV)

Hannah's faith, as shown in her dedication of Samuel to God, is all the more remarkable if you consider the world in which she lived. The last verse of the book of Judges describes that world: "In those days Israel had no king; everyone did as they saw fit" (Judg. 21:25). The people lived largely without reference to the law of God. They were on the verge of reaping the consequences that Joshua warned about many years before: "If you violate the covenant of the LORD your God, which he commanded you, and go and serve other gods and bow down to them, the LORD's anger will burn against you, and you will quickly perish from the good land he has given you" (Josh. 23:16).

The people had access to God's Law and the stories of his gracious work with their ancestors, but they didn't pay much attention. It was as if they had received no revelation from the LORD—the same sort of situation Solomon would refer to in this proverb: "Where there is no revelation, people cast off restraint, but blessed is the one who heeds wisdom's instruction" (Prov. 29:18). God revealed himself and his law for Israel, but it was mostly ignored or rejected. As a result, not many of God's chosen people experienced the blessedness that Hannah found.

In our world too so much blessing awaits those who pay close attention to what God wants and who try to honor him in every part of their lives. But too many either disdain or trivialize God's revelation and cast off all restraint. They do so because they don't want restrictions on their lives but want the freedom to live as they please. However, casting off restraint implies a coming disaster; it leads to what Proverbs 29:18 says in the King James Version: "Where there is no vision, the people perish."

June 11

The Failure of Israel's Priests

1 Samuel 2:12–17, 27–36

Her prophets are fickle, treacherous men; her priests profane what is holy; they do violence to the law.
Zephaniah 3:4 (ESV)

Israel's priests bore at least some of the responsibility for the spiritual conditions among God's people. God gave specific rules about the sacrifices his priests were to bring to him. The Bible uses the term "fat of the land" to describe the required offerings. Literally, this was the fat of the best lambs, but it also symbolized the best of the best. The priests were allowed to eat from the sacrificed animals, but only after the fat was burned as an offering to the LORD. But Eli's sons, Hophni and Phinehas, took the best meat for themselves; "they were treating the LORD's offering with contempt" (1 Sam. 2:17).

Eli's sons also committed adultery with the women who performed some of the tasks around the temple. Although Eli rebuked his sons, he did not exercise proper control over them, and he ate what they ate. God's designated representatives did not fulfill their leadership mandate but instead modeled the popular philosophy that everyone should do as they saw fit. God warned Eli but, when Eli ignored his warning, God promised to make Hophni and Phinehas pay for their contempt with their lives and to make Eli suffer in other ways. God also said that he would raise up a line of faithful priests to serve him.

Do you think the church and its leaders today ever show contempt for God? Do we ever go through the motions of religion, concerned mainly with self-preservation instead of repentance for sin or expectancy for God's work? If so, then just as much as Eli's sons, we show contempt for God's honor and purposes. God will still find a way to advance his kingdom, but the question for us is, "Will we be more like Eli's sons, or like the one whom the LORD was raising up as Israel's prophet and priest—Samuel?"

June 12

Samuel's Growth in Wisdom

1 Samuel 2:18–21, 26

The fear of the LORD is the beginning of wisdom;
all those who practice it have a good understanding.
Psalm 111:10 (ESV)

Scripture says that Samuel grew up in the presence of the LORD. Speaking literally, everyone does this because God is everywhere. But the Bible means to say more than this; it means that even at a young age Samuel drew close to God to love and honor him and to learn how to serve him. He learned to recognize God's way in an evil world and practiced following that way. He did his work so well that Eli gave him a priestly garment to minister in. Although little Samuel was no priest, Eli gave him this linen ephod because he saw that God was with him.

The idea that Samuel did well in God's service is strengthened in verse 26, which summarizes his progress: "The boy Samuel continued to grow in stature and in favor with the LORD and with people." Luke later said something very similar of the boy Jesus. The favor of the LORD is a sign of growth in biblical wisdom, which, in part, is knowing the truth about how things are.

Mere growth in knowledge, however, does not necessarily lead to increased wisdom. Despite a common notion in our world that education is the solution to delinquency, the Bible tells us that the fear of the LORD is the beginning of wisdom. While knowledge is important, it must be integrated with a proper humility before God so that we always come before him in reverence and worship, obedient to his commands. Wisdom involves coming to know the truth and then living according to that truth, both with regard to the LORD and with regard to his world.

That's what everyone in our world needs just as much as did all of the nominally religious people in the days of both Samuel and Jesus. May God grant that we grow in wisdom that so God's favor might be seen more clearly in us and in our world.

June 13

A Call to Service

1 Samuel 3

We are his workmanship, created in Christ Jesus for good works, which God prepared beforehand, that we should walk in them.
Ephesians 2:10 (ESV)

In looking at Samuel's call to service, it is interesting to reflect on how the LORD calls people into his service today. We should note at the outset that God does not merely call those whom we ordinarily label as ministers or missionaries, but also people for every category of service in his kingdom. As to how this call comes, it may be that some still hear something as clear as an audible voice. Many others, however, sense the leading of God through the experiences of their lives and the comments of other people. Some answer God's call quickly while others, like Jonah, run the opposite way until there's no longer any place to go.

Since none of us know in advance how or to what service God will call us, each of us needs to seek to stay close to God through attention to his word and Spirit. We must also develop our ability to serve God while keeping our ears and eyes open to the opportunities he places before us. Then, knowing that he will never lead in a manner contrary to his revealed will, we may say with Samuel, "Speak, for your servant is listening" (1 Sam. 3:10)

When we really hear the LORD and do his will then what Scripture says of Samuel will be true for us too: "The LORD was with Samuel as he grew up, and he let none of Samuel's words fall to the ground" (1 Sam. 3:19). Because Samuel listened carefully to God and did what God wanted him to do, his words were not frivolous or wasted but true and helpful. People could tell that he was a prophet of the LORD and spoke with the LORD's authority. Not everyone liked what he said and did; some still ignored or opposed him. But that wasn't Samuel's problem. Nor is it ours if we follow his example; the LORD will always use true service for his glory.

June 14

The Ark of the Covenant is Captured

1 Samuel 4:1–11

The ark of the covenant...[contained] a golden urn holding the manna, and Aaron's staff that budded, and the tablets of the covenant.
Hebrews 9:4 (ESV)

God's word had been coming to Israel through Samuel for some time and he was recognized as a true prophet. Even so, no one thought to ask him how Israel might prevail in their war with the Philistines. Israel's elders thought they knew what to do; they would take the ark of the covenant into battle because the ark with its contents was the preeminent reminder and symbol of God's presence with his people. As God had told Moses, "There above the cover between the two cherubim that are over the ark of the covenant law, I will meet with you and give you all my commands for the Israelites" (Ex. 25:22).

Consequently, when the ark was brought into Israel's camp, the soldiers were sure that victory was imminent. The noise of their celebration was heard as far away as the enemy camp. The Philistines, having learned the cause for Israel's celebration, became as terrified as Israel had been happy. They remembered the stories of how Israel's God had led his people out of slavery and struck down their enemies. Now that this god had been brought to the battlefield they dreaded what would happen in battle. The Philistine commander did the only thing he could—tried to make his men so afraid of being Israel's slaves that they would fight with desperation, no matter what the odds against them.

That address might afterwards have been acclaimed as the best motivational speech of Philistine history, for the outcome of the battle was shockingly different from what both sides had pictured: Israel's army was slaughtered and its priests killed. Both sides had thought that the LORD was with Israel, but it turned out that he wasn't, as shown by the capture of the ark. How could that be?

June 15

Why the Ark's Presence Didn't Help

1 Samuel 4:12–22

[God] delivered his power to captivity, his glory to the hand of the foe.
Psalm 78:61 (ESV)

Some of you will recall that the Nazis in the movie *Indiana Jones and the Raiders of the Lost Ark* believed that the ark had invincible powers. That was proved when the Nazis finally secured the ark and took off the lid. Then they were consumed by flames and piercing firebolts from inside. The good guys were saved only because they had enough respect and sense to look away.

That, obviously, is not what happened in Israel's battle with the Philistines. The Israelites had forgotten and the Philistines did not know that God cannot be kept in a box. The Philistines moved their gods from place to place, but Israel could not. Their God was the one whose knowledge and omnipotence Samuel's mother had praised when dedicating her miracle child. There was no one else, Hannah said, who could take credit for creating the earth and no one else who would judge the deeds of everyone from one end of the world to the other (1 Sam. 2:3–10).

Israel should have tried to discover what God wanted and then done that. But no one asked God or his prophet Samuel. Nor did they get any good advice from Hophni and Phinehas who, along with Israel's leaders, behaved as though God could be kept in a box and made to obey their wishes. They all forgot that they were servants and that God was in charge. No one considered the central thrust of that book of the Law inside the ark—the need for wholehearted love for God and obedience to him (See one of Moses's sermons on this in Deuteronomy 10:12-22).

Now the nation really was in a desperate way. Eli was shocked and dismayed by the death of his sons, but even more so by the capture of the ark, at which news he fell backward off his chair and broke his neck. As Eli realized, without God he and his people really were doomed.

June 16

God Cannot Be Manipulated

1 Samuel 4

Jesus increased in wisdom and stature and in favor with God and man.
Luke 2:52 (ESV)

The desperate plight of Israel is illustrated in the story of what happened when Eli's pregnant daughter-in-law heard of the ark's capture and the death of the men in her family. She went into labor early and gave birth to a son she named Ichabod, which means "the glory has departed." It was an appropriate way to recognize that, aided and abetted by Israel's disobedient priests, the glory of the LORD had departed from Israel.

It was not that God was compelled to leave the country when the ark was captured by the Philistines; the ark's capture was just symbolic of what had already happened because of disobedience. The leaders of Israel hadn't even considered asking God what he wanted, but assumed that the presence of the ark meant they could do whatever they wanted. Therefore, in contrast to Samuel's God-inspired words, none of which fell to the ground, all of Israel's plans came to nothing. Israel suffered defeat because they did not listen to God or his servant Samuel with the ears of humble servants of God.

More than a thousand years after this abortive attempt to manipulate God, God sent another message of grace in the person of Jesus. He reminded people of God's rigorous requirements, not so they would focus on the minor points of God's law as the Pharisees did, but so they'd understand and remember that God requires devotion that is true and wholehearted, inside and out. Jesus became more than another Samuel who spoke with God's authority; he became the one through whom God boxed himself in, so to speak, making binding promises to those who accept his gift of grace. Apart from this grace our destiny is Ichabod, "the glory has departed." With it our destiny is Immanuel, "God is with us."

June 17

A Caution for Leaders in Christ's Kingdom

Psalm 106

Whoever would be great among you must be your servant,
and whoever would be first among you must be slave of all.
For even the Son of Man came not to be served but to serve,
and to give his life as a ransom for many.
Mark 10:43–45 (ESV)

Positions of authority in the church and elsewhere in society come with a significant risk, that those who have power to say how things will go will forget their own constant need for humility before the LORD and instead seek the power and prestige that comes with authority. It is too easy to forget whose agenda we are to pursue. A sign of this is when we try to get God on our side rather than making sure we're on his side.

It's pretty clear that the first of these is what Israel was attempting by bringing the ark of the covenant into camp. Even if some of Israel's priests and leaders started off with the right perspective and motives, they began to look at the service of the LORD as a way to gain power and privilege. But, of course, it was never their desires, programs, plans, and leadership that needed to be served. Titles, forms, and arks mean nothing if God is not served. How much Israel's leaders could have used the humility and devotion to God that is displayed in Psalm 106. Note particularly the confession of sin expressed in verse 6 and the confession of failure to wait for God's counsel expressed in verse 13.

We must never forget whose kingdom it is, nor that everyone in God's kingdom is called to humble service while living constantly by the instruction and admonition of the Word. Those servants who are called to leadership must pay all the closer attention to this. We can accomplish absolutely nothing of value in God's kingdom without his direction and strength. He will not follow us; rather we must follow him if we are to gain the victory over Satan and his hosts. It's only as we submit to God that we are assured of his presence and blessing.

June 18

Ichabod Reversed

1 Samuel 5–7

Be exalted, O God, above the heavens! Let your glory be over all the earth!
Psalm 108:5 (ESV)

The Philistines scored a great triumph with the capture of the ark but got more than they bargained for when they put the ark in the temple of their god. Within two days, Dagon fell off his perch twice, the second time breaking off his head and hands. The ark was moved to Gath, but the people there developed tumors. A similar thing happened at Ekron, but with much death. Finally, the Philistines decided to send the ark laden with gifts back to Israel. They used two cows that left their calves behind, thus proving the LORD's hand in what had happened, and took the ark straight to its destination.

God did not act only against the Philistines. He also put to death seventy Israelites who dared to get too familiar with the ark of the LORD as it was being returned to its proper place. This was not, as previously thought, because there was some power inherent in the ark. It was rather a severe object lesson illustrating the holiness of God, who had accommodated himself to live with his people by giving them a holy priesthood and precise rules for them to follow. These events made quite an impression on the people; they heeded Samuel's call to fasting and repentance and for some time thereafter served the LORD alone, giving him the reverence they owed him.

The Philistines continued their periodic attacks over the next twenty years but didn't have much success. As long as Samuel lived, the LORD led Israel to victory against the Philistines. Israel even retook the towns that had been captured. The people submitted themselves to the leadership of Samuel, prophet of the LORD. The glory of the LORD that had previously departed the land (as commemorated in the naming of Ichabod) was now back for all to see.

June 19

The People Ask for a King

1 Samuel 8; Deuteronomy 17:14–20

[The king] shall read in [the Law of God] all the days of his life, that he may learn to fear the LORD his God by keeping all the words of this law and these statutes, and doing them.
Deuteronomy 17:19 (ESV)

The life path taken by Samuel's sons was a sad reprise of that taken earlier by Eli's sons; they took bribes and perverted justice. It makes me wonder if there was a problem with the parenting of Eli and Samuel. Perhaps they bore no blame; after all, children will make up their own minds about whether to serve God or themselves. But it at least bears notice that godly parents must do everything in their power to help their children make their own commitment to love and serve the LORD.

The failure of Samuel's sons was partly why Israel's leaders asked Samuel to appoint a king over them. That appeal, however, broke with the long-standing tradition of Israel being ruled directly by God himself using priests and prophets who did nothing on their own, but sought his will in every decision.

Samuel did not like the request, taking it to be a rejection of the kingship of the LORD. At God's command, Samuel warned the people about the problems of having a king like the other nations. But the people had made up their minds, convinced that a king, with all of the accoutrements of his office, would raise their status among their neighbors. They may have been correct in this. However, the danger was that with a king the people would become even less bound to God and his word.

God was not unalterably opposed to the appointment of a king for Israel; he had spoken to Moses about this long before. But he also had warned that such a king was to revere the LORD and closely follow the words of his law. So it was with this understanding that the LORD told Samuel to listen to the request of the people that they be given a king.

June 20

Saul Anointed as Israel's King

1 Samuel 9–11

You...shall anoint them and ordain them and consecrate [Aaron and his sons], that they may serve me as priests.
Exodus 28:41 (ESV)

The LORD revealed the identity of Israel's new king to Samuel through a series of miraculous coincidences. Saul certainly seemed to be the perfect king for Israel; Scripture emphasizes both his physical impressiveness and his humility. So, at the LORD's command, Samuel anointed him with oil.

Anointing with oil had long been part of life in the ancient world; oil mixed with perfume was used on special occasions for personal grooming and for showing honor to guests. It had a more important place in sacred rituals. Robertson Smith writes in the International Standard Bible Encylopedia article on anointing that sacred anointing originated in the ancient custom of smearing the best parts—the fat—of the sacrificed animals on the altar. This helps explain the Scriptural assessment of Eli's sons; their seizure of the meat of the sacrificed animals before the fat was burned off constituted contempt for the LORD's offering (see 1 Sam. 2:15–17).

Up until this point in Israel's history, the sacred ritual of anointing with oil was used to mark Israel's priests, along with the tabernacle and its furnishings, as set apart for the service of God. Now, in this anointing ceremony, Samuel marked Saul as set apart for God's service in the office of king. Saul was confirmed as God's choice when, shortly after, the Spirit of the LORD came upon him in power, enabling him to prophesy with the prophets of God.

Before Saul's coronation the Spirit of the LORD again came upon him in power, this time to enable him to unify the tribes of Israel to meet the threat posed by the Ammonites. It was an auspicious beginning for this new period in the life of God's people.

June 21

Warnings and Signs of Trouble

1 Samuel 12:1–13:15

Strive...for the holiness without which no one will see the Lord.
Hebrews 12:14 (ESV)

Like Moses and Joshua before him, Samuel called Israel together for a farewell speech. In it he emphasized the great mercy shown by the LORD in that God had not given them the punishment they deserved for all their sins, including the sin of asking for a king in place of God's direct rule. Samuel concluded with an admonition and a warning—that they serve the LORD with all their hearts or else be swept away, together with their king, for their persistent sinfulness.

Shortly after this, Saul's willingness to serve the LORD was tested. Saul's anxiety is not difficult to understand. The army was very afraid of an impending attack by the Philistines, and Saul realized that he must make a move soon or his men might desert. But he couldn't attack before Samuel the prophet came to offer the pre-battle sacrifices that demonstrated Israel's dependence on the LORD.

Saul probably wanted to do the right thing. But when Samuel didn't show up at the expected time, he took matters into his own hands and made the offering himself. In doing so Saul took upon himself more responsibility than his office allowed. He forgot for whose service he had been anointed and decided that for the sake of his own success he would violate God's law.

Saul showed disdain for the elaborate provisions God had made to live with his people. God had provided a holy priesthood and a holy tabernacle with holy furnishings together with repeated warnings, most recently in Samuel's farewell speech, to pay close attention to his laws. But Saul seems to have abandoned the humility he had in the beginning. Nor did he repent when confronted by Samuel, but offered excuses instead. It was an ominous sign of things to come.

June 22

Jonathan's Unusual Faith

1 Samuel 13:16–14:12a

We look not to the things that are seen but to the things that are unseen. For the things that are seen are transient, but the things that are unseen are eternal.
2 Corinthians 4:18 (ESV)

Prior to Saul's disobedient sacrifice he was facing the Philistines with an army of three thousand men and few, if any, chariots. It's no wonder that he'd been anxious then, for the Philistines vastly outnumbered the Israelite army and had three thousand chariots, which were the ancient equivalent of the modern tank. Things soon deteriorated even more, and Saul's army was reduced to six hundred men. Moreover, except for Saul and Jonathan, none of them had the iron sword or spear that every Philistine soldier possessed. It was truly an impossible situation, and the Israelites were hiding in the hills and caves, frightened and faithless.

However, in the midst of Israel's predicament, Jonathan had a different perspective—that numbers were nothing to the LORD. The "uncircumcised fellows" label that he applied to the Philistines was already evidence of his faith, for he understood that circumcision was a sign and seal of God's covenant with Israel. By implication, then, it was also a sign that the Philistines, who had not covenanted with the LORD, had no valid claim to the land.

Jonathan's armor bearer didn't have had a lot of choice in the matter, but it appears that he shared his master's perspective. All of Israel's soldiers had been circumcised, but only these two had the faith to see what this meant. They remembered what King Saul seems to have forgotten: It's what the LORD wants that matters. God's chosen people did not need to fear their enemies but to follow Samuel's counsel to fear the LORD and serve him faithfully with all their hearts. Apparently, that's just what Jonathan had been doing, and here too in this difficult situation he determined to proceed in faith.

June 23

The LORD Makes Israel Victorious

1 Samuel 14:12b–23

The horse is made ready for the day of battle,
but the victory belongs to the LORD.
Proverbs 21:31 (ESV)

It isn't easy to translate faith into action; fears pile up the most at the point of action. Sure, Jonathan got the sign that he asked the LORD for, but he might have second-guessed it. Moses had not been content with only one sign from the LORD (see Ex. 4). And neither had Gideon (see Judges 6:36–40). However, with the confidence that victory rests with the LORD, Jonathan and his armorbearer immediately acted upon what they saw God calling them to do.

Jonathan didn't even have his sword out; he needed both hands and feet for climbing. But faith overcame fear, and they finally made it to the top. And then God gave him and his armorbearer a great victory. Amazing! Twenty well-armed men overpowered by two with only one sword between the two of them. What would have happened, I wonder, if Jonathan had not been close enough to God to act upon the reality that he saw by faith?

It was not Jonathan's faith that delivered Israel. But God certainly used Jonathan and his faith and, in the process, renewed the faith and spiritual vision of a nation. Previously, while Jonathan and his armorbearer were clambering up the steep slopes to answer God's call to action, the rest of Israel's army was shivering in dread anticipation of what the Philistines would do next. But the consequences of Jonathan's faithful obedience suddenly made things very clear for them. They didn't even need eyes of faith, for what they saw physically corresponded to reality. Those outside-of-the-covenant intruders, those uncircumcised fellows, were on the run. The panic of the Philistines, together with the ensuing devastation of their army, was God's doing. It was the LORD who rescued Israel that day.

June 24

Saul's Foolish Oath

1 Samuel 14:24–52

The lips of the righteous feed many, but fools die for lack of sense.
Proverbs 10:21 (ESV)

Saul repeatedly wavered between seeking his own glory and that of the LORD. On this occasion he failed to recognize just how completely indebted he was to God for Israel's victory over the Philistines. As a result, he was not content simply to take advantage of the opportunities God put before him, but foolishly bound his army with an oath that they must not eat until victory was complete.

What Saul did not know, however, was that he thereby condemned his own son; Jonathan had not heard of his father's oath and had regained some energy by eating honey he had found. How ironic that the life of the one whom the LORD had most used to give Israel the victory over their enemies was endangered by the one who benefited most from that victory. Jonathan later had to be rescued from the hand of his own father.

In certain respects Saul still seemed to want to follow the LORD; he told his men not to sin against God by eating meat with blood in it. He knew what God had told Moses, "It is the blood that makes atonement for one's life" (Lev. 17:11).

The king's concern for law-keeping was correct. But he should have remembered another law too: "If anyone thoughtlessly takes an oath to do anything, whether good or evil (in any matter one might carelessly swear about)... when anyone becomes aware that they are guilty in any of these matters, they must confess in what way they have sinned (Lev. 5:4–5).

Saul himself had been partly to blame for the impatience his hungry and exhausted men showed in improperly draining the blood of the butchered animals. He would have done well to confess his own foolishness and mixed motives.

June 25

Saul Rejected as King

1 Samuel 15

For I desire steadfast love and not sacrifice,
the knowledge of God rather than burnt offerings.
Hosea 6:6 (ESV)

In one of Israel's celebrations of Saul's kingship, Samuel warned: "Be sure to fear the LORD and serve him faithfully with all your heart; consider what great things he has done for you. Yet if you persist in doing evil, both you and your king will perish" (1 Sam. 12:24–25).

Saul's declining willingness to serve faithfully is illustrated in this chapter. He got a clear command from the LORD to attack and totally destroy the Amalekites, together with all they owned. This was consistent with the repeated instructions of God regarding this nation; Moses had reviewed them in some of his final words to Israel: "When the LORD your God gives you rest from all the enemies around you in the land he is giving you to possess as an inheritance, you shall blot out the name of Amalek from under heaven. Do not forget!" (Deut. 25:19).

But, Saul had what he thought was a better idea. He kept the Amalekite king alive and decided to destroy only the poorest of the animals. Saul's rationale with Agag was unclear, but his ostensible reason for keeping the best animals was so they might be sacrificed to the LORD. Whether or not Saul was sincere in this is beside the point. Samuel later put it to Saul like this in an often quoted nugget of Scripture: "To obey is better than sacrifice, and to heed is better than the fat of rams" (1 Sam. 15:22).

The LORD took Saul's actions to be a rejection of him. Saul repented, but the LORD rejected him as Israel's king. Leaders in God's kingdom are especially responsible for the quality of their obedience. Saul's sin is equally important for all of us to avoid. Those who compromise and rationalize in their obedience to God are not faithful and trustworthy servants.

June 26

David Anointed to be King

1 Samuel 16

The LORD has sought out a man after his own heart, and the LORD has commanded him to be prince over his people.
1 Samuel 13:14 (ESV)

Soon after God rejected Saul as king, Samuel was instructed to anoint one of Jesse's sons to succeed him. Samuel was hesitant about this call to anoint Saul's replacement, fearing that if the king found out he would have Samuel killed. Nevertheless, he proceeded by inviting Jesse to join him in making a sacrifice to the LORD. There, Samuel was impressed by Jesse's oldest son. But here again, as happened so often in redemptive history, the LORD's choice was the unexpected one. In fact, Jesse's youngest son was the last one that Jesse and Samuel considered. Not that something was lacking in David's character or appearance; it was just that to human eyes he was not as well suited as his older brothers for this important position. But the LORD saw something that others didn't see nearly as well; he saw David's heart.

David had a few things Saul lacked, among them a persevering faith in God and concern for God's honor and law. David wasn't perfect, of course; to the contrary he would do some very shameful things. But he always repented of his sin and came back to the LORD. The essential thing about David, unlike Saul who did pretty much as he wanted when he thought he could get away with it, was that he always returned to do what the LORD wanted him to do. Paul testifies to this in Acts 13:22, referring to 1 Samuel 13:14. What God wanted more than anything was to live with his people. As king, David would show his concern for this by preparing to build a temple for the LORD in Jerusalem.

God confirmed his selection of David by filling him with his Spirit from the day of his anointing. Afterwards, David grew in the power of the Spirit while Saul succumbed more and more to the influence of a different spirit.

June 27

David and Goliath—Part 1

1 Samuel 17:1–37

Some trust in chariots and some in horses,
but we trust in the name of the LORD our God.
Psalm 20:7 (ESV)

There had already been many battles in the ongoing war between Philistia and Israel. Here again their armies assembled to fight although neither side was pressing the battle. Israel certainly had reason to fear the better equipped Philistines with their iron weapons of war and the intimidating Goliath. But the Philistines remembered their losses against Samuel (1 Sam. 7:13) and Saul (1 Sam. 14:22–23, 47). This time, however, they appeared to be as sure of victory as the Israelites were fearful of defeat.

Then David appeared in camp. He was less impressed with the formidable Goliath than he was astonished by the giant's willingness to defy the armies of the living God. He was taken aback as well by the criticism he got for his observation—and rightly so. For if God was as irrelevant in this battle as everyone seemed to think, then Israel was in deep trouble indeed.

Of all of the people in Israel, David had the faith to remember who God was—the Creator and true Master of heaven and earth. And of all the people in Israel, David remembered God's promises and believed that what God wanted would actually be done. He had already seen God at work in the desperate situations of his own young life—in the success God had given him against the predators of his sheep. And he had no doubt that God would do the same here with this giant predator of God's people.

For this perspective and for what would follow, David is often portrayed as a great hero and model for us. However, his faith and courage, though exemplary, points us to the real hero of the story—the living God. David knew that God would vindicate trust in his goodness and power by delivering Israel from this current threat.

June 28

David and Goliath—Part 2

1 Samuel 17:38–58

For not in my bow do I trust, nor can my sword save me.
But you have saved us from our foes.
Psalm 44:6–7a (ESV)

Having no other options, Saul accepted David's proposal that he take on the champion of the Philistines. Saul then unsuccessfully tried to dress David in his personal armor. Afterwards, David went down into the valley to meet Goliath armed only with his shepherd's staff, slingshot, and rocks from the stream bed.

Goliath could not believe his eyes and swore by his god to make short work of this foolish boy. David responded to him with a Holy Spirit–inspired statement of faith that by day's end everyone would recognize the supremacy of the God of Israel. And with what happened next, everyone did. When the Philistines saw their champion killed they suddenly knew the hopeless panic that Israel had previously felt. Israel's army, in turn, found the courage to hand the Philistines a terrible defeat.

The events of that day set the stage for the transition of power from Saul to David—a significant advance in the realization of God's purposes for his chosen people. It is as God had told their forefathers long before: "Although the whole earth is mine, you will be for me a kingdom of priests and a holy nation" (Ex. 19:5–6). In other words, the vindication of David's trust in the LORD helped Israel better recognize its task to give a witness to the rest of the world of God's sovereign power and glory.

That witness would be frustratingly inadequate. Still, what happened with David and Israel was a taste of the greater salvation and fulfillment of God's purposes that would come through Jesus Christ and his church—whom Galatians 6:16 calls the "Israel of God." As with David and Israel, we still face many threats, but we may do so with even greater assurance that God will have his way and achieve all of his purposes in this world and the next.

June 29

Preparation for Service

1 Samuel 16:13; 17:34–37

It is God who…has anointed us, and who has also put his seal on us and given us his Spirit in our hearts as a guarantee.
2 Corinthians 1:21b–22 (ESV)

As we've noted before, the primary focus of Scripture in this story is less on David than on the LORD. Even so, it is worthwhile to note the ways in which David was prepared for service to God; these are instructive for us as well.

First, David was anointed by Samuel for the kingship of Israel. The anointing that happened with him happens even more fully with every believer today; we too are anointed by God so that his Holy Spirit resides with and in us. This is the same Holy Spirit who came upon David in power enabling him for service. The power of God's Spirit is essential for the spiritual warfare to which all of God's children are called. Paul addresses this matter of the Spirit's enablement in Ephesians 6.

Second, although David would become famous for his exploits, he was prepared for service to God by his faithfulness in the routine tasks of ordinary life. In the menial tasks of a shepherd David gained the experience and skills necessary to help him defeat Goliath. Years of training in obscurity are what most people need to help them acquire the courage and skills for success in meeting bigger and more public challenges.

Third, there is David's faith and devotion to the law of God. This becomes clearer in the Psalms he wrote. It is also evident in the astonishment he expressed on this occasion, that anyone should dare to defy the living God, and in his attribution of his success as a shepherd to God's enablement.

It took all of these things—God's anointing, practicing and training in obscurity, and learning to know and love the law of God—to prepare David for the service to which God called him. Such things are essential for us as well.

June 30

Saul's Envy of David

1 Samuel 18

Righteousness guards him whose way is blameless,
but sin overthrows the wicked.
Proverbs 13:6 (ESV)

After the victory over Goliath and the Philistines, Israel's dominance continued, often with David as the most successful of Saul's commanders. David's victories were good for Saul. And yet, it troubled the king deeply when he heard the songs comparing his own successes to the greater successes of David.

At the same time, Saul depended on David for the music that could soothe his troubled spirit. In his better moments Saul appreciated David, but in his worse ones envied and hated him, even trying to kill him on certain occasions—when an evil spirit came upon him. (By the way, this puzzling statement about an evil spirit from the LORD does not mean that evil can be traced back to God, but simply that all spirits are subject to the sovereign God, and nothing can happen without God's permission.)

Saul hoped that the problem of David's popularity might eventually be solved by David's death in battle with the Philistines. The offer of his oldest daughter Merab was an attempt to obligate David to continue to expose himself to danger in Saul's service. When that marriage fell through, Saul offered David another daughter, even while hoping that he would be killed in his attempt to fulfill the dowry that Saul required.

Contrary to Saul's hopes, David did not die, but returned with proof of double the required number of Philistines killed. Saul had no choice but to keep his word. But his resentment grew and, except for brief periods, for the rest of his life he considered David his enemy. Saul's envy of the one whom God had chosen to replace him represented a persistent rebellion against God himself. Saul's real enemy was the LORD against whom he sinned and to whose will he refused to submit.

July 1

David's Friend Jonathan

1 Samuel 19–20

A friend loves at all times, and a brother is born for adversity.
Proverbs 17:17 (ESV)

When David came to court following his defeat of Goliath, Jonathan not only celebrated his victory, but made a covenant of friendship with him and gave him clothes and other symbols of his own authority (see 1 Sam. 18:3–4). When Jonathan's father Saul later became upset by the repeated successes of David against the Philistines, Jonathan never shared his father's concern to preserve his own status. Even though he was the next in line to the throne, he became David's advocate. That's because, as with his own success against the Philistines (see 1 Sam. 14:12), Jonathan attributed David's victories to the LORD.

Jonathan went beyond this too. At considerable risk to himself, he tried to allay Saul's concerns and secretly helped David evade capture. Jonathan only narrowly avoided being killed by his own father for his outspoken support for David. He had such fierce anger and deep grief over Saul's conduct in this matter that he didn't eat for the rest of that day. It was not that he felt sorry for himself, although no son should ever be so mistreated by his father. Rather, Jonathan's anger and grief was over his father's shameful treatment of David; he saw Saul's behavior as sad evidence of his rebellion against God and his lack of God's Spirit.

Along with Joseph, Jonathan is one of the few biblical characters Scripture has nothing negative to say about. As with Joseph, Jonathan consistently tried to follow the leading of the one he knew to be sovereign. He was content with the LORD's choices about his future and the future of his people. He was unwilling to assume the prerogatives of power if it meant acting with injustice or going against what God wanted. Jonathan knew that meaning in life comes not by way of power, wealth, or fame, but from faithful service to God.

July 2

On the Run—Part 1

1 Sam 21:1–9; 22:6–23

You love evil more than good...
I trust in the steadfast love of God for ever and ever.
Psalm 52:3, 8 (ESV)

Following his escape with Jonathan's help, David spent the next few years trying to avoid capture and death. Over time he became the leader of a few hundred men who were in similar straits or discontented with Saul for other reasons. But he began virtually alone, with neither provisions nor weapons. His first stop was at the house of Ahimelech the priest, who had no food except for some bread that had been consecrated as an offering to God. In view of the emergency, Ahimelech gave it to David along with the sword of Goliath that had been in safekeeping with him.

One of Saul's men, Doeg the Edomite, saw the transaction and later reported it to gain favor with the king. Ahimelech had not known that David was a fugitive; nevertheless, Saul held him accountable for aiding an enemy and ordered his execution. To their credit, Saul's guards were not willing to kill a priest of the LORD, but Doeg did not share their scruples. He killed Ahimelech together with the other priests of Nob, as well as the citizens of the town; only one priest escaped. It was both an atrocity for which Saul was guilty, and the fulfillment of God's judgment against the house of Eli, as prophesied by Samuel (see 1 Sam. 2:33).

This was the beginning of a very dark time for David who felt some responsibility for the massacre. In Psalm 52 he expresses his hope that the LORD will call Doeg to account for the evil he has done. David speaks of the laughter of the righteous at the prospect of this judgment. It's not selfish revenge that David wants, but he wants God to make things right, for God's honor is at stake. Indeed, it is right for all God's people to pray that in the end God will vindicate his honor and make things right—judging evil and rewarding righteousness.

July 3

On the Run—Part 2

1 Sam 21:10–22:5; 23:1–29

Strangers have risen against me; ruthless men seek my life…
Behold, God is my helper; the LORD is the upholder of my life.
Psalm 54:3, 4 (ESV)

David thought that he didn't have many good options for escaping capture. At first he went to Philistine territory, feigning insanity to escape imprisonment or death. Then he went to Moab until a prophet of the LORD told him to go back home. There it became clear that David had a real heart for his people and didn't blame them for Saul's persecution. He even wanted to risk himself in the defense of Keilah against the Philistines and asked the LORD for permission to do so. His men made him get double confirmation from the LORD on this matter, but then agreed. David and his men defeated the Philistines and saved the town.

Saul heard about what happened and went to Keilah to capture David. David went back to the LORD to inquire whether he could count on the people he had saved to protect him and his men. When told that they would betray him, he left for the Desert of Ziph. There Jonathan secretly met David to renew their covenant and encourage him to keep trusting in God.

That undoubtedly made David feel better until he heard that the Ziphites also planned to betray him to Saul. In fact, he would have been captured then if Saul had not needed to respond to a more immediate threat from the Philistines. David penned Psalm 54 as an expression of his distress. Here again he asked that the LORD would vindicate him by judging evil and saving his life.

Since then, many others who have likewise been betrayed or abandoned have used this Psalm in their own prayers. Often there is little else we can do in such situations than bring all of our problems to the one who both Scripture and experience tell us will be sure to help because it's in his character to save those who love and trust in him.

July 4

Waiting for God's Timing

1 Samuel 24; 26

When he was reviled, he did not revile in return; when he suffered, he did not threaten, but continued entrusting himself to him who judges justly.
1 Peter 2:23 (ESV)

The psalms that David wrote during his years of exile suggest that he was content to wait for God's timing in the matter of his restoration to his homeland. Certainly that was true of David's best impulses as illustrated in the events of these chapters.

Twice David had the opportunity to deal with Saul in the way that Saul had been attempting to deal with him. The first time, David was deep in the cave into which Saul had come alone to relieve himself. It was his chance to kill Saul and seize the throne that God had promised him. But David did not dare harm the one whom God had anointed as Israel's king; he even felt guilty for cutting off a piece of Saul's robe. Another time David sneaked into Saul's camp while Saul and his men lay sleeping. But here again he refused to kill the king, and only took Saul's spear and water jug to prove that he had been there.

Both times when David revealed to Saul that he had not taken advantage of his opportunities for revenge, Saul was shamed by his distrust and aggression against David. The first time, in a moment of honesty, Saul even admitted that he knew that God had chosen David to be king. He asked David to swear that when he became king he would not take the expected action of killing off Saul's descendants. The second time Saul expressed remorse again and promised never again to try to harm David. However, David knew better than to trust Saul's promise, and on both occasions each man went his own way.

David's distrust would be proved right. Even so, he was content to wait for God to fulfill the promises made at his anointing. As with the Christ to come, David entrusted himself to him who judges justly.

July 5

Impatience with God's Timing

1 Samuel 25

Wait for the LORD and keep his way,
and he will exalt you to inherit the land.
Psalm 37:34 (ESV)

David was not always as content to wait for God to give him justice as he had demonstrated in his two personal encounters with Saul. While living in the Desert of Maon he and his men were not far from the property of Nabal in Carmel. As Nabal's servants later testified, David and his men treated them well and protected them from the predations of others. Yet, when David sent men to politely ask for some payment for services rendered, Nabal, whose name means "fool," insulted them and intentionally slighted David by questioning his lineage.

David was furious and prepared to kill Nabal and all his servants. It was a rash decision made in the heat of the moment, as David himself later confessed. His vengeance was averted only by the quick thinking of Nabal's much wiser and more gracious wife, Abigail, who intercepted David with apologies and gifts. With this, David, who seemed to have forgotten his desire to let God vindicate him, withdrew, expressing his regrets and thanking God for Abigail's good judgment. A few days later, God himself put Nabal to death; David would later marry his widow.

God continued to preserve David in the time that remained before until Saul's death. Some of David's decisions were questionable during this time. One was his decision to seek refuge with the Philistines (see 1 Sam. 27). Nevertheless, God used David and his men to meet the threat to Israel posed by the Amalekites (see 1 Sam. 30). As an added benefit, David used the plunder from his victories to enlarge his base of support among the towns of Judah. The LORD came through on his promises to David, not because David's actions were always blameless, but because God always keeps his promises.

July 6

Saul's Decline and End

1 Samuel 28:3–24, 31

"In returning and rest you shall be saved; in quietness and in trust shall be your strength." But you were unwilling.
Isaiah 30:15 (ESV)

The downward spiral of Saul's life seems to have begun when he refused to destroy the Amalekites as the Lord had commanded. For that rejection of the word of the LORD, Saul was rejected as king over Israel (1 Sam. 15:26). Even so, Saul could have repented. He could also have repented on any further occasion when the signs of envy and other sins rose in him. But any sorrow he felt over sin was temporary at best. He still worshiped God on occasion but his heart was not in it. As 1 Samuel 16:14 puts it, "Now the Spirit of the LORD had departed from Saul, and an evil spirit from the LORD tormented him."

What happened with Saul seems similar to what is spoken of in Romans 1:21–29. Paul uses the phrase "gave them over" three times in the space of a few verses to describe what eventually happens to those who know God but persist in dishonoring him. God gives them over, abandoning them in their foolishness, with the result that they sink ever farther into wickedness.

Saul became more anxious and depressed. David had been a good servant but Saul, in jealousy, repeatedly tried to have him killed. Nor was he above using his own children in his plots, once even threatening to kill the righteous and innocent Jonathan. Saul's spiritual low point came the day before his death when he resorted to a pagan practice that he himself had outlawed: going to a spiritual medium to consult with spirits of the dead. The next day the Philistines defeated Israel's army, and Saul and his three sons died in the battle—Saul by suicide. It was the end of a life distinguished by many failures to obey God—failures that kept Saul from fulfilling his commission to lead Israel in unreserved service to God.

July 7

David's Coronation

2 Samuel 1:1–2:7

O LORD, in your strength the king rejoices, and in your salvation how greatly he exults! You have given him his heart's desire and have not withheld the request of his lips.
Psalm 21:1–2 (ESV)

David might have been expected to receive the news of Saul's death with relief if not joy. It meant that he would no longer have to remain in hiding, but could return to live among his people. The death of Jonathan was a different matter, of course; he was a dear and faithful friend to David, and he would be greatly missed. Still, the death of these two meant that David had a much easier path to the throne.

David's reaction, however, was unexpected for one who had been on the run for so long; he had the Amalekite who had a hand in Saul's death executed. Besides that, he grieved not only over Jonathan, but over Saul as well because of the office that he had held by the appointment of God. David thought more of what these deaths meant for Israel's status among its neighbors than about what they meant for his own future.

The glory of Israel and Israel's God was at risk. The opponents of God and his people were sure to rejoice. David even called for the mountains and the fields of Israel to join him in grieving.

David did not rush home to fill the vacancy left by Saul; here again he showed the patience and willingness to trust that he had shown before in his personal encounters with Saul. David waited, and then, only after the LORD's direction, he went to Hebron to be crowned.

David anticipated the conflict that lay ahead of him. Power transitions are never easy, and in spite of the death of Saul and his closest heir, there were others in the royal family who had aspirations to the throne of Israel. But David knew that he had the LORD's blessing.

July 8

The City of David

2 Samuel 5:1–10

Let my tongue stick to the roof of my mouth, if I do not remember you, if I do not set Jerusalem above my highest joy!
Psalm 137:6 (ESV)

After seven years of war between Saul and David, all of Israel agreed that David was the LORD's choice and united under his kingship (see 1 Chron. 11:2). One of David's first official acts was to lead his army against the Jebusite stronghold of Jerusalem. The Jebusites were confident of their ability to withstand David's siege; they considered their city to be impregnable. But that very quality made it an ideal capital for David, and he found a way to take it, perhaps through the water shaft mentioned in verse 8.

Afterwards, although the LORD had given Israel the whole land, Jerusalem came to be seen as the chief symbol of the fulfillment of God's promises. *Jerusalem* even became a metaphor for the people chosen to be God's treasured possession (see Ex. 19:5).

- Zephaniah 1:12 speaks of the LORD searching Jerusalem with lamps and punishing the complacent—obviously referring to all of God's disobedient people.
- Jesus lamented Israel's sin this way: "Jerusalem, Jerusalem, you who kill the prophets and stone those sent to you, how often I have longed to gather your children together, as a hen gathers her chicks under her wings, and you were not willing" (Matt. 23:37).

At this time, the future looked bright. Jerusalem became the political and spiritual center of a united people; it was known as the city that Yahweh had chosen. Just one place we see this is in Solomon's prayer of dedication for the temple, where he refers to what the LORD had told his father: "I have chosen Jerusalem for my Name to be there" (2 Chron. 6:6). Thus it was that "David became more and more powerful, because the LORD Almighty was with him" (1 Chron. 11:9).

July 9

The Ark Is Brought to Jerusalem

2 Samuel 6

Arise, O LORD, and go to your resting place,
you and the ark of your might.
Psalm 132:8 (ESV)

David knew that the secret to continue to experience the blessings of the LORD on himself and his people was God's presence in their midst. So after his coronation he made plans to bring the ark of the covenant from Kiriath Jearim to Jerusalem. As a sign of the ark's importance, he did this with an army of men and great fanfare. But the transfer did not go off quite as planned.

The ark was transported, as it had been earlier by the Philistines, on a new cart drawn by oxen. That former transfer had gone well until some men of Beth Shemesh looked into the ark and died for their disregard for the honor and respect that God demanded for this sign of his presence. This time too, Uzzah was killed when he dared touch the ark. His intentions were probably good, but his action clearly violated God's command that no one but his priests, the Levites, handle the ark. David became very angry, although it's not clear whether this was at God or at himself for failing to honor God's directions. But a few months later he did things properly, using the Levites to carry the ark with poles on their shoulders as God's law commanded (see 1 Chron. 15:15).

David himself led the celebration, leaping and dancing before the LORD. But not everyone shared his joy; his own wife, Michal, was disgusted by his actions. This was not merely because she thought he did not behave with the dignity of a king. The implication is that she did not share David's heart for God or his desire that Yahweh be an integral part of the life of Israel. So, for refusing to join the celebration of God's presence with his people, Michal suffered the worst indignity possible for a woman of that time; she had no children to the day of her death. She herself became a sign that life is impossible without the LORD.

July 10

David's Concern for God's House

2 Samuel 7:1–2

My soul longs, yes, faints for the courts of the LORD*;*
my heart and flesh sing for joy to the living God.
Psalm 84:2 (ESV)

David had brought the ark of the covenant to Jerusalem but had no permanent home for it. That bothered him, especially as he became less preoccupied with defending Israel against enemies.

David's desire to build a house for God was not unique in his time. Temples of some kind are found in every civilization; they are expressions of the innate human impulse to know and please God. Even apart from God's self-revelation in Scripture, there's a sense in the depths of human souls that there exists one who is far greater, one to whom humanity is responsible for worship and service. People disagree on what God is like, but everyone senses the need to communicate with him. It is just this for which a temple is important. Temples represent a point of contact between God and people; they represent fellowship with the one who is greater than all we see.

Israel, even more than other nations, was interested in fellowship with God; after all, Israel had God's special revelation to illumine their inbuilt impulse to worship. The patriarchs set up sacred places and altars to commemorate the appearances of God. Shechem, Bethel, and Hebron were important because these were the places where God had showed himself.

The idea of a house for God gained traction at the time of the Exodus when God gave instructions for a tabernacle to serve as a meeting place between him and his people. But that had been a temporary provision for a nomadic people; now David wanted something permanent. He certainly knew what his son Solomon would later confess, that the LORD could not be contained in any human structure (1 Kings 8:27). But David was still concerned about the lack of a temple.

July 11

God's Message for David

2 Samuel 7:3–17

We are the temple of the living God; as God has said: "I will make my dwelling among them and walk among them, and I will be their God, and they shall be my people."
2 Corinthians 6:16 (ESV)

When David spoke to Nathan about his desire to build a house for the LORD, the prophet liked the idea and told him to do it. But God gave Nathan a different message that night and he quickly relayed it to David. The message was that God was not upset with the lack of a permanent home. He was more concerned with making a home for his people where they would no longer be disturbed. That was why God had relieved David of his duties as a shepherd of sheep and installed him as the shepherd of God's people. It was under David, God said, that he would his give his people rest from their enemies.

David would have seen this as the fulfillment of God's promise made to Moses and repeated to Joshua after Israel had entered into the Promised Land: "My Presence will go with you, and I will give you rest" (Ex. 33:14). But the most surprising part of God's message was still to come. God told David that instead of receiving a house from him, God would build David a house—a dynasty that would last forever. Furthermore, David's offspring would build the temple that David wanted to build.

David would later see Solomon as the guarantor of his dynasty and the one who fulfilled God's promise. And Solomon did build the temple that David had in mind. But David could not have foreseen an even greater offspring who would himself be the temple of God—the perfect point of contact between God and people (see John 2:19–21). Nor could he have imagined what Scripture claims for the spiritual offspring who comprise Christ's body: "Don't you know that you yourselves are God's temple and that God's Spirit dwells in your midst?" (1 Cor. 3:16).

July 12

A Proper Response to God

2 Samuel 7:18–29

Do you not know that your body is a temple of the Holy Spirit within you, whom you have from God?
1 Corinthians 6:19 (ESV)

Even with the limited perspective he had about what God was promising, David proclaimed his astonishment that the sovereign God would treat him and his family so favorably. He then went on in his prayer to rehearse the great things God had done and was doing for him and for all his people. His prayer concludes with this expression of confidence in God: "With your blessing the house of your servant will be blessed forever" (2 Sam. 7:29).

Let me reiterate that this blessing has come and is coming true through Jesus Christ who is the ultimate offspring of David. The temple that Jesus is building is not a building at all, but a people who are a suitable dwelling place for God. "You also, like living stones, are being built into a spiritual house" (1 Peter 2:5). Since Jesus has an eternal kingship (see Luke 1:32-33), this is a house that will last forever.

We may wonder how the LORD can stand to use us as his house. After all, God's house is supposed to be holy. To be sure, Christ's sacrifice makes people legally righteous and holy before God. But we know that this demands from us a holy lifestyle that proves the reality of our salvation. Besides that, the way that God mediates his blessing to the people of this world is through his house—his self-examined and purified people who minister in Jesus's name, and by the power of his Spirit. We can't limit God's work in this world to what we do, but it is primarily through our lives that God shows his presence in his creation.

Can you believe that God chooses to live in me and you? Can you believe that God chooses to live in your spouse, your family, and your neighbors? We may say in astonishment and gratitude with David, "Who are we that you have brought us this far?"

July 13

David's Victories and Righteous Rule

2 Samuel 9

Keep your heart with all vigilance, for from it flow the springs of life.
Proverbs 4:23 (ESV)

Chapters 8 and 10 describe the consolidation of David's power over the surrounding nations. This is summarized twice in Chapter 8 with these words: "The LORD gave David victory wherever he went." David saw these victories as evidence that God was fulfilling the promises he had given through the prophet Nathan.

Both friends and enemies of David would have expected him to remove internal threats by having Saul's descendants killed. However, David remembered his covenant with Jonathan and also his promise to Saul not to destroy Saul's name or children when he became king (see 1 Sam. 24:21–22). David might have been excused for reneging on his commitment because of the assassination attempt made against him by Saul's son Ish-Bosheth (see 1 Sam. 4:8). But David remained committed to being kind to Saul's family.

When told about Jonathan's son Mephibosheth, David brought him to Jerusalem to be treated like one of his own sons. Mephibosheth was undoubtedly happy not to be killed. He humbled himself, showing David that he knew his place. A few years later, when David came under attack from his son Absalom, Mephibosheth was accused by a servant of harboring the ambition to be king (1 Sam. 16:3), for which David granted his property to the servant. But this was still later proved to be a false accusation (2 Sam. 19:24–30). At that time Mephibosheth declined the king's offer to restore his property, being content to resume his former position at court.

Through the events of this time David mostly behaved as the godly king God had called him to be. However, although it was not yet apparent, future actions would show that he did not take enough care to guard his heart.

July 14

David's Sin

2 Samuel 11

Desire when it has conceived gives birth to sin,
and sin when it is fully grown brings forth death.
James 1:15 (ESV)

We might infer from the way this chapter opens that David should not have been in Jerusalem and living in comfort in his palace, but with his men on the battlefield. However, while we can't know for sure that David had no legitimate reason to stay in Jerusalem, it is clear that his conduct there was dishonorable, to say the least.

It was not the fact that he was tempted one night as he caught a glimpse of a beautiful woman bathing. It was his self-indulgence in giving that first glimpse time to ripen into lust, and then into an invitation that Bathsheba could not have refused. David's conduct was not unusual for a king of that time; he could do as he pleased. But it was especially disgraceful for a king who wanted to serve the LORD God as the head of a nation called to that same purpose.

David knew in his heart that his actions were wrong, but he thought he'd gotten away with his evening tryst until Bathsheba sent word that she was pregnant. That was a problem; Uriah would know that he was not the father for he had been with the army on the field of battle for some time.

So the cover-up began. David recalled Uriah to Jerusalem on a pretext, thinking that he would naturally take the opportunity for a conjugal visit. But Uriah would not in good conscience do this while his men endured hardship on the battlefield. So David took the next step, instructing Joab to put Uriah where the fighting was the worst. There, Uriah was killed just as David hoped. Soon after, the king added Bathsheba to his harem.

Coveting, lust, adultery, lying, and murder—each sin gave rise to others. Plainly, David deserved God's judgment.

July 15

God's Judgment

2 Samuel 12:1–12

God will bring every deed into judgment, with every secret thing, whether good or evil.
Ecclesiastes 12:14 (ESV)

God sent the prophet Nathan to David with words of judgment. Nathan told him a story that would help him realize the enormity of his sin. But, the king didn't recognize himself in the story. In fact, he reacted in righteous indignation against the rich man who had done such a despicable thing. David had rationalized his behavior so much and managed to repress his guilty conscience so well that what Nathan said next came as a total shock to him: "You are the man!"

In earlier days, David had written this of his own mistreatment: "The face of the LORD is against those who do evil, to blot out their name from the earth" (Ps. 34:16). I doubt that David ever dreamed then that he would someday be accused of doing evil. Nor did he dream that the words with which he judged the rich man in the prophet's story would be used against him. But David was guilty of great evil and, as Nathan told him, he was placed under the judgment of God. In mercy, however, God eventually brought one piece of good out of the whole mess—the birth of another son: Solomon.

Are you surprised by how easy it is for us to see David's guilt and yet how far it was from his own mind? If so, do you think that David was unique in his capacity for self-deception? Or could it be that all humans have the same capacity? Don't we also underestimate our own inclination toward sin and evil? For that matter, how can we be surprised by the murders that others carry out when we consider the seeds of murder that live in our own souls? Let us be quick to recognize the sins within that, if given room, will become full grown and death-dealing to both ourselves and others. And let us be wise to deal appropriately with them.

July 16

A Proper Answer for Sin

Psalm 32

If we confess our sins, he is faithful and just to forgive us our sins and to cleanse us from all unrighteousness.
1 John 1:9 (ESV)

It is not unusual for people who are confronted with evidence of their wrongdoing to offer a lame apology rather than a statement of contrition. A lame apology might be followed by a "but" that offers an excuse, or by substituting "I didn't mean it" for "Forgive me." The former suggests that what was said or done was just an excusable slip; the latter says that what was said or done was wrong and asks for the grace of forgiveness.

What is sin anyway, and when does it become bad enough to confess? A popular idea is that sin is just moral blemishes, nothing that requires radical reconstructive spiritual surgery. In a pinch we can compare our own morals and conduct to that of people whose standards are obviously lower, and come off quite well by comparison. You might know people who imagine that God is happy with them just the way they are and wants nothing more than to make them happy with themselves. If that's so, then of course, sin doesn't require any radical solution—nothing like the cross of Christ.

The truth of our moral and spiritual condition is evident when we compare ourselves to Christ. In his light we look awful. Not many of us have grisly crimes as part of our history, but what about all the neglect of the good we're capable of doing? How many more physically, emotionally, and spiritually needy people would be helped and filled with hope if we embraced all the opportunities to do good that God gives us? When we see ourselves in light of Christ, even our best righteousness, the Scripture tells us, is like "filthy rags" (Isa. 64:6). Therefore, it is foolish to offer excuses or try to cover it up. The path of wisdom and life is to confess our sins and ask God for forgiveness.

July 17

David's Repentance

2 Samuel 12:13–25; Psalm 51

Create in me a clean heart, O God, and renew a right spirit within me.
Psalm 51:10 (ESV)

After David's eyes were opened to what he had done, he confessed that he had sinned against the LORD. We see this emphasis also in his expanded confession in Ps. 51.

I don't think we can conclude from David's words that he failed to recognize that he'd also sinned against many people—not only Uriah and Bathsheba, but also the whole nation that he had been called to shepherd. But David came to see what each of us must also see, that every sin is first of all against God. As appropriate as it to confess our sins to each other, and especially to those we've wronged, we must first be reconciled to the holy and righteous God through repentance and confession.

King David was a deeply flawed man. But he was perhaps better than many of us at doing the appropriate thing once his sin was uncovered. He provides a good example of how to respond once the Spirit of God makes clear what has been done. In fact, I think that one of the main reasons that David is called a man after God's heart is his godly sorrow and repentance. He proved willing to admit and confront the sickness in his own soul.

Are you? Have you confessed your need of Christ's forgiveness? With the help of his Spirit do you watch for and regularly confront the continuing sickness to which your soul is prone?

Don't be over-protective of your heart in that regard; at times it will require Holy Spirit surgery. Learn to recognize compromises with sin early and take care of them right away so the compound interest of sin will not surprise you with its awful consequences. Then you will truly be a person after God's own heart and someone who, with God's help, finds victory in the spiritual battles of life.

July 18

David's Children

2 Samuel 13

Teach [my words] to your children, talking of them when you are sitting in your house, and when you are walking by the way, and when you lie down, and when you rise.
Deuteronomy 11:19 (ESV)

In the custom of the kings of his day, David had several wives. This was not by God's will; he had warned that the king must not take many wives (see Deut. 17:17). Although David had a heart for the LORD, one might wonder how many of his family problems were traceable to the difficulties inherent in maintaining a harem and raising the children of multiple mothers.

Two sons in particular caused problems for David. First was Amnon, who raped his half-sister Tamar and then disgraced her even further when he refused to salvage her honor by marrying her. Second was Absalom, brother to Tamar and half-brother to Amnon, who waited for two years and then seized his chance to kill Amnon in revenge for what he had done to his sister. Absalom then fled to avoid punishment for his unlawful action.

When David heard about what Amnon had done he was furious, but unaccountably did nothing about it. His own equivocation may have strengthened Absalom's resolve to seek revenge. When David heard about the revenge murder he was further distressed, although he could not punish Absalom, who had left the country.

We can only wonder to what degree David's own moral failings contributed to his inability to discipline his children and impress God's commandments upon them. Admittedly, it couldn't have been easy to consistently parent and discipline all of his children; I suppose that's part of the reason for God's prescription against multiple wives—even kings must take care that their children are nurtured in the fear of the LORD. To do that, they need close and continuing involvement and interest in their progress and in their discipline.

July 19

Absalom's Rebellion

2 Samuel 15:13–16, 23–26; Psalm 3

I believe that I shall look upon the goodness of the LORD in the land of the living! Wait for the LORD; be strong, and let your heart take courage; wait for the LORD!
Psalm 27:13–14 (ESV)

David grieved over the necessary exile of Absalom But after three years David allowed him to return to Jerusalem, and then, after just two more years, to return to court (see 2 Sam. 14). Absalom, however, had designs on David's throne and over the course of time he won a considerable following among those who felt they had not received justice from the king. Eventually Absalom's support grew to alarm David so much that he gathered some of his supporters and fled the city in fear for his life.

David knew that he was still the anointed king of Israel, something Absalom apparently had little regard for. But Absalom's supporters seemed so many at this time. David speaks of that in Psalm 3, which was written about the difficulties of this very occasion. His many foes thought that his kingship was over. David, however, hoped that the LORD would bring him back to see Jerusalem even though he was ready to accept whatever the LORD would do (see 2 Sam. 15:25–26).

David's flight from Jerusalem wasn't very glorious. His supporters along the path of his journey wept aloud. David himself went up the Mount of Olives barefoot and weeping—mourning with his head covered. How can one rest in such circumstances? But it is David's testimony in the psalm that he does that, and even wakes refreshed because he finds his strength in the LORD.

The psalm also speaks of glory bestowed on him by the LORD. David did not experience that glory in his flight but he was confident that God would be sure to answer his prayers, judging the sinners and delivering the faithful. It's the same confidence in the LORD to which we also are called in all of our difficulties.

July 20

The LORD Works on Behalf of David

2 Samuel 16:15–17:23

If it had not been the LORD who was on our side when people rose up against us, then they would have swallowed us alive.
Psalm 124:2–3 (ESV)

Absalom's chief advisor was Ahithopel. But David's former chief advisor, Hushai the Arkite, sought that same post with Absalom. When questioned about why he hadn't left with David, Hushai said that he wanted to serve the one chosen by God and by Israel. It was a somewhat ambiguous reply, but Absalom considered himself to be the chosen one, so he added Hushai to his staff.

Ahithopel advised Absalom to show his authority by taking over David's harem. He also said that Absalom should move quickly to pursue David and finish him off. Ahithopel's plan was widely supported until Hushai proposed waiting for more soldiers to be mustered. Hushai's advice won the day, with the result that Ahithopel was disgraced and later committed suicide.

What no one knew, however, was that the LORD had sent Hushai to frustrate Ahithopel's good advice in order that Absalom's plans might fail. Hushai contributed further by sending a secret message to David telling him to hurry and leave Israel proper by crossing to the east side of the Jordan. His messengers providentially avoided capture and got the message to David. Once across the river, David went to the city of Mahanaim and gathered supporters in preparation for the coming battle.

Later on, as recorded in 2 Samuel 18, David's army defeated Absalom's. It was a great victory, but it came with great cost, for, contrary to David's instructions, Absalom himself was killed. For a time, David's sorrow over the death of his son overwhelmed his joy at the victory he had prayed for. Joab finally got David's attention only when he warned that he was in danger of losing the support of his army. With that, David again assumed the responsibilities of his position.

July 21

David Returns to Jerusalem

2 Samuel 19:8b–15, 39–20:2

Pray for the peace of Jerusalem! "May they be secure who love you!"
Psalm 122:6 (ESV)

After Absalom was defeated, the northern tribes of Israel, remembering the quality of David's previous leadership, wanted him to resume his rule over the country. David, seeing that they seemed more enthusiastic about this than the members of his own tribe, exhorted the men of Judah to show more initiative in making preparations for his return. This they eagerly did, moving just across the Jordan River to Gilgal, where David waited to be welcomed back into the Promised Land.

This move back into the land was of equal and opposite significance to David's previous departure from the land. At that time, God's promise of perpetual rest from all his enemies seemed very elusive. Now, David's spirits were restored as he anticipated his return to the throne.

David was conducted back into the land by all the men of Judah and half the men of Israel. This became a bone of contention for the Israelites, who thought that Judah had not waited for them because Judah wanted the prestige of being David's primary escorts. They argued about it, the men of Judah touting their kinship with David, and the men of Israel claiming that they were ten tribes as opposed to one, and also that they had been the first to want David back as king.

The argument concluded badly with harsh words between the two factions. As a result, the men of Israel defected for a time. They would return, but resentment within Israel would linger and return with a vengeance years later, at the end of Solomon's life. David would always be regarded as the greatest king of Israel, but not even he had an answer for the spiritual malaise that plagued humankind ever since sin entered the world. That would await the coming of Jesus, the final king of David's line.

July 22

David's Foolish Act of Pride

1 Chronicles 21:1–22:1

When pride comes, then comes disgrace,
but with the humble is wisdom.
Proverbs 11:2 (ESV)

This story differs only slightly from that found in 2 Samuel 24. Both describe David's decision to take a census of Israel. The reasons for God's disapproval are not very clear to us; perhaps after his victories over the Philistines (1 Chronicles 20), David started to believe the press reports about himself and wanted to catalog his power. It was quite clear to Joab that David was desperately wrong in ordering the census; he pled with the king not to bring guilt on Israel by going through with his plans.

However, David insisted and Joab complied. But Joab refused to include the tribes of Levi or Benjamin. The Levites, entrusted to be Israel's priests, had previously been excluded by God from any census (see Ex. 30:12). Joab excluded Benjamin too, perhaps (as noted in the NIV Study Bible) because the tabernacle in Gibeon and the ark in Jerusalem both fell within its borders.

Scripture calls David's command evil, saying that Satan incited him. But, the corresponding account in 2 Samuel 24 says the LORD incited David. This is not to blame the LORD, but is merely a testament to God's sovereignty; not even Satan can act without his permission. In response to David's disobedience, God sent a plague that resulted in much loss of life and even threatened to destroy Jerusalem. Before that, however, God took pity on his people and relented. David and his leaders repented then, and at God's command, secured a property that would eventually serve as the location for the LORD's temple.

It is such a short step from praise to pride—from taking refuge in God to self-satisfaction. It was clear that not even David, whom later generations would extol as a model of service to God, could achieve the perfection and consistency that God demanded.

July 23

David's Rock and Fortress

2 Samuel 22

We have this [confidence that God will honor his promises] as a sure and steadfast anchor of the soul.
Hebrews 6:19 (ESV)

David may have written the words of this song of praise earlier in his life to celebrate his deliverance from Saul. But this song (also found in Psalm 18) was appropriate for this occasion too, near the end of David's forty years as king. He had experienced many difficulties, some of which just came with the territory—Absalom's attempt to kill him and usurp the throne, a revolt led by Sheba, a man of Saul's tribe (2 Sam. 20), a three-year famine (2 Sam. 21:1), and yet another war with the Philistines (2 Sam. 21:15). But David brought some difficulties upon himself, most recently those connected with his census of Israel.

One might think that David would cry, "I can't take any more!" Instead we find a psalm of praise to God, whom he calls his rock and deliverer. David recounts many things that God had done for him, but doesn't say much about the reasons for God's grace. His words in verses 21–28 almost seem to be a boast about his righteousness, as if this had earned him the favor of God. But a better explanation of why God was so gracious is simply that he wanted to be. David says in verse 20, "He rescued me because he delighted in me." And in verse 51 he connects his experience of God's kindness to his anointing by God. David had done nothing to merit God's delight or anointing; he simply reveled in it.

What David is really saying in verses 21–28 is that as one to whom the LORD had shown such favor, he was determined to recognize his total dependence on God and do his best to keep God's ways. He recognized his absolute need to stay close to God. With a few exceptions, he repeatedly called out to God; he repeatedly took refuge in the rock. It was the LORD's favor and the certainty of his promises that was the anchor for David's soul.

July 24

The LORD's Choice to Succeed David

1 Kings 1:1–53; 2:13–25

The LORD loved [Solomon] and sent a message by Nathan the prophet. So he called his name Jedidiah, because of the LORD.
2 Samuel 12:24b-25 (ESV)

The members of David's court knew that Solomon would be the next king. Already at Solomon's birth God instructed that he should also be given the name Jedidiah; this was both a sign of God's favor and an indication to David that here was his dynastic successor. Another confirmation of this is Bathsheba's reference in 1 Kings 1:13 to a previous promise David had made to her about Solomon's future.

In David's delay to make the appointment official, another son—Adonijah—put himself forward as David's successor. As with Absalom, Adonijah surrounded himself with a retinue of men, together with chariots and horses. When David, to his discredit, said nothing, Adonijah went farther, arranging his own coronation ceremony. That he did not invite Bathsheba and Solomon to it is a sign that he knew God's intention, but chose to ignore it.

Bathsheba and Nathan reminded David of his promise regarding Solomon. David agreed and proceeded to make it official. Of course, that left Adonijah and his supporters in fear for their lives. But Solomon showed mercy to Adonijah, requiring only that he make no further attempts to usurp the throne. But Adonijah's promise was a hollow one, which he showed by his request to be given Abishag as his wife. Because she was officially a member of David's harem, Adonijah's request was really an attempt to strengthen his claim to the throne.

Nor was his offense merely against Solomon—it also dishonored the LORD, who had chosen Solomon to be king. Solomon's order to have Adonijah killed, therefore, was not merely a personal vendetta, but a judgment of the LORD upon one who disdained his covenant.

July 25

Solomon's Request and God's Answer

1 Kings 2:1–4; 3:4–28; 4:20–34

The beginning of wisdom is this:
Get wisdom, and whatever you get, get insight.
Proverbs 4:7 (ESV)

Before David died, he gave final instructions to Solomon. His main concern was that his son live and rule according to God's law. But David also asked him to deal with a number of unfaithful men he had not had the heart to discipline. This Solomon did, with the result that his rule over Israel was solidified.

Solomon showed his love for the LORD by his obedience to the Law and by the sacrifices he made. He further showed his heart for God by the request he made when the LORD appeared to him in a dream; he asked for the ability to do what he knew he could not do without God's help—to govern his people with wisdom.

Wisdom is not the first thing people usually think of when told they can have anything they want. For the old and sick the most popular request might be for life and health. Others may desire wealth, power, or fame. But Solomon already showed much wisdom with his request, for wisdom is more important than all the rest. It's what helps people keep first things first. More than anything this involves knowing and doing the will of our Creator and Redeemer. We will lose everything when we die, if not before. But any knowledge and love of God that we gain on earth, we can take with us into eternity.

Everyone in Israel was astonished with the wisdom by which Solomon determined the rightful mother of the baby that two women were fighting over. His reputation spread far beyond Israel. People came from around the world to meet him. He became famous, but even better was the growing fame of the one who had given him such wisdom. Many, like the queen of Sheba, praised God for what he was doing though Solomon (see 1 Kings 10:9).

July 26

Solomon Builds the Temple

1 Kings 6 (2 Chronicles 3)

One thing have I asked of the LORD, that will I seek after:
that I may dwell in the house of the LORD all the days of my life,
to gaze upon the beauty of the LORD and to inquire in his temple.
Psalm 27:4 (ESV)

One of the best things Solomon did as Israel's king was to complete his father's dream of building the LORD's temple. David had wanted it built on a threshing floor on Mount Moriah where the LORD had appeared to him (2 Chron. 3:1). This was also where Abraham, at God's command, had gone to sacrifice Isaac (see Gen. 22:2) and where God had graciously provided a ram to die in his place. It was thus an appropriate building site for the temple, which would serve as the main religious symbol of God's presence with his people.

The careful attention to the plan of the temple, like that of the tabernacle before it, reflected an appropriate concern for God's conditions for dwelling with his people. However, despite the care taken with the materials and workmanship, as was appropriate for this little bit of heaven on earth, the temple remained a poor imitation of the place where God dwells in all his glory. As Hebrews 8:5 puts it: Priests "serve at a sanctuary that is a copy and shadow of what is in heaven."

Before the throne of God in heaven, as it also was in the Garden of Eden before sin, there is nothing to offend God's holiness. Considering both the reality of sin and God's unwillingness to abandon his imagebearers, we may be thankful that in the past God accommodated human sinfulness by arranging for temples and sacrifices. This arrangement, however, was inherently unsatisfactory (see Heb. 10:11–13). It was also temporary, as Paul makes clear in Romans 3:25 when he speaks of God's forbearance in leaving the sins committed beforehand unpunished. However, God's arrangement did anticipate the perfectly satisfactory and once for all sacrifice of Christ.

July 27

The Temple Furnishings

1 Kings 7:13–51 (2 Chronicles 4)

*These are a shadow of the things to come,
but the substance belongs to Christ.*
Colossians 2:17 (ESV)

The temple furnishings, like the temple itself, pointed to a reality beyond themselves. There were many decorations and utensils of gold to indicate the glory that belonged to God. The most important representation of God's glory and presence was the ark of the covenant in the Most Holy Place.

In the temple's holy place were several items of gold: the table for the bread of the presence, the altar of incense, and the lampstands, all of which showed God's willingness to communicate and fellowship with his people. They all anticipate Jesus.

- Jesus is the bread of life, who gives us life and access to God.
- Jesus is the one in whose name our prayers are heard and who constantly intercedes for us before the throne of God.
- Jesus is the light of the world, in whose light we share by virtue of his sacrifice and through the gifts of the Holy Spirit.

In the temple courtyard was the sea, a huge bronze basin supported by twelve bulls. As with the smaller and more portable bronze basin used in the tabernacle, the water of this basin was used by the priests for their ritual cleansing. There were also ten bronze basins with stands for washing offerings. Such cleansing was necessary for Israel to approach the LORD. As imperfect as this cleansing was, it foreshadowed the cleansing that we have obtained through Christ (see Heb. 9:11–14).

Also in the courtyard was a bronze altar for the burnt and fellowship offerings. The sacrifices offered here were necessary because, as God told Moses, "The life of a creature is in the blood, and I have given it to you to make atonement for yourselves on the altar" (Lev. 17:11). Hebrews 9:22 reinforces this emphasis: "Without the shedding of blood there is no forgiveness."

July 28

The Temple Is Completed

1 Kings 8:1–21 (2 Chronicles 5:2–6:11)

Moses was not able to enter the tent of meeting because the cloud settled upon it, and the glory of the LORD filled the tabernacle.
Exodus 40:35 (ESV)

When the temple was completed, Solomon brought the ark of the covenant to it with extravagant celebration and sacrifices—so many that they could not be counted. Knowing what had happened on two previous occasions, Solomon was very careful in the arrangements he made to transport the ark. The priests of Israel carried it according to God's instructions, using long poles strung through rings on the ark (see Ex. 25:15).

This centerpiece of the temple at one time contained a gold jar of manna, Aaron's staff that had budded, and the stone tablets of the covenant (see Heb. 9:4). Now, however, it held only the major sign of the LORD's covenant with his people, the stone tablets inscribed with the Ten Commandments given to Moses. The atonement cover (or mercy seat) of the ark had carved cherubim at either end; they represented the real ones who guarded against Adam and Eve's reentry into Eden after their sin, and still guard access to the throne of God in heaven.

Afterwards the LORD filled the temple with his glory. It was just what had happened in Moses's day when the tabernacle was dedicated. The glory cloud was so thick that the priests could not perform their service. Ezekiel later had a similar experience in a vision (see Ezek. 10:4). And still later, Jesus predicted his own return in a cloud with power and great glory (see Luke 21:27).

Solomon rightly saw the presence of God's glory cloud as confirmation that the LORD really was with his people. God's promise that David's son would build the temple was now fulfilled. Although there was still a more complete fulfillment to come through Christ, this was the high point in the life of Israel under the old covenant.

July 29

Solomon's Prayer of Dedication

1 Kings 8:22–53 (2 Chronicles 6:12–42)

Call upon me in the day of trouble;
I will deliver you, and you shall glorify me.
Psalm 50:15 (ESV)

Solomon's prayer of dedication shows his full awareness that the Almighty God cannot be confined to any earthly dwelling, even such a magnificent one as this. In fact, God cannot even be confined to the highest heavens. Although Solomon makes no mention here of God's creation of the heavens and the earth, he clearly realizes that God is not restricted by created reality, and that he deigns to dwell with his people only by his grace.

Solomon is aware as well of God's faithfulness to his covenant despite the checkered history of Israel's faithfulness to him. It is something for which Solomon is very grateful. And yet, knowing that his own people are likely to forget this awesome and celebrative occasion, he presumes to ask the LORD to honor the future prayers made from this place.

Knowing that people are less likely to pray when things are going well, Solomon asks that God will hear the prayers raised after his people have been judged for disobedience. He speaks of injustice perpetrated within Israel, of defeat by enemies, and of drought, famine, and plague. Solomon knows that these need not happen if the people live by God's laws, but he knows they will happen because of willfulness. He asks that when the people repent, God will listen to their prayers and forgive and restore them.

Nor does Solomon pray only for Israel, for he knows that God's heart for the whole world has prompted his promise that Israel will be a blessing to the nations. So he prays as well for God to hear the prayers of believing foreigners so that the whole world may know and fear the LORD. From beginning to end, Solomon's prayer is one that fits this occasion and honors the LORD who made it possible.

July 30

The Dedication and God's Response

1 Kings 8:62–9:9 (2 Chronicles 7)

I have set before you life and death, blessing and curse. Therefore choose life, that you and your offspring may live.
Deuteronomy 30:19 (ESV)

The dedication of the temple involved still more days of feasting and sacrifice. The parallel passage in Chronicles says that God's power was manifested in the fire that fell from heaven and consumed the sacrifices. Again, the glory of the LORD so filled the temple that the priests were hampered in their duties. For two weeks the people celebrated, and then Solomon sent them home. They were overwhelmed with joy for the good things the LORD had done for his people.

Later, the LORD appeared to Solomon in a vision with an answer to his prayer of dedication. In an earlier vision, Solomon received the gift of wisdom. This time as well, God responded positively. He promised an enduring kingdom if Solomon would continue to walk with him in integrity and with a pure heart.

But as God did so often before in his long history with Israel, along with the words of blessing he warned of the curses that would befall outright disobedience or even any negligence of true worship. God said that disobedience would make Israel an object of ridicule among the nations and it would make his temple as unimpressive as it was now imposing. In that case Israel could not possibly be a blessing to the nations.

2 Chronicles 36 tells of Israel being in the very predicament God had warned against. By this time God's laws had been neglected for many years, including his commands about keeping him first and about Sabbath rests for the land. Finally, for mocking his messengers, despising his words, and rejecting his prophets, God handed Israel over to the Babylonians who, after confiscating its treasures, set fire to the temple. Only then did the land enjoy its Sabbath rests, which had been neglected for so long.

July 31

The Way Back to God

2 Chronicles 7:14

You are the salt of the earth... You are the light of the world.
Matthew 5:13, 14 (ESV)

This part of God's answer to Solomon's prayers is one of the most beloved of God's pledges in Scripture and is profitable for his people of every time and place. It presumes a failed love relationship with God and the inevitable experience of the disintegration that follows sin.

2 Chronicles 7:14 says that restoration is possible; it begins with a humble willingness to face the pain of self-examination and to confess sinful pride. All evil has its root in pride, the unwillingness to give God the central place that he deserves in our lives. It is a humble spirit that helps us deal with the root sin of pride and position ourselves to submit to God's rule in our lives.

Prayer is the expression of such humility of heart. In prayer, humility of attitude becomes an action of faith. True prayer by its very nature demonstrates humble dependence on God. If done persistently in a life open to examination and correction, it transitions into what Scripture calls "seeking God's face."

Repentance must inevitably follow. This is not merely an awareness of sin or a change in attitude; that has already been manifested in humility and prayer. Repentance is turning from evil ways to walk in God's way; it is a change in behavior.

Although God's prescription is of value to all people, he addresses it to those he calls his own—to Solomon and all of Israel. But it also applies in a particular way to followers of Jesus today. We have been called by God to love him and serve our world, but the first and most important thing to do is to let him make us what we should be. When we, individually and communally, follow God's turnaround steps, not only will God forgive and restore us; he will use us to bless and heal our world.

August 1

The Beginning of Wisdom

Proverbs 1:1–7

Behold, the fear of the LORD, that is wisdom,
and to turn away from evil is understanding.
Job 28:28 (ESV)

Solomon was renowned for his wisdom, some of which is found in Scripture; he wrote much of Proverbs, and most theologians also attribute the Song of Solomon and Ecclesiastes to him. In these books are found many wise sayings and proverbs about human behavior and how one ought or ought not live. However, they are not laws like the Ten Commandments, which always need to be obeyed. Some proverbs are universally true. But others are more like stereotypes and don't fit every occasion; what is wisdom in one situation may be inappropriate for another. So besides knowing a proverb, you have to know when to use it. Even so, the Bible's wisdom is inspired and "useful for teaching, rebuking, correcting and training in righteousness" (2 Tim. 3:16).

Solomon's introduction to Proverbs indicates the kind of help he hopes to give. He wants to give practical instruction in how to live—how to conduct oneself in everyday situations of life. The name for this knowledge he wants to impart is wisdom and it begins with the fear (knowledge and love) of the LORD.

The best course to follow in any given situation may not immediately seem the most attractive, given the human propensity to prefer short-term gratification over long-term benefit. But wisdom helps us to live a disciplined and prudent life—one that pursues what is right, just, and fair. Many people who lack wisdom have the perception that such a life cannot be very happy or satisfying. Just the opposite is true. Being happy in life and pleasing God are not at odds; God created us to be happy and fulfilled in our service to him and each other. In both this life and the next, our quality of life depends on wisdom—discerning what pleases God and living as we were created to live.

August 2

Wisdom or Folly?

Proverbs 9

In everything the prudent acts with knowledge,
but a fool flaunts his folly.
Proverbs 13:16 (ESV)

Wisdom and Folly are portrayed in this chapter as persons who invite simple people (those who need wisdom about how to live) into their houses to be fed (instructed).

- Wisdom's house is big, well-stocked, and prepared for her guests, while loud and noisy Folly has a disordered house that contains nothing for guests except what has been stolen from elsewhere. Folly has no life or property of her own; she is a parasite of Wisdom.
- On Wisdom's table are the food and drink of understanding how to live, while what Folly serves up are sweet tasting things that appeal to the senses but offer no real nourishment.

It's an important choice that the simple have—that all of us have, for everyone needs wisdom for living. By the end of this chapter we can see it's a life and death choice. More than one horror movie is based on the idea that some ghoul disguised as a beautiful person lures naive people to torment and death. Although anyone should be able to see through Folly's deceit, some do not want to understand; they want to do whatever feels good from moment to moment, and it is these whom Folly snares.

One course of action leads to understanding and life; the other leads to ignorance and death. Those who choose for folly end up fatally deceived. Everybody dies sooner or later, but it is not this grave that Proverbs means. The grave to which fools ultimately go is the grave of eternal destruction. That's why the fear (knowledge and love) of the LORD is the beginning of wisdom. And remember, the instruction of wisdom is good for more than the avoidance of eternal death. It helps us to avoid many foolish and sorrow-producing choices in this life.

August 3

The Foolish Neglect of the Essentials

Proverbs 24:30–34

But I say, walk by the Spirit,
and you will not gratify the desires of the flesh.
Galatians 5:16 (ESV)

This proverb makes practical sense: a farmer's inattention to weeds can lead to poverty. But it makes good spiritual sense too: we must keep our spiritual focus and keep our souls "weed-free." Not that anyone should withdraw from the affairs of this world, but we need to understand that there are consequences to how one lives. Each decision people make impacts their character and their relationship with God. Those who neglect that relationship or shun it are headed for a bad end.

Wealth, fame, and power pose special challenges to the nurture of one's soul. If you long after such things, be especially careful; your dream can be your undoing. Know too that foolishness can trap anyone. Many people have tried, at least in some sense, to live for God. But all of those who ended up fools flirted with danger more than they should have. They all thought they could get away with some compromises to their character or faith but they couldn't and they didn't. Those who appear to be getting away with embracing, or even flirting with, evil are not, no matter how long it takes for the consequences to show up.

It's what you do with the myriad seemingly insignificant challenges in your life that determines your path and end. Keep the weeds out of your field. Keep them out while they're small, for who knows which ones will grow too big for you to handle.

Certain sins pose particular challenges. Centuries ago, Christians composed a list of what they considered to be the most deadly sins. Although these sins are not grouped in any such list in Scripture, the wisdom of the Bible gives strong warnings against each one. We'll look at these sins and their corresponding virtues over the next few days.

August 4

The Deadly Sin of Pride

Proverbs 3:34; 11:2; 18:18–19; Isaiah 14:12–14

Whoever has a haughty look and an arrogant heart I will not endure.
Psalm 101:5 (ESV)

The first of the so-called deadly sins is pride, perhaps because Scripture mentions it more than any other sin. Pride is neither mere self-esteem nor finding pleasure in one's accomplishments, which Scripture commends (see Eccl. 3:22). It is unfitting self-esteem, an unreasonable estimation of one's own qualities. Other words for it are conceit, selfishness, arrogance, vanity, egotism, and boastfulness. Pride is never part of wisdom, but it is found in every fool. There's nothing good in pride and God is resolutely opposed to all who persist in it.

Here's why: Pride is a resentment of and rebellion against Almighty God, who created everything—from rocks to humans—to depend on his continuing grace. Without that grace, the whole universe would again become the nothingness from which God created it. We have a measure of authority and independence in God's world but absolute independence is simply death.

According to Isaiah it was pride that caused Satan's fall from heaven. It also prompted Adam and Eve's first act of disobedience. Pride is destructive of community. Babies cannot yet know that the world does not revolve around them. But grownups should know better, whether their pride manifests itself as arrogance or a false humility that demands that they be the center of attention. The only antidote is a proper humility before God and others; such humility is always part of true wisdom.

Pride (which is really the will to be independent of God) is the first thing that must go before one can come to Jesus. The proud cannot get into the kingdom of heaven—not until they are humbled to recognize their need of salvation and their utter inability to save themselves or even live without God's help.

August 5

The Cultivation of Humility

Proverbs 3:34; 15:33; 18:12; Zephaniah 2:3

This is the one to whom I will look: he who is humble and contrite in spirit, and trembles at my word.
Isaiah 66:2 (ESV)

If pride overrates one's importance or qualities, humility truly assesses them. False humility does not; it is more like pride in that it draws attention to itself. But true humility gives tribute where it is due. This may involve giving other people credit, but the primary credit for all that is praiseworthy must go to God who entrusts everyone with certain opportunities and gifts.

People often take comfort in comparing themselves to others whose problems are more obvious than their own. But Scripture calls us to compare our attitudes and actions to God's standards. The remedy for pride is getting to know both God and ourselves better.

Getting to know God better involves prayerful reflection on God's Word—both individually and communally—by which we come to greater appreciation of his redemptive actions in the world. Besides this, listen to his Holy Spirit in the circumstances of your life and while you engage in deliberate acts of selfless service. Such listening and doing can help you to subdue the pride that will separate you from God's grace.

A better knowledge of yourself will help too. Can you find yourself in one of these stories Jesus told about pride and humility?—that of the guest who took a better seat than he deserved at a feast (Luke 14:7–11), or that comparing the prayers of a proud Pharisee with those of a humble tax collector (Luke 18:10–14)? Jesus's conclusion to both stories paraphrases Proverbs 3:34: "Those who exalt themselves will be humbled and those who humble themselves will be exalted" (Luke 14:11). God wants us to know both that we're unworthy and helpless without him, and that with him, we have no excuse for not obeying his commands.

August 6

The Deadly Sin of Anger

Psalm 4:4; 37:8; Proverbs 29:22; Ecclesiastes 7:9

Be angry and do not sin; do not let the sun go down on your anger, and give no opportunity to the devil.
Ephesians 4:26–27 (ESV)

Anger is too often associated with foolishness, sin, and evil. But it may not start out that way; it may begin with humiliation or frustration, or even by imitation: "Do not make friends with a hot-tempered person...or you may learn their ways" (Prov. 22:24–25). Anger is infectious. That is easily seen in families; if one person comes home angry, that person's anger can be enough to set off the other family members. And even if anger is not sinful or foolish in its initial impulse, it too often becomes that.

God's anger is different; it is righteously directed against the sinful persons or practices that are destructive of his good plans. Sin violates God's intentions for the world and his creatures. God's anger is a statement from one who knows all things that he won't put up with those who ignore or oppose him. This also explains Jesus's anger at those who tried to turn God's good laws for the Sabbath into legalistic rules that forbade the healing and peace he wanted for his sin-plagued and broken people (see Mark 3:1–5).

It is appropriate for us to get angry at such things too; we may share God's anger with injustice and other sin. If we were less self-centered, we would share even more of God's anger against all that is unrighteous. Most of the time, however, our motives are not as pure as God's and our anger is not as righteous. Our anger is usually more concerned with some perceived wrong to ourselves—some violation of our rights. It quickly moves us beyond sulking to being violent in spirit and vengeful. We want the one who offended us to suffer as we have suffered, or to suffer even more. How quickly anger becomes sinful and a deadly foothold for the devil's work in us.

August 7

Assuaging Anger

Proverbs 15:1; 19:11; 29:11; 1 Samuel 25:28

Be quick to hear, slow to speak, slow to anger; for the anger of man does not produce the righteousness of God.
James 1:19–20 (ESV)

Each of the Scripture passages listed above offers wisdom about how to prevent or deal with the problem of sinful anger. The first involves the art of the gentle answer. A wise person can sometimes defuse the anger of another by not responding in kind to an angry outburst. This is usually contrary to one's inclination, which is to take immediate offense. But a hard answer to another's anger typically supplies more ammunition for that anger and also feeds one's own perception of being mistreated.

Patience enables the gentle answer and also helps calm the anger people sense rising in themselves. Patience is being able to wait without complaining in the face of reasons to do precisely that. It is difficult to delay the satisfaction of expressing one's anger; it requires the help of the Holy Spirit to do it. But that very delay can give anger a chance to subside and a better response to be made. That connects patience to a related fruit of the Spirit—self-control. Self-control is the self-discipline to act in a manner better than one feels like acting. We don't expect self-control from infants or animals; what looks like self-control in animals is simply training. But it is a crucial virtue for humankind.

Prayer really helps all of these ways of dealing with anger. Besides the special help that God's Spirit offers in response to sincere prayer, it is almost impossible to hold on to anger against one that you are praying for. Prayer is especially important for the most difficult and most important of the godly responses to anger: forgiveness. Forgiveness is not making light of offenses but deciding to show grace to those who don't deserve it. It's what Abigail asked of David and what Jesus himself modeled and commended for those who love and follow him.

August 8

The Deadly Sin of Envy

Genesis 26:12–15; Proverbs 14:30; 24:17–18

We ourselves were once foolish...slaves to various passions and pleasures, passing our days in malice and envy.
Titus 3:3 (ESV)

The deadly sin of envy is commonly mistaken for jealousy and covetousness; but it differs somewhat.

- Jealousy is the desire to protect what one possesses.
- Covetousness goes beyond admiration to become an excessive desire for something that belongs to another.
- Envy finds displeasure at the successes achieved by others. In an even more malicious form, it finds pleasure in their failures.

Proverbs 24:17–18 warns against taking perverse pleasure in the failure or downfall of others. Admittedly, other Scriptures speak with hope about the coming judgment of the wicked. But such hope is not envy; it is rather the godly desire for evil to be judged so that justice and righteousness can prevail. God's first desire is not for judgment, but that the wicked will be converted: "Do I take any pleasure in the death of the wicked? declares the Sovereign LORD. 'Rather, am I not pleased when they turn from their ways and live?" (Ezek. 18:23).

That was God's desire for Cain and Saul. Cain's envy is implied by his anger with Abel following God's evaluation of the relative merits of their offerings (Gen. 4). Saul's anger with David was likewise a sign of envy (1 Sam. 18). Envy was also the reason for what some Philistines did to Isaac upon seeing his blessings and wealth. They couldn't be as successful as Isaac so they tried to bring him down to their level.

Envy is destructive of community. That is reason enough to shun it. But another good reason is the welfare of the one who envies. Not only does peace elude those who harbor envy (see Prov. 14:30), the bitterness of envy often does more damage to those who indulge it than it does to the objects of their envy.

August 9

Gratitude and Contentment

Job 5:2; Psalm 23

We, though many, are one body in Christ, and individually members one of another. Having gifts that differ according to the grace given to us, let us use them.
Romans 12:5–6a (ESV)

Envious people resent the inequalities of life. To be fair, sometimes inequality does indicate injustice. However, the concern of the envious is not with justice; they resent only those inequalities by which they themselves do not profit. They don't want equality with the poor and defeated, just with those whom they consider their equals, but who have enjoyed more wealth and success.

Gratitude and contentment are two antidotes of such attitudes. These are no easier to cultivate than envy is to root out. We need God's help for both—that we may confess our sin, pray for the will to change, and take to heart what God teaches in his word.

Scripture teaches that in God's sight we are all equally valuable, although unequal in the gifts and opportunities we receive. This inequality is actually God's generous way of providing the whole community of his people with the gifts needed to partner with him in his redemptive mission. The comments of Karl Olsson are relevant here: "Everything I envy is God's gift to someone: intelligence, grace, wit, artistic genius, personal attractiveness. And what others find enviable in me—that is also a gift. Hence [envy is really a despising of the grace of God to another, and] sanctification begins in praising God for the gifts he has given."
Seven Sins and Seven Virtues, 26

Think about how many undeserved benefits you receive by the grace of God. "He does not treat us as our sins deserve or repay us according to our iniquities" (Ps. 103:10). Instead, he tenderly shepherds us through the valleys of life, providing for us in this life and promising to be our security in the next. That understanding can fuel our gratitude and contentment.

August 10

The Deadly Sin of Greed

Ecclesiastes 5:10–15; 2 Kings 5:20–27

Take care, and be on your guard against all covetousness, for one's life does not consist in the abundance of his possessions.
Luke 12:15 (ESV)

Money is often blamed for being the root of all evil. But it is actually the love of money (greed) that Scripture identifies as the root of all evil (1 Tim. 6:10). Money is a good tool, but to love it or other material things goes beyond proper enjoyment to let them, in a sense, replace God as one's master. As Jesus said, "No one can serve two masters" (Matt. 6:24).

One frequent result of greed is injustice in society.

- Ahab's greed for Naboth's vineyard led to the deception of his people, a kangaroo court and death for an innocent man, and to God's judgment upon Ahab's house (see 1 Kings 21).
- Israel's prophets regularly opposed the schemes of the powerful to profit at the expense of the powerless (see Micah 1:15).
- In every age, injustice too often prevails where power is concentrated in the hands of a few.

Greed does not always perpetrate injustice; even so, it yields a miserable harvest in the lives of the greedy.

- The greedy are never satisfied. To the contrary, increased abundance usually brings increased anxiety about how to keep it. The love of money—which is by definition excessive—harms those who indulge in it.
- The greedy increasingly divert resources and energy meant for family and community to achieve material goals.
- The greedy are progressively enslaved by their desires. In part, this means a decreasing ability to take pleasure in anything else (like the fabled Midas). Nor are only the rich susceptible, for greed is found in every social class, driving the poor to be rich and the rich to be richer. Wherever possessions become an idol, it is the possessor who ends up being possessed.

August 11

Liberating Generosity

Deuteronomy 15:11; Proverbs 14:21; 19:17; 22:9

You will be enriched in every way to be generous in every way, which through us will produce thanksgiving to God.
2 Corinthians 9:11 (ESV)

Greed is a harsh master, and all the more so when we remember that we can't take any of our possessions with us when we die (see Eccl. 5:15). Understanding this, why in the world would otherwise clear-thinking people devote their lives to the excessive accumulation of things that lose every bit of value to the accumulator at death? It doesn't make sense.

On the other hand, we do take with us the spiritual fruit that is produced in a life changed by Christ. Galatians 5:22 speaks of the fruit of goodness, which can also be translated as generosity. This is not a new emphasis of Scripture. God's people are repeatedly counseled not to be hardhearted or tightfisted toward the poor, but open-handed (see Deut. 15:7). The generosity God counsels is in imitation of his generosity toward us. The world gives in order to get. We give because we already got; we got everything we have as a gift. Our generosity confirms that we understand and appreciate God's.

We need to understand that generosity is not merely giving from our leftovers. Our concept of what's essential and what's leftover constantly changes to reflect our own circumstances. We may think that we will be able to be more generous when we get a little more. But when we get there, we find that we aren't satisfied after all, and we recalculate that mythical contentment figure, once again putting off giving until our greed is satisfied.

The only rescue from the sin of greed is with the help of God. Seek first his kingdom and his righteousness. And with the help of his Holy Spirit, practice the discipline of giving. That will help with both your deliverance from the deadly sin of greed and your dedication to attend to the things in life that last forever.

August 12

The Deadly Sin of Gluttony

Proverbs 23:1–3, 19–21

Many...walk as enemies of the cross of Christ. Their end is destruction, their god is their belly, and they glory in their shame, with minds set on earthly things.
Philippians 3:18–19 (ESV)

Gluttony is like greed in its love of things, but its desire is to consume rather than possess. This applies to food and drink, and also to other consumer goods. Gluttony does not care about the difference between enough and too much and actually has more to do with one's attitude than with one's shape or dress or possession of luxuries. Gluttony is seen in overeating and in many other things people do to excess: smoking, drinking, use of drugs, and also shopping or attention to various diversions.

Not all gluttony has to do with excess; C.S. Lewis spoke of the gluttony of delicacy—eating with too much fuss or too expensively. This is not to scorn excellence in food preparation, which is good, but not the most important good and never to be an idol that diverts one from prioritizing God and service to him.

Gluttony is an evil master and reaps evil rewards:

- Lack of self-control in eating can lead to obesity, about which no more needs to be said. But it can also lead to obsession with fat, dieting, and exercise.
- The overconsumption of food, drink, and drugs can deprive families of necessary goods.
- There are health and moral costs from such things as promiscuity, alcoholism and drug abuse, improper eating, and so on. One way or another, gluttony is destructive of community.

Gluttony inevitably leads to poverty, if not physical, then emotional and spiritual poverty. This is especially evident when gluttony crosses the line into addiction. By God's grace there are ways out of gluttony and addiction. However, the hold of sin is always easier to avoid than it is to escape.

August 13

Combating Gluttony

Proverbs 25:27–28; Ecclesiastes 8:15

Whether you eat or drink, or whatever you do, do all to the glory of God.
1 Corinthians 10:31 (ESV)

Godly wisdom commends enjoying eating and drinking, but it also warns against lack of self-control in that enjoyment. Other words are sometimes used in place of self-control—moderation, restraint, and temperance (which applies to more than alcohol consumption). But they all point to the same reality: some things that taste good—like honey—aren't so good when consumed in excess. Combating gluttony involves forgoing some pleasures for the sake of others that, although more distant, may be better.

Self-control is best formed early in life. It does not come naturally, but is fostered by the discipline of loving parents. Still, external discipline must eventually give way to self-discipline. This does not come naturally either, but is helped by the consideration of what's best in the long run. It helps to count the costs of consuming to excess: health costs, emotional costs, family costs, and so on. But primarily, we need to understand that gluttony is a spiritual problem, an idol that serves to alienate people from healthy relationships with God.

The very blessings of God can become the downfall of one who is blessed. God warned Israel about that, knowing that their enjoyment of good things from him could lead them to pride and forgetfulness (Deut. 8:10–14). For that reason, it can help to fast on occasion—both from food and from other things often consumed to excess. How can we be properly grateful if we are so devoted to satisfying our appetites that we never have the experience of unfulfilled desire? Paul answered those who proclaimed that their freedom in Christ permitted them to "do anything" by saying "but not everything is beneficial" and "I will not be mastered by anything" (1 Cor. 6:12).

August 14

The Deadly Sin of Lust

Job 31:9–12; Proverbs 6:20–29

This is the will of God, your sanctification: that you abstain from sexual immorality; that each one of you know how to control his own body in holiness and honor, not in the passion of lust like the Gentiles who do not know God.
1 Thessalonians 4:3–5 (ESV)

Desire is good, even strong desire. Sexual desire too, is a gift of God. But it is to be consummated in the context of marriage, in which a man and woman are bound together in an exclusive pledge of faithful love. The deadly sin of lust is the precursor to fornication (involving unmarried people) and adultery (involving a married person and one who is not that person's spouse). Jesus made clear that God's command against these acts is already violated by the lust that gave rise to them (see Matt. 5:27–28). We should note that the temptation to lust is not sin in itself. But when invited to linger, the temptation becomes the sin of lust, whether or not the lust leads to improper physical intimacy.

Adultery is destructive of marriage, which is foundational to the continued existence of stable families and societies. But premarital sex is not friendly to marriage either. It is often associated with promiscuity and increases the risk of contracting a sexually transmitted disease. It also interferes with the development of the well-rounded intimacy that is an essential foundation for marriage. As Proverbs indicates, those who play with fire get burned.

Sexual liberation is anything but; unrestrained indulgence leads ultimately to perversion and obsession, turning the good things of sexual desire and appreciation for beauty into objects of worship. Lust ends in idolatry. Witness the growing acceptance of pornography as normal. Pornography is commonly thought to serve sexual interests, but it gets bored easily and craves more and more degradation to satisfy. Lust is as demonic for some people as alcohol is for alcoholics. Its hold can be broken only with repentance and the sanctifying help of the Holy Spirit.

August 15

Conquering Lust

Job 31:1–12

The grace of God has appeared, bringing salvation for all people, training us to renounce ungodliness and worldly passions, and to live self-controlled, upright and godly lives in the present age.
Titus 2:11–12 (ESV)

As difficult as it may be, abstinence is the God-approved course of action for the unmarried. It is also one of the best ways to build the trustworthiness and character that helps marriage last. Too many consider abstinence, and even steadfast faithfulness in marriage, to be unrealistic and foolish. C.S. Lewis called chastity "the most unpopular of all the Christian virtues." But as difficult as it may be, Christ calls us to this spiritual discipline.

Lewis also speaks of men without chests, which, in this context, means those without the will to submit themselves to the LORD's commands regarding chastity. The development of will might involve such things as cold showers, avoiding situations in which temptations are likely, and making a covenant with one's eyes—a decision to turn away immediately when tempted. But chastity requires more than that too; lust is best conquered by replacing improper sexual desires with the desires of what Scripture calls true religion.

We have all sinned and fallen short of God's expectations. But our sexual brokenness is not beyond the sanctifying power of the Holy Spirit. Augustine, whom we know as one of the church fathers, was promiscuous in his youth. But, convicted by Romans 13:14, "Clothe yourselves with the Lord Jesus Christ, and do not think how to gratify the desires of the flesh," he acknowledged his sinfulness and accepted Jesus as his Savior. One day after this, a former "playmate" saw him as he walked along and called, "Augustine, it is I!" He took one look at her and, reminding himself of his new position in Christ, quickly turned and ran away, answering, "But, it's not I!" Then he quoted Galatians 2:20—"I no longer live, but Christ lives in me."

August 16

The Deadly Sin of Sloth

Proverbs 6:6–11; 24:30–34; 26:13–16

[We urge you to] work…so that you may walk properly before outsiders and be dependent on no one.
1 Thessalonians 4:11–12 (ESV)

Several Proverbs address the foolishness of sloth, particularly as it shows itself in laziness. Sloths fail to take advantage of good times to make provision for bad times. They allow thorns and weeds to infest their fields and do not attend to the breaks in the walls that protect their property. Proverbs 26:13 suggests that fear may be a factor in this neglect. But whether fearful or lazy, sloths are shortsighted and all too often end up in poverty.

The physically slothful take unfair advantage of others' hard work and generosity. This is self-destructive, harmful to society, and offensive to God, who wants people to use their gifts and talents.

Another form of sloth is even worse and deadlier—spiritual laziness. In fact, it is this that got sloth included in the list of deadly sins. Spiritual sloth may be displayed as a lukewarm or apathetic spirituality, as was the problem in the church of Laodicea (Rev. 3:14–21). It may also be evident in an individualistic hyper spirituality. The apostle Paul criticized certain Christians in Corinth for focusing on gifts meant for personal edification while neglecting those meant for the strengthening, encouraging, and comfort of others (see 1 Cor. 14). Either way, spiritual sloth is as selfish as the physical kind; it is interested only in what feels good in the moment. And it is another form of idolatry.

Dorothy Sayers made these cogent remarks about sloth: "In the world it calls itself Tolerance, but in Hell it is called Despair...the sin which believes in nothing, cares for nothing, seeks to know nothing, interferes with nothing, enjoys nothing, hates nothing, finds purpose in nothing, lives for nothing, and remains alive because there is nothing it would die for." "The Other Six Deadly Sins", Address to the Public Morality Council, Caxton Hall, Westminster, Oct 23, 1941.

August 17

Mission Minded

Proverbs 13:4; 21:25–26; 28:19

Jesus said to them again, "Peace be with you.
As the Father has sent me, even so I am sending you."
John 20:21 (ESV)

If the slothful crave and get nothing, the ideal must be to crave and get something. The unslothful don't crave to excess, like the greedy, gluttonous, or lustful. They crave to honor the LORD by engaging in the work he has created us for. God has equipped us to provide for our own livelihood by the work of our hands and minds. This does not negate our responsibility to be generous and share with those who genuinely need help, but neither does it foster an unhealthy dependency in them.

Besides providing for ourselves and helping the helpless, God wants us to participate in other aspects of his mission in the world. He has a kingdom to grow in our midst and people whom he wants to hear the gospel. He has other people who need to learn more about how to apply the gospel to their everyday life, people who need to learn to bring everything to him in prayer and "demolish arguments and every pretension that sets itself up against the knowledge of God, and…take captive every thought to make it obedient to Christ" (2 Cor. 10:5).

God looks both at your heart and at the deeds of your life. No matter how active you are, you are a spiritual sloth if you do not attend to your relationship with the Lord. There is no substitute for a deep and personal walk with God. But given that, there is no way that you should remain spiritually inert, or too spiritually joyless and hopeless to let God's love shine through in the deeds of your life. God wants passionate partners for his ongoing mission to the world. His Spirit will motivate and equip you for that; he will keep your hope alive or revive it as you work and pray while taking nourishment and direction from the word and Spirit of God.

August 18

God's Heart for the World

Psalm 67

The LORD has made known his salvation; he has revealed his righteousness in the sight of the nations.
Psalm 98:2 (ESV)

The command to bring the news of God's grace to the world is emphasized more in the New Testament than the Old. But, from the beginning, God had more than Israel in mind. His promise to Abraham was not only of blessing for Abraham and his descendants, but of blessings for the nations of the earth through them. Continuing this theme, Psalm 67 begins by asking for God's blessing on Israel. Next it indicates the larger reason for which God's people were to be blessed—so that God's salvation might be known throughout the world. "May God bless us still," the Psalm ends, "so that all the ends of the earth will fear him."

The world desperately needs a witness of God; too many people "do not know what makes them stumble" (Prov. 4:19). Consider:

- The physical problems brought on by unholy lifestyles.
- The emotional immaturity displayed in the sinful nature, and with this, the compulsion to seek poor substitutes to placate a lack of peace and fear of death.
- The thinking disabilities of those separated from God: Many allege that there are no universal standards, no essential differences between men and women, and no clear divisions between animals and humans, and so on.
- The bondage of the will that leaves people susceptible to self-destructive behavior and a lack of self-control.

Not all stumbling immediately disappears when one becomes a Christian; too many Christians walk more closely with the world than with the Lord. Still, God has the answer; he wants everyone to come to him through Christ and get supernatural help from the Holy Spirit so they may experience and celebrate the blessings meant for those who submit to God's guidance and just rule.

August 19

Sharing God's Heart for the World

Proverbs 4:18–19

I heard the voice of the LORD saying,
"Whom shall I send? And who will go for us?"
Then I said, "Here I am! Send me."
Isaiah 6:8 (ESV)

Sin affects the physical, the emotions, the understanding, and the will. It throws the whole person into deep darkness. However, such people are vulnerable in a healing way to the light in the hearts and lives of those who personally know the light of the world. Our faith may not be as strong as we would like, but it does gives us hope and healing for every aspect of our lives. Will you, therefore, share it with others who need it?

Perhaps you want to but feel inadequate. If so, you're not alone. But there is help; one of several books on the topic is Paul Little's *How to Give Away Your Faith*. He describes friendship evangelism, which is not anything like an armed invasion but more like the making of a friend who hopefully will see real faith in action.

Throughout history the church has grown and flourished only where ordinary Christians learned to give away their faith. Sometimes people are so hungry for the gospel that everything seems to work. At other times, the opposite is true. Today, although interest in spirituality is high, too few people think that the Scriptures will answer their needs or questions. Such people are more likely to listen to friends and especially those in whose lives the light of wisdom and love shines.

By God's grace the faith that gives us hope and healing can be given away so that it enlightens the lives of those around us who are in trouble and darkness. This will help us as well, for faith is strengthened by giving it away. Don't underestimate the effect that your little words and actions, with the help of the Holy Spirit, can have in introducing others to the Light of the World.

August 20

Cover-up versus Confession

Psalm 32:1–5; 139:23–24; Ecclesiastes 12:14

Whoever conceals his transgressions will not prosper,
but he who confesses and forsakes them will obtain mercy.
Proverbs 28:13 (ESV)

The good news that God wants the world to know and embrace begins with bad news: We are all sinners and deserving of judgment. The response to that news is crucial. Will we deny or cover-up what God calls sin, or will we confess it and ask God for forgiveness?

David tried both. Whether Psalm 32 was written after his sin with Bathsheba or on some other occasion, David's first impulse was to deny and cover-up what he'd done. His lack of success with that is familiar to all whose consciences will not let them be after willful sin; he could not rest until he confessed. Only then did he experience the relief and freedom of God's forgiveness.

In this world some people get away with hiding their sins and maintaining the illusion of spiritual health. But that's unusual, because secrets have a way of unraveling and sins have a way of betraying the sinner. It's too difficult to keep secrets and lies straight. Even if it can be done, it exacts a harsh toll. Suppressing the accusations of conscience eventually results in a heart that nothing can get to—no conscience, no feeling, no mercy, no sorrow—a robotic, or even worse, a demonic heart.

Even if sins can be concealed until the time that sinners can no longer be held accountable by any earthly court, concealment is not possible from the Lord of heaven and earth. Breaking the secrecy of sin allows you to get ready for the great accounting when everything will be out in the open. The course of wisdom is to be honest with God and resist all temptations to conceal your sin from him. Pray for forgiveness and for him to correct what is offensive in your heart and life. Only then can you stop compromising the mission that God has for you.

August 21

A Good Name

Proverbs 22:1; Psalm 125

The memory of the righteous is a blessing,
but the name of the wicked will rot.
Proverbs 10:7 (ESV)

It has been said that you shouldn't talk about yourself in a group; it will be done after you leave. That means you have a reputation—what people think about you. And what a shame when someone ruins another person's reputation. In the long run, however, what Abraham Lincoln once said rings true, "Character is like a tree and reputation like its shadow. The shadow is what we think of it and the tree is the real thing."

Solomon speaks in Proverbs 22:1 not about the shadow (reputation) but about the real thing (character)—who you really are. In sum, he says that a good name is a good character, and a good character is worth more than any jackpot.

Character begins with sincere trust in the LORD, and it manifests itself in a consistent integrity. Psalm 125 indicates that such a person refuses to participate in evil, or even crooked ways, but rather maintains a steadfast commitment to what is good. Character is inevitably built and proved by the choices we make in daily life, the cumulative effect of which is life or death. As Proverbs 11:3 puts it, "The integrity of the upright guides them, but the unfaithful are destroyed by their duplicity." According to Psalm 125, the former endure while the latter are banished.

The name Christian is no guarantee, for some who bear the name do so under false pretenses. Witness the fate of Ananias and Sapphira, who bore the name but betrayed God and their community by their actions (see Acts 5). True Christians are true followers of Christ. Does that describe you? To what things do you say "yes" and to what things "no"? How do the choices you make every day reflect on the one whose name you bear?

August 22

The LORD Is My Shepherd

Psalm 23

I am the good shepherd; I know my own and my own know me...and I lay down my life for the sheep.
John 10:14–15 (ESV)

Psalm 23 is a favorite of many people for its assurance of God's comfort and help that accompanies us through the trials of this life and, afterwards, ushers us safely into his presence in eternity. In a sense the LORD does what any good shepherd does. He provides, he protects, he directs, and he disciplines. But the implication is that he doesn't do this for all sheep. That's why the personal pronouns of this Psalm are important. It doesn't say, "The Lord is **a** shepherd." but "The LORD is **my** shepherd." With that relationship, we are assured of these things from God:

- Provision: I will have everything I need to get me home where there will be no more hunger or thirst or pain or homelessness or destitution.
- Protection: No harm will come that will last longer than the brief years of my present life.
- Direction: I'll never be in a place where God isn't nearby, and I'll never be without a clue as to what he wants me to do because he's left written instructions.
- Discipline: I have someone who will warn me if I even think about striking off on my own, and who will not give up on me, but will always bring me back to his side.

What a difference it makes to have the promise of such blessings. We need fear no evil for nothing can separate us from the provision, protection, direction, and loving discipline of our shepherd and savior Jesus Christ. He does more than release us from our fears; he offers a sense of fullness and prosperity in the presence of the enemies that usually rob us of such things. The oil of God's presence covers all of his sheep. His love and mercy envelops each one—now, right here no matter what our current situation, and also for the unending future.

August 23

Can God Trust You?

Proverbs 3:1–12

It is required of stewards that they be found faithful.
1 Corinthians 4:2 (ESV)

"The LORD is my shepherd" is a statement of trust in God. As important a claim as that is, however, it doesn't mean much if it's not backed up by action. Proverbs 3 indicates some of the attitudes and actions that confirm the extent of your trust in God, or to put it another way, that confirm that God can trust you.

- Are you teachable; do you accept and learn from his discipline?
- Do you acknowledge the LORD in all your ways?
- Do you bow to God's wisdom when it differs with yours?
- Do you honor God with the firstfruits of your wealth?

Some people wonder whether the trouble they face is from Satan or is part of the LORD's discipline. But it's really both. Satan tries to use trouble to separate you from God. But when God allows it, it's because he wants to use it to draw you closer to himself. So if there are identifiable ways that you've ignored or disobeyed God, then take trouble to be God's loving discipline, meant to get you back to where he wants you. If, on the other hand, you can't identify particular sinful ways, there's still more to learn about trusting God. So, no matter where your trouble comes from, cultivate your relationship with the LORD and let him see that he can trust you in the bad times as well as the good times.

Pay special attention to how you use your gifts and abilities and the material rewards that come from using them well. Perhaps God has given you the ability to make lots of money. Or maybe not. Either way, with the understanding that you are not the owner but merely the steward of the possessions God has given you, prove your trustworthiness by living a life of gratitude and generosity. If you want to trust God and to have him trust you, then be the best manager you can be with the life and possessions that God has given you.

August 24

Irresponsible Debt

Psalm 37:21; Proverbs 22:7

If then you have not been faithful in the unrighteous [earthly] wealth, who will entrust to you the true riches?
Luke 16:11 (ESV)

Noah Webster, in his 1828 dictionary, used biblical and moral illustrations in defining terms. He said this about debt: "It is a common misfortune or vice to be in debt." Today, debt may be considered a misfortune but it is rarely considered a vice. But Proverbs 22:7 is correct: debt puts you in a type of bondage. This is not necessarily an argument against all kinds of debt. However, too often people go into debt simply because they cannot say "no" to their desire to accumulate things.

Irresponsible debt creates many problems:

- It gives the illusion of financial security and success.
- It frequently causes worry and family problems.
- It invites temptations—whether to postpone or avoid repayment or to cheat in order to save or get money; such things put additional burdens on honest people.
- It ties up money in principle and interest payments that could be better used for necessities or to help others.
- In the case of irresponsible debt by governments, it puts future generations in bondage to debts that they did not incur.

There's help for those who need it. The only trouble is, it has to do with self-discipline, which is not very pleasant to those who aren't used to it. Monetary self-discipline includes such things as learning the ability to postpone pleasure, not spending money on sin, living within one's means by adherence to a budget, accepting responsibility, etc. Each of us needs to consider whether or not our lives show godliness with contentment. Irresponsible debt and irresponsible spending, whether or not that incurs debt, hampers our life and witness and, as Jesus said, our ability to receive the true riches that God wants to give his people.

August 25

The Value of a Friend

Proverbs 17:17; 27:5–6, 17; Ecclesiastes 4:9–12

A man of many companions may come to ruin,
but there is a friend who sticks closer than a brother.
Proverbs 18:24 (ESV)

Good friends are of great value in helping us become the people God wants us to be; they can help us avoid what God hates and pursue the things that God loves and desires for us. Bad friends, on the other hand, hurt us through their weakness of character or lack of wisdom by not holding us to account for our poor choices. We all want and need friends. But we have a choice in that regard: "Walk with the wise and become wise, but a companion of fools suffers harm" (Prov. 13:20).

The desire and need for friends finds its origin in God's creation of humankind. God made us not only to relate to him, but to love and be loved, and to help and be helped by each other—we were created to live in community. Marriage is one of the most intimate expressions of friendship, but certainly not the only one. You can also be supported and learn about yourself and your life in conversation with friends. Intelligence and zest for living are stimulated and sharpened by such interaction. As you verbalize your disappointments, aspirations, failures, and victories, you come to a fresh sense of purpose and strength to meet challenges.

To be so vulnerable is disastrous with enemies and with false friends, whose only interest is in what they receive or who love only in good times. False love indiscriminately affirms every decision, whether good or bad, and refuses to mention or, worse, praises sinful living. Even enemies can flatter people and tell them what they want to hear, but true friends will tell the unpopular and difficult truth, even at some hazard to themselves. They love, support, and stimulate us to be better than we are and correct us when we're wrong. No wonder the Bible advises wisdom in the matter of choosing our friends.

August 26

Finding a Marriage Partner

Proverbs 5:15–23

A man shall leave his father and his mother and hold fast to his wife, and the two shall become one flesh. So they are no longer two, but one flesh. What therefore God has joined together, let not man separate.
Matthew 19:5b–6 (ESV)

If biblical wisdom is important for choosing friends—and it is—then it is doubly so in marriage. God has ordained marriage to be permanent; the *one flesh* bond is meant to last until death. The pain at the loss or betrayal of friendships is multiplied in the dissolution of marriage. It is critical not to enter into marriage too quickly or for the wrong reasons.

As with friendship, men and women seeking a marriage partner should evaluate their potential mate according to the standards put forward by God in his word. Besides the aforementioned deadly sins and contrasting virtues, Proverbs advises women to pay particular attention to a man's patience (Prov. 19:11), willingness to learn (Prov. 19:25, 12:15), interest in listening as opposed to talking (Prov. 18:2), and faithfulness (Prov. 5:8). Proverbs also advises men on what to look for: a woman's discretion (Prov. 11:22), true demeanor (Prov. 21:19), and inner nobility as compared to outer charm (Prov. 31:29–30). Actually, both women and men might be evaluated by the same standards, and above all, by their fear of the LORD (Prov. 1:7, 19:23).

Once married, men and women must be wise about nurturing and protecting their commitment, both for mutual benefit and to please the Lord (Prov. 5:21). Just don't count your own satisfaction of greater worth than God's word and honor. As much as you must value the satisfaction of your marriage partner, don't even count that of greater worth than God's glory. For the former is served by the latter. When, for God's sake and with Christ's help, you nurture and protect your marriage as God intends, then you'll find happiness in marriage and be sanctified in preparation for eternity.

August 27

When Sex is Good

Song of Solomon 8:5–7

Let your fountain be blessed, and rejoice in the wife of your youth...be intoxicated always in her love.
Proverbs 5:18–19 (ESV)

Manicheanism was a third-century heresy that viewed the physical (the body in particular) as evil, and salvation as a way of escape from the prison-like nature of earthly existence. It also considered spirituality to be more concerned with thoughts and emotions than with physical existence and desires. The Manicheans thus thought of sex as something shameful—to be endured rather than enjoyed. They read the Song of Solomon as an allegory about spiritual love and not as the celebration of sexual love in the context of lifelong, heterosexual marriage.

However, the love described in this book is physical and strong enough to break a person if it is not expressed appropriately. Hence the refrain we hear throughout the book, "Do not arouse or awaken love until it so desires." This is why God insists that sex belongs only in marriage, which begins in a public ceremony where two people vow to maintain a lifelong commitment to one another—body and soul. To have sex without that commitment is selfish. It often raises false hopes and undermines the development of genuine intimacy and stable relationships.

Those who sleep with someone to whom they aren't married need to ask what prevents them saying with the rest of their life what they say with their body. True love won't tolerate a halfway commitment because it is as strong as death. The truth of this is apparent in the negative effects—promiscuity, pornography, and family breakdown, etc.—that result from the refusal to treat love as it deserves. Men and women are made to delight in and enjoy each other. Sex is good, healthy, and wholesome in the context of a marriage commitment between a man and a woman, especially if they've joined together in a mutual commitment to the LORD.

August 28

The Necessity of Parental Discipline

Deuteronomy 6:1–9; Proverbs 5:23; 6:23; 29:17–18

Train up a child in the way he should go;
even when he is old he will not depart from it.
Proverbs 22:6 (ESV)

Supernanny was a reality TV show that featured parents at their wits' end about how to control their unruly children. A professional nanny responded to their pleas for help and most of the time was able to give parents enough guidance and skills so that order could be restored in their households.

It's not difficult to see how such chaos originates. It arises whenever parents allow their children freedom without consequences for abusing that freedom. Besides physical care, children need parenting to help them to attain emotional and spiritual maturity. By nature we would all like to be kings and queens in our own little universe; it's discipline that helps us learn the self-control that, perhaps counter-intuitively, leads to a more peaceable and happy life. To really prosper—physically, emotionally, and spiritually—we must obey the laws under which God created us to live, foremost of which is to love him above all

Positively, discipline involves instruction, training, and rewarding proper behavior. But there's a negative side too, which addresses improper behavior with correction and punishment. The goal of both is the same—to bring our children to the obedience and self-discipline necessary for life. Often that means they must learn to sacrifice what may appear to be in their immediate interests for the sake of more valuable and longer term goals. Success in this can mean the difference between a good end and a bad one. The least negative result of the failure to learn self-discipline is the loss of potential blessing, but much greater losses and even death can result. So God says, "Discipline your children, for in that there is hope; do not be a willing party to their death" (Prov. 19:18).

August 29

How to Discipline

Psalm 78:1–8; Proverbs 3:11–12; 13:24

Those whom I love, I reprove and discipline.
Revelation 3:19 (ESV)

A research study from some years ago highlighted how the improper balance of support and control hampered the effectiveness of parental discipline. The kind of discipline children need is more like that we receive from God—always high in loving support and offered with the goal of helping us to reach maturity in our attitudes and actions toward God and our neighbors.

How parents show that support and control may differ in families; Scripture does not require identical parenting styles or complete agreement about the place of physical punishment in discipline. Perhaps we can agree, however, that children must never be punished in anger but always in love, appropriately, and with an eye to what will support them and help them to maturity.

At the risk of oversimplifying the very difficult task that God has given parents, let me offer a few guidelines:

- Model the behavior you want, and pray continually.
- Make rules that are defensible and enforceable. Say what you mean and mean what you say. Discipline is not about winning, but about what's right.
- Clearly communicate what you expect or how you were disappointed but don't lose your self-control.
- Use natural/logical consequences when you can. That ties actions to consequences and helps children learn before the consequences get too big and dangerous.
- Offer unconditional love communicated physically and verbally, and with control that is age-appropriate—high in infancy, but decreasing with age and maturity. The goal after all, is to entirely replace parental control with self-control through proper guidance and loving correction so that children become equipped to offer their own obedience to God in all of life.

August 30

The Beginning and End of Wisdom

Ecclesiastes 12

The fear of the LORD is the beginning of wisdom,
and the knowledge of the Holy One is insight.
Proverbs 9:10 (ESV)

Much of Ecclesiastes is taken up with Solomon's concern for the apparent meaninglessness of life: everything eventually passes away: work, pleasures, wealth, etc. Even the search for wisdom seems futile: "For with much wisdom comes much sorrow; the more knowledge, the more grief" (Eccl. 1:18). What's more, it appears that any advantage of wisdom can be negated by misfortune or by the foolishness of others: "The race is not to the swift or the battle to the strong, nor does food come to the wise or wealth to the brilliant or favor to the learned; but time and chance happen to them all" (Eccl. 9:11).

Yet, Solomon never suggests that life isn't worth living; rather he commends "the enjoyment of life because nothing is better for a person under the sun than to eat and drink and be glad. Then joy will accompany them in their toil all the days of the life God has given them under the sun" (Eccl. 8:15). This is not the "eat, drink, and be merry for tomorrow we die" godless philosophy of the self-satisfied man in Luke 12:19. Rather, it's that despite all of life's uncertainties, God is still in control. So Solomon confesses, "I know that everything God does will endure forever; nothing can be added to it and nothing taken from it. God does it so that people will fear him" (Eccl. 3:14).

True wisdom is to remember our Creator from youth into old age and death—"until the spirit returns to God who gave it" (Eccl 12:7). Solomon concludes by reinforcing what he has emphasized in all of his writings on wisdom: "Fear God and keep his commandments, for this is the duty of all mankind" (Eccl. 12:13). And as one additional incentive, he reminds us of the coming day when our lives will be judged by God.

August 31

Solomon's Problem

1 Kings 10:23–11:8

I passed by the field of a sluggard, by the vineyard of a man lacking sense...it was all overgrown with thorns; the ground was covered with nettles, and its stone wall was broken down.
Proverbs 24:30–31 (ESV)

Later in life, Solomon lost some of the wisdom for which he was reputed. Wisdom gave way to foolishness as his attention was diverted from the LORD, the original object of his devotion, to his possessions, building projects, and wives. The signs of trouble surfaced already at the start of Solomon's reign, when, ignoring God's command against such things (see Deut. 17:16–17), he began to accumulate horses, wealth, and wives of foreign birth.

Solomon's marriages were mostly political arrangements and not unusual for his time. But most of the time they violated God's command against intermarriage with idol worshipers. What happened was just what God had said would happen; Solomon's wives turned his heart to their gods.

This turning of Solomon's heart was also connected to his failure to write out a copy of God's law for himself and to read it every day as instructed in Deuteronomy 17:18–20. If the king did this, the LORD promised success for him and a long reign in Israel for him and his family.

By secular standards, Solomon was a great ruler. Yet, he did not take enough time to worship in the temple that he had built for God. Nor did he pay enough attention to the commandments and warnings that God had given. Solomon took care of many things, but he neglected his heart and soul. He wrote about the sluggards who neglected their property, but he himself was a spiritual sluggard who permitted his life to go to ruin. If Solomon did repent it was too late to avoid all the consequences of his sin and neglect, and so he stands as a perpetual warning that we also must always keep first things first.

September 1

The Beginning of Israel's Decline

1 Kings 11:9–43

And you, Solomon my son, know the God of your father and serve him with a whole heart and with a willing mind...If you seek him, he will be found by you, but if you forsake him, he will cast you off forever.
1 Chronicles 28:9 (ESV)

There were many significant milestones in Israel's journey to find all of the blessings that God had promised Abraham's descendants. But the pinnacle, so far as anyone could see, was reached during the reign of King Solomon. Palestine was strategically positioned for trade over land and by sea. It was especially under Solomon that Israel's economy flourished.

It was also under Solomon that the temple was built as a permanent structure to replace the moveable Tent of Meeting that had been positioned at the center of Israel's encampment during their years in the desert. The temple was meant to reinforce and make permanent the truth that all of Israel's life and blessings were attributable to the LORD, without whom Israel's people had neither purpose nor hope for a future.

Although Solomon was faithful to the LORD in building the temple, he became unfaithful in both his personal walk with God and his official responsibilities. He tolerated and even built worship centers for idol gods. As a result, God told him that he would no longer rule over a united Israel, but only over one tribe—Judah. Although the division would not happen until Solomon's death, the fracturing of Israel began already during his life. The LORD raised up adversaries against this increasingly foolish son of David.

It was the beginning of a sad chapter for the tribes of Israel, whose unity the LORD had wanted so much. The civil wars would not only make things difficult for Israel, they would also prevent Israel from blessing the rest of the world as God had promised Abraham they would.

September 2

The Sins of Jeroboam

1 Kings 11:44–12:33

What is this breach of faith...against the God of Israel in turning away this day from following the LORD by building yourselves an altar this day in rebellion against the LORD?
Joshua 22:16–17 (ESV)

The precipitating event for civil war within Israel was the refusal of Solomon's successor to listen to the advice of his elders. They advised the king to reduce the forced labor and taxes that had financed Solomon's projects. But King Rehoboam refused; as a result Jeroboam led the other tribes in a revolt against Judah.

Jeroboam was afraid, however, of the long-term viability of his kingdom if his people kept going to Jerusalem to offer their sacrifices at the temple. His solution was to set up alternate worship centers outside of Jerusalem. This was the very problem that had so concerned Joshua and God's people hundreds of years before. Then, they had perceived the altar built by the trans-Jordan tribes to be for the purpose of providing an alternate place for worship. Civil war was averted that time when they learned that the altar was not for alternate worship, but simply as a testimony that the LORD alone was God and deserving of worship.

To compound Jeroboam's problem, he appointed priests who were not authorized by God. In place of the ark of the covenant he made golden calves to put in his shrines. The calves were meant to symbolize the LORD's presence, but this act constituted idolatry; it was the very deed by which Aaron had brought God's anger down on himself and the people at the time of the giving of the law through Moses (Ex. 32).

These allowances for false worship became known after this as "the sins of Jeroboam." The verdict for each subsequent king of Israel was: "He did evil in the eyes of the LORD and did not turn away from any of the sins of Jeroboam son of Nebat, which he had caused Israel to commit; he continued in them."

September 3

The Time of the Prophets

Deuteronomy 18:14–22; 1 Kings 14:1–18

If there is a prophet among you, I the LORD make myself known to him in a vision; I speak with him in a dream.
Numbers 12:6 (ESV)

After Solomon's death and the split of his kingdom into two, the LORD made clear to both Israel and Judah that he still expected wholehearted service. To that end, God often sent prophets to tell the people what he wanted. Sometimes they reminded the people of God's will as previously revealed through Moses and his successors. But sometimes, too, as with Ahijah who predicted the loss of Jeroboam's kingdom and the death of his son, they were given new revelations that were specific for the person, place, or time. Either way, they could and did say with conviction, "Thus says the LORD."

There was a plethora of false prophets as well—those who pretended to speak for God even if they had not been sent by him. These were usually in the employ of a king who really did not want to hear the word of the LORD. Moses had made clear long before that such prophets could be identified by the discrepancies between God's words and their words, and by the failure of their predictions. True prophets, on the other hand, didn't have to worry about either of these outcomes; true prophets had only to be faithful to the calling and word of the LORD.

There were prophets in Israel before the split; Moses, Aaron, and Miriam were all prophets, as was Samuel, who, at God's command, anointed both Saul and David as king. Among those who worked during David's lifetime were the prophets Nathan and Gad. But prophets became particularly active during the time of Israel's decline in faithfulness—between Solomon's death and the exile of God's people from the Promised Land. They did not call the people to some new and unknown task, but simply told them to recall what God had done for them, and return to his service.

September 4

The High Calling of the Prophets

1 Kings 13

Walk in a manner worthy of the calling to which you have been called.
Ephesians 4:1 (ESV)

This story illustrates the typical response that Israel's kings would give on hearing the prophetic word of the LORD. They would usually ignore it or resist it instead of repenting and bowing to the LORD's will.

The truth of the message Jeroboam received was proved as soon as the king tried to silence the man of God. Jeroboam immediately recognized his mistake and pled with the prophet to ask the LORD for the restoration of his crippled hand. He was granted this request and was grateful for it. But his gratitude neither lasted nor went far enough. Later on Jeroboam "appointed priests for the high places from all sorts of people. Anyone who wanted to become a priest he consecrated for the high places. This was the sin of the house of Jeroboam that led to its downfall and to its destruction from the face of the earth" (1 Kings 13:33-34).

This story also illustrates the absolute faithfulness required of those who were called to bring the word of the LORD; the prophets had to be very careful to do and say only and exactly what God directed. The man of God, who gave Jeroboam God's message but didn't obey the LORD's command not to eat or drink until he got back home, paid for his disobedience with his life. However, from the respect accorded him by the other prophet, it appears that he was not entirely rejected by God for his failure. Nor was his previous message to the king compromised.

What happened to the man of God remains somewhat puzzling. But at least this much is clear: those who bring the word of the LORD are themselves subject to its demands. The apostle Paul confirms this in his warning that believers must live a life worthy of their calling. This is a warning, moreover, that applies doubly to those in leadership in Christ's church.

September 5

Asa's Response to Prophetic Warning

2 Chronicles 15

Return to me, and I will return to you, says the LORD of hosts.
Malachi 3:7 (ESV)

Asa's father Abijah trusted in God and led the people to follow the LORD's requirements, but left some foreign altars and high places in the land. Asa had the wisdom to destroy these when he became king, and to call on the people to seek the LORD, the God of their fathers, and to obey his laws and commands. In doing so, King Asa illustrates the sort of response that God wanted his people to make to the warnings of his prophets.

At first things went well under Asa; God blessed Judah and gave them victory over their enemies. But gradually the devotion of the people waned, at least partly through the influence of Asa's idol-worshiping grandmother. As a result, the LORD's altar fell into disrepair while the altars of idol gods were rebuilt.

God allowed the people to suffer the consequences of their sin. Crime increased so that it was not safe to travel. Nations and cities waged war against each other. God was troubling the people to get their attention. He sent the prophet Azariah to Asa with the message that the LORD had not left his people; rather they had left him. If the people persisted in their disobedience, the LORD would leave them in their misery. However, if they would seek him, he would be found by them.

Asa took God's word seriously. He removed the idols, repaired the LORD's altar, and called all the people together. They came eagerly. Convicted of their sin, they sought the LORD with all their heart and soul. And true to God's word, the LORD was found by them, and their repentance was followed by the great joy of revival. God's loving discipline worked. At least temporarily, his royal representative and the people he ruled experienced the joy that God intended for the citizens of his kingdom.

September 6

Ahab's Idolatrous Kingdom—Part 1

1 Kings 16:15–33

You shall bear the penalty for your sinful idolatry,
and you shall know that I am the Lord God.
Ezekiel 23:49 (ESV)

Israel, Judah's northern neighbor, did not demonstrate Judah's sensitivity to God's warnings through the prophets. This is extensively illustrated in the biblical record of the confrontations between Israel's King Ahab, who allowed the worship of Canaanite idols, and the prophet Elijah, who represented the LORD's claim to Israel's worship.

Ahab's course was influenced by the example of his father Omri, a talented leader whose building projects in Samaria rivaled those that Solomon had previously carried out in Jerusalem. The surrounding world was undoubtedly impressed by Omri. However, the LORD was not; Scripture says that he did evil in the LORD's eyes and sinned more than all those before him.

Ahab, who succeeded his father after twelve years, was worse: "He not only considered it trivial to commit the sins of Jeroboam son of Nebat, but he also married Jezebel, daughter of Ethbaal king of the Sidonians, and began to serve Baal and worship him" (1 Kings 16:31).

The main gods of Jezebel and the Canaanites were the fertility gods, Baal and Asherah, to whom sacrifices were made in the hope that they would bless the people with good harvests and many children. Ahab not only tolerated the worship of his pagan wife, he took an active role in leading Israel in her false religion, enabling the hold of sin to become stronger and stronger.

The ensuing spiritual warfare would be intense; reminiscent of one that took place centuries before between Pharaoh, false claimant to Israel's worship, and Moses, who represented the true claim of the Creator. In the end, however, the LORD would prevail.

September 7

Ahab's Idolatrous Kingdom—Part 2

1 Kings 16:23–33

When Noah awoke from his wine and knew what his youngest son had done to him, he said, "Cursed be Canaan; a servant of servants shall he be to his brothers." He also said, "Blessed be the LORD, the God of Shem; and let Canaan be his servant."
Genesis 9:24–26 (ESV)

As descendants of Noah's son Shem, the Israelites were heirs to a rich blessing. By contrast, Ham and his son Canaan were told that they would be dominated by Noah's other sons, and particularly by Shem and his offspring. This prophecy had started to come true already with Abraham, who prospered in what was called the land of Canaan. Further fulfillment came under Joshua when God brought Israel back to the land of Canaan.

However, by Ahab's sponsorship of the worship of Baal and Asherah, he effectively made his people subject to the Canaanites. It wasn't that Ahab wanted to outlaw the worship of the LORD—not like his wife Jezebel, who wanted that and wanted also to destroy God's prophets and even God himself, if she could. Yet, Ahab was doing something suicidal in compromising Israel's worship of the LORD. If this continued, it really wouldn't matter how much Israel prospered, because they would be separated from God, apart from whom they had no identity or future.

Ahab violated many of God's commandments, but the first and greatest one especially: "You shall have no other gods before me!" This was God's fundamental rule for life. Ahab also broke another long-standing command of God, the command to leave the broken walls of Jericho as a perpetual reminder to keep Israel's worship pure.

But God would not give up his claim on his people so easily, for he had made a sacred covenant with them. For centuries nations tried to conquer or subvert the loyalty of Israel, but the LORD always brought them back. He would do that this time as well.

September 8

The Sinful Rebuilding of Jericho

1 Kings 16:34

Joshua laid an oath on them at that time, saying, "Cursed before the LORD *be the man who rises up and rebuilds this city, Jericho. 'At the cost of his firstborn shall he lay its foundation, and at the cost of his youngest son shall he set up its gates.'"*
Joshua 6:26 (ESV)

Since Joshua's time, Jericho had remained an unfortified settlement. But, being a border city on a well-traveled route qualified it as an important line of defense against Israel's enemies. So Ahab commissioned Hiel to rebuild Jericho's walls. As much political sense as that made, it was a big mistake. The moment Hiel went to work he unleashed the curse that the LORD had put on Jericho and its rebuilders centuries earlier.

Perhaps it was partly out of fear that the previous kings of Israel had left Jericho unfortified. However, they also knew the lesson Jericho's ruins told. They reminded everyone of God's judgment against the Canaanites and their false worship. The ruins also proclaimed to both Israel and the world the grace and power by which God had settled his people in the Promised Land.

Ahab, and much of Israel with him, had become deaf to this message. Instead, Ahab proclaimed another message. Whether or not he put his name on Jericho's rebuilt walls, he meant them as a testament to his own success and glory. But Hiel paid a big price; he lost what an Israelite treasured above all—children to ensure that his family would not die out. It may even be that, encouraged by Ahab, Hiel sacrificed his own sons in pagan rituals. However he lost them, he suffered for disobeying the LORD; he lost his inheritance in the Promised Land.

Ahab showed more concern for building his own legacy than he did for what God wanted. But, in the effects of the curse, he got a preview of the lesson that Elijah would reinforce: "No one can prevail against the LORD."

September 9

Covenant Blessings Disappear

1 Kings 17:1

If you will not obey the voice of the LORD your God or be careful to do all his commandments... the LORD will make the rain of your land powder. From heaven dust shall come down upon you until you are destroyed.
Deuteronomy 28:15, 24 (ESV)

God sent his faithful prophet Elijah, whose very name means "My God is Yahweh," to bring Ahab to his senses over his leadership of Israel. Drought was a particularly appropriate consequence, given Ahab's idolatrous worship of the Canaanite fertility gods.

The ensuing famine was severe. Even King Ahab had trouble finding enough food to keep his animals alive. The nation staggered under the LORD's judgment. Nor was it only Israel's idol worshipers who suffered. We find out later that there were at least seven thousand people in Samaria who did not worship false gods. However, as part of the disobedient nation, they also suffered the consequences of the sins of the majority. They too had to watch their land dry up and their animals die. That's often the way sin works. Until Christ comes again, those who are righteous may not escape the impact of the sin of which they are innocent.

Elijah disappeared after he announced the drought, withdrawing to allow the effects of the LORD's judgment to become fully apparent. The people found out what misery it was to live without God; they had a little taste of hell.

Yet this was not a final judgment for them. Elijah had said, "There will be no more rain **except** at my word," implying that such a word would eventually come. So then, each day that went by was a learning aid to help the people realize how important God was and how powerless were the false prophets and false gods in the face of such a catastrophe. This drought was an opportunity and incentive for Israel, and for Israel's King Ahab, to repent and return to the LORD.

September 10

Patient Waiting and Prayer

1 Kings 17:2–6

Elijah was a man with a nature like ours, and he prayed fervently that it might not rain, and for three years and six months it did not rain.
James 5:17 (ESV)

In the midst of this time of judgment, the LORD took care of Elijah. He provided food and water for his servant in this time of scarcity. We do not know exactly where the brook Cherith was, or how the birds fed Elijah, or where they found the food, or even if Elijah had scruples about receiving nourishment from birds that God had labeled unclean. All we know is that the LORD took care of him.

The point of this story is not that true believers will never go hungry or thirsty. There were other believers in Israel who suffered along with the unfaithful. Yet, it is true that the grace the LORD showed to Elijah is a sample of the grace that he shows to his covenant people throughout history—his church of all ages. As the LORD kept Elijah alive, he was keeping his word alive, and with it, the hope of a future when things would be different.

Elijah was surely aware that he was being preserved because there was still more for him to do. However, it seems that he was in the dark about what that was. He didn't know how long the drought would last, nor how long it would be before the LORD sent him to Ahab again. As he had followed God's orders in his speaking, so also he would have to wait and trust without knowing just how or when God might use him next.

As a faithful prophet, however, Elijah also took what initiative he could; he prayed. It's the same initiative that Scripture repeatedly impresses as necessity upon all God's people, no matter how limited our other courses of action. Prayer is sometimes the only action we can take, as it likely appeared to be to Elijah during this time of waiting. So we may be sure that Elijah kept praying that Ahab and Israel might learn their lesson from God.

September 11

Grace Outside of Israel

1 Kings 17:7–16

Is God the God of Jews only? Is he not the God of Gentiles also? Yes, of Gentiles also...through faith.
Romans 3:29-30 (ESV)

Zarephath was in Queen Jezebel's homeland of Sidon. The religion of this place was the very reason that Israel was in trouble now, for with his marriage to Jezebel, Ahab had contaminated the covenant community with false religion. But now, God unexpectedly imported true religion into Sidon. This would be a twofold lesson:

- Israel should not take God's grace for granted.
- God had a bigger prize than Israel in mind. This foreign woman was to help restore God's own people and also to help make God's power known to a people who were not his own.

The widow's hospitality to Elijah was no small matter; she was in desperate circumstances. All that she owned had been used up. She and her son had only one meal left, and yet Elijah required even that of her. For that matter, the demand that God, through Elijah, made on this widow was not really different from the demand that God makes on everyone he calls into relationship with himself. God always asks for everything. He demands complete faith, complete trust. At the same time, his demands are always accompanied by his assurance of sufficient grace.

Neither the widow nor Israel could participate in the life God offered or in the covenant blessings without putting their faith and their lives on the line. And that's just what the widow did; she believed that the word of God was worth more than food. Her belief was confirmed by the miracle of God's provision.

Israel had forgotten that connection between worshiping God and eating well. If you put the LORD first, he will take care of the food. But if you put food before the LORD, as disobedient Israel had done by worshiping fertility gods, that is your ruin.

September 12

Brought to Complete Trust

1 Kings 17:17–24

Who will not fear, O LORD, and glorify your name?
For you alone are holy. All nations will come and worship you,
for your righteous acts have been revealed.
Revelation 15:4 (ESV)

God miraculously provided for Elijah and his hosts. However, it was a big challenge to their trust when the widow's son became ill and died. Neither one of the survivors doubted that the LORD's hand was in it. They knew that it was God who had taken the boy away in death. But they didn't understand it and cried out, "Why LORD! Why are you doing this?" The widow knew that she was a sinner; that's clear from her question to Elijah. But she still felt deceived by the LORD and his prophet. What had been the use of that unending supply of food if her son was now dead of something else? More than that, what was left to cling to if the LORD had turned against her? She had lost her son, the joy of her life.

Elijah was confused and anguished as well. He was sure, however, that the kingdom of the LORD would somehow be advanced through the boy's death. In that assurance Elijah went to work. He struggled in prayer for a miracle in which death would be reversed. Elijah was concerned not merely for the widow, but for the truth, power, and glory of God to be revealed.

The LORD heard Elijah's prayer and brought the boy back to life. This no doubt confirmed Elijah's faith, but the widow's increase in faith was even more spectacular. Her declaration of complete trust in God and his prophet was a sign that she had come to true faith. Her declaration would also be a witness to Israel from one who'd been outside of God's covenant of grace, but now had benefited from God's grace. Israel would see again that in the face of privation and death, everyone is powerless, everyone except the true Lord of heaven and earth. He is the only one through whom life can be sustained and restored.

September 13

Elijah Reappears in Israel

1 Kings 18:1–19

When the poor and needy seek water, and there is none, and their tongue is parched with thirst, I the LORD will answer them; I the God of Israel, will not forsake them.
Isaiah 41:17 (ESV)

Although Obadiah probably was not very vocal about his faith, he was one of the truly devout and God-fearing people remaining in Israel. One time he risked his life to save the lives of a hundred of the LORD's prophets. So he was probably pleased to see Elijah back in Israel. Even so, Obadiah was hesitant to arrange a meeting with Ahab; he was not sure that the LORD would not take Elijah away again, leaving Obadiah to suffer the consequences of Ahab's disappointment.

Ahab had been desperate to find Elijah in the hope that the accursed drought might be lifted. Still, when they met, he called Elijah a "troubler of Israel." This indicates that he was still only grudgingly ready to admit that the fertility of the land and the prosperity of Israel would not return except by the LORD's command. What Ahab says sounds very much like what schoolchildren sometimes say of a teacher who reacts to their misbehavior with appropriate measures: "My teacher got me into trouble." At a later time, Ahab calls Elijah his enemy. That's someone who gets you in trouble once too often.

It galled Ahab that Elijah responded by saying that Ahab was the one who had troubled Israel by abandoning the LORD's commands. However, as much as Ahab found Elijah to be a pain in his royal neck, it was the prophet who had announced the devastating drought and whose consent was needed for the rain to return. So Ahab knew he had no choice but to obey Elijah's order to assemble representatives from all of Israel together with the prophets of the Canaanite gods on Mount Carmel. There, as Ahab would find out, the LORD would correct Ahab's false leadership of Israel in a very public way.

September 14

Elijah's Discomfiting Question for Israel

1 Kings 18:20–21

O men, how long shall my honor be turned into shame?
How long will you love vain words and seek after lies?
Psalm 4:2 (ESV)

The question that Elijah asked the assembled multitude was one that reminded the Israelites of the covenant that God had made with their nation. The people of Ahab's day may not have known their history very well, but they knew of the pledge of exclusive loyalty to the LORD that their ancestors had made. They also knew about the curses that would come to the disobedient—specifically the curse of Deuteronomy 28:23—"The sky over your head will be bronze, the ground beneath you iron."

That's just what had happened in the drought; the fertility of the soil and the livestock that Israel had counted on Baal and Asherah to provide had dried up along with the rain. So far, however, the people had not rejected those Canaanite gods. So Elijah's question about how long the people would waver between allegiance to the LORD and Baal was very appropriate.

The people did not answer. Some were no doubt fuming with anger, some were probably resentful at being forced to account for their behavior, and some were likely feeling guilty because of Elijah's question. Perhaps some of those gathered on Carmel did not even know what the right answer was; their faith was weak after so much neglect and false worship.

Psalm 135 testifies to the unspeaking mouths, unseeing eyes, unhearing ears, and lack of breath of the silver and gold idols of the nations. Verse 18 of that chapter further claims, "Those who make them will be like them, and so will all who trust in them." That's just what had happened: Israel had become dumb, blind, deaf, and dead, like its idols. The power of the LORD would have to be displayed before the people could discern the truth and give an obedient response.

September 15

The Contest Begins

1 Kings 18:22–29

They are turned back and utterly put to shame, who trust in carved idols, who say to metal images, "You are our gods."
Isaiah 42:17 (ESV)

The prophets of the Canaanite gods had the first chance to win the contest proposed by Elijah. Some probably believed they had a chance of success—not the con artists who just told people what they wanted to hear but—those who seriously believed they could harness occult powers. These prophets hoped and tried to believe that their gods would respond. Indeed, if it were possible anywhere, it should have been on Mount Carmel where the power of Baal to nurture life was supposed to be the strongest.

But Baal's prophets took nothing for granted. They never tried harder than they did that day. They did everything they knew to do: frantic, mindless dancing, cutting themselves, loud and urgent chants and spells, some of which may have been drug-induced. But it wasn't enough; there was no response from Baal.

As I read this story, I think about all the things that modern people do to make God do what they want him to do, or otherwise try to control their destiny. Too many act as though salvation or utopia can be achieved by human effort and technique.

If it could, those hard-working prophets would likely have succeeded. But human effort can never manufacture something from nothing. Watching them, Elijah began to laugh. God also mocks such pretended wisdom; it would be the supreme joke if it weren't so tragic.

Wherever such godless ideas still appear as wisdom, the end of the day has not yet come. But it did come for those false prophets. By evening, their bodies caked with blood, they were exhausted, miserable, and silent, with no sign of success. Their foolishness was exposed. It can be no other way with those who will not bow to the LORD.

September 16

Elijah's Turn in the Contest

1 Kings 18:30–37

Are there any...false gods of the nations that can bring rain?
Or can the heavens give showers? Are you not he O LORD our God?
We set our hope on you, for you do all these things.
Jeremiah 14:22 (ESV)

Elijah began by repairing the altar of the LORD, which, in its present state of disrepair, was a silent testimony to the present distance between Israel and the LORD. The twelve stones Elijah used pointed to the importance of the unified worship still demanded of Israel. This altar was the foundation upon which true sacrifice could be offered.

When the altar had been repaired, Elijah prepared the sacrifice. There was no great difference between what he did and what Baal's prophets had done. But with the water that he poured over the altar, Elijah ensured that the impact of the coming proof would be as great as possible.

Even so, the water poured over the altar was not the fundamental difference between the two sides. That difference was in the results to come, which followed from the respective gods to whom the sacrifices were made and prayers were offered. Elijah, confident that he was following the will of the one and only God of the universe, prayed for the LORD to demonstrate his authority over the nothing idol gods. The LORD responded with an answer that left no doubt about who was the true God. Elijah's prayer was effective because only Elijah's God was real.

Since Elijah's time, Christ Jesus has become the ultimate sacrifice for sin and the only path to the Holy God. There is no way to catch God's ear or to enjoy his mercy as long as his approved sin-bearer is neglected or rejected. However, when Christ is at the center of our lives and worship we, like Elijah, may be sure that God will reveal himself in power and mercy to answer our hopes and prayers.

September 17

Israel's Response to Revealed Truth

1 Kings 18:39–40

With the heart one believes and is justified,
and with the mouth confesses and is saved.
Romans 10:10 (ESV)

The fire that God sent in response to Elijah's prayer was meant to remind the people of God's previous revelations to their nation and to recall them to whole-hearted service. If the LORD's voice had thundered from heaven, things could not have been clearer.

The response of the people was similar to that of their ancestors when the tent of meeting was dedicated at Mount Sinai. At that time, "Fire came out from the presence of the LORD and consumed the burnt offering and the fat portions on the altar. And when all the people saw it, they shouted for joy and fell facedown" (Lev. 9:24). Here too, the people knew they were in the presence of Almighty God and they fell flat on their faces before him. Their faith returned with strength and they cried out, "The LORD, he is God! The LORD, he is God!"

Not everyone came to faith by God's revelation. The crowd of false prophets and priests who had vainly cried out to their gods for hours did not repent. Therefore, what repentant Israel experienced that day as a miracle of Almighty God, the unrepentant prophets of false gods experienced as the beginning of God's judgment. The now-faithful people seized the idol prophets and put them to death. It was the only possible end for those who persisted in defying the LORD God.

Their sad end is a sign for all people that there is no grace and no salvation without judgment, and no love without justice. As Elijah was God's agent in rescuing God's people from disaster, so he was God's agent in dispatching the enemies of God. It's the same thing that will happen eventually to all who do not acknowledge Jesus Christ as Savior and Lord of their lives; those who will not repent will be caught in God's awful judgment.

September 18

The Blessings Return

1 Kings 18:41–46

If you faithfully obey the voice of the LORD your God...
[he] will open to you his good treasury, the heavens, to give the
rain to your land in its season and to bless all the work of your hands.
Deuteronomy 28:1, 12 (ESV)

With divine help the people finally sorted out who the real God was and how awful had been their rebellion against him. With repentance and confession, the way was open for a restoration of the covenant with all its blessings. The blessed rain could now return, both the physical rain and the rain of spiritual blessings.

However, as Elijah knew, the blessings would not come without prayer. At first, his servant saw no results from Elijah's prayers. Nor did he see any results the second time Elijah sent him to look, nor the third, fourth, fifth, or sixth times. Only after the servant's seventh trip from the place where Elijah was praying to where the servant could look out over the distant western horizon did he see a little cloud rising from the sea. He reported it to Elijah, who knew that it was the sign of the imminent return of God's covenant blessings. It wouldn't be long now before Ahab and his people would enjoy the favor of God.

Elijah told Ahab to get going before the rain stopped him. By the power of the LORD whom he represented, Elijah ran ahead of the king. Ahab had gone up the mountain following hundreds of false prophets, only to have his misguided plans fail. Now he was on his way back down, but this time following Elijah, the true prophet of the LORD. Hopefully Ahab had learned that he could continue as king only by truly following the LORD.

What was true for Ahab and Israel is still no less true today. Real and continuing life is possible only when you follow the Lord; every other path is destined for failure. God will always win over those who oppose him and sooner or later vindicate those who put their trust in him.

September 19

Elijah's Model Prayer—Part 1

1 Kings 18:36, 38

Be still, and know that I am God. I will be exalted among the nations, I will be exalted in the earth!
Psalm 46:10 (ESV)

Elijah's prayers were obviously effective and well-suited to the challenges of his day. What may not be quite as clear is how well they serve as a model for us to follow. I'm confident that whether or not we see equally spectacular results, we cannot go wrong praying as Elijah prayed.

The first thing Elijah asked for was that the LORD God would make himself known as the one true God: "LORD, the God of Abraham, Isaac and Israel, let it be known today that you are God in Israel."

Elijah wasn't asking the LORD to do something new and different here, for God had a history of revealing himself as the true God and worthy of all praise, adoration, and obedience. So really what Elijah was asking was that God would do it again. The people had forgotten; they no longer believed. So Elijah wanted the LORD to show himself again to be God and to make what he had done in the past relevant and immediate to his people of that day. Elijah asked that God would light the fire, not for Elijah's sake but for God's sake, so that the people would get beyond a merely formal understanding of God and get to know him as their LORD.

What an excellent prayer for us today—that the church and the world both will know that the LORD God is the true God. The continuing existence of God's people today is dependent upon the knowledge of God, upon God making himself real and known. God wants to do that, so we can pray that prayer with confidence, sure that God will confirm himself to his people as their sovereign creator and redeemer, and that he will also help the unbelieving world know this truth.

September 20

Elijah's Model Prayer—Part 2

1 Kings 18:36, 38

The LORD God helps me; therefore I have not been disgraced; therefore I have set my face like a flint, and I know I shall not be put to shame. He who vindicates me is near.
Isaiah 50:7–8 (ESV)

The second part of Elijah's prayer followed from the first: "[And] let it be known…that I am your servant and have done all these things at your command." God had called Elijah to be his servant and to speak for him. So Elijah was quite properly praying for God to validate him: *LORD, prove that I'm not just making all this up out of my own head, but that I've been acting at your direction. I'm just speaking your Word. I don't have in myself the power to bring your promises to fulfillment; you have to do that. Validate that the word I speak is your word.*

Elijah's prayer for God to validate him was not a self-seeking or proud prayer. He could have become proud when Ahab credited him with bringing the country to a standstill in the drought. But he didn't; he had only God's glory in mind. He knew how unimportant he was, but also how important his work was—his work to reveal the glory and promote the honor of God. Only as a servant on a mission did Elijah demand the people's attention; he wanted everyone to recognize they were all called to be the servants of the Most High God.

We can and must also pray for the LORD to support and defend his true church as servant and agent of his saving work. We can pray boldly and confidently for this because God tells us that this is his desire. God lifts up his church not so it will get the glory, but so the attention of the world will be focused more and more on Christ. What is to be glorified is not the persons of the church, but the work and the service of the church, which is for Christ's sake. May the world come to realize, in its encounters with God's people, that they are dealing with God himself.

September 21

Elijah's Model Prayer—Part 3

1 Kings 18:37–39

[John the Baptist] will go before [the Messiah] in the spirit and power of Elijah, to turn the hearts of the fathers to the children, and the disobedient to the wisdom of the just, to make ready for the Lord a people prepared.
Luke 1:17 (ESV)

The third part of Elijah's prayer was for a proper response—for the people to recognize God and confess him. "Answer me, LORD, answer me, so these people will know that you, LORD, are God, and that you are turning their hearts back again."

Elijah knew that every revelation of God—whether of mercy or of power—demands an answer from the people who witness it. He also knew that people would not necessarily be changed by such a revelation. That is, not all hard-hearted people who see God's miracles become believers. For example, Pharaoh's heart had not become soft when he had seen the LORD's power in Egypt. Nor did the prophets of Baal get soft hearts when they saw fire from the LORD. It's not enough for people merely to recognize the might and power of God; they must also accept his rule with a willing and believing heart.

The long drought had made the people sad, to be sure, but it had not made them recognize that the LORD was God and return to him. At this point, they were still faithless. So along with the outward and visible revelation of God in fire, Elijah prayed for an inward revelation, a change of heart, demonstrated by repentance and conversion.

This prayer was magnificently answered in all respects. God did just what Elijah asked. He revealed himself as Lord, he proved that Elijah was a faithful prophet, and he brought the people to repentance and devotion. We must likewise pray that people today not only recognize God's power, but that they also respond to his call to put away their idols and come over to his side.

September 22

Elijah's Model Prayer—Part 4

1 Kings 18:41–45

I will pour water on the thirsty land, and streams on the dry ground; I will pour out my Spirit upon your offspring, and my blessing on your descendants.
Isaiah 44:3 (ESV)

God's answer to the first parts of Elijah's prayer testified to the power and grace of God. Yet, a most important thing was still lacking. So, after his prayers for God's glory, his own vindication, and the people's response had been answered, "Elijah climbed to the top of Carmel, bent down to the ground and put his face between his knees." He was ready to ask now for the return of the covenant blessings and specifically the blessing of rain.

Elijah prayed seven times, the number seven symbolizing the fullness of the rich communion possible between the LORD and his people. But that repeated prayer also shows Elijah's persistence in prayer. It is possible, after all, to miss out on God's blessings by giving up too easily.

God's answer began in the form of a little cloud that grew and finally brought an end to the drought. Neither the fire nor the rain came automatically, but only after prolonged prayer. Elijah prayed so intensely that a watcher might have thought that the blessing was entirely dependent on his prayer. In a way it was; it was what God expected and desired from his servant partner—Elijah raising the needs of the people to their sovereign LORD, just as Christ would later do and teach his followers to do.

I wonder how often our prayers are like Elijah's. We are invited to approach God with pitiful cries for help, painful prayers of repentance, and joyful prayers of thanksgiving and praise. But, also, as partner-servants of Almighty God, we need to pray the bold, working prayers of Elijah. The more we get to know the Scripture in which God reveals so much of his plans, goals, and promises, the more we can pray like this.

September 23

Why Elijah's Prayers Worked

1 Kings 18:25–46

Pray then like this: "Our Father in heaven, hallowed be your name. Your kingdom come, your will be done on earth as it is in heaven."
Matthew 6:9–10 (ESV)

Before leaving this story, I want to emphasize the main factors that ensured the success of Elijah's prayers. On the surface the prayers of the idol prophets had much in common with Elijah's prayers. They were offered to someone unseen, they asked for similar things, and they were energetic. Elijah's prayer does seem to have been offered with more confidence. And yet, it was not his confidence that made the prayer work; it was God. Prayer only works for the ones whose God is real. That was the first factor in Elijah's success.

A second factor of equal importance was that Elijah prayed according to God's directions. He knew in advance that God wanted the very things for which Elijah prayed.

- God wants it known that only he is God.
- God promises to validate those who do his bidding.
- God repeatedly makes clear the results he intends from the revelation of his power.
- God's blessings are meant for those who are in a proper relationship with him.

It's no wonder Elijah's prayers worked. But don't make the mistake of thinking that they were unnecessary because they just summarized what Elijah already knew God wanted to do. Elijah understood that the prayers of believers are part of the process by which God advances his kingdom and fulfills his promises.

May our prayers be as urgent, knowledgeable, to the point, confident, and persevering for our world. As God's partner-servants, let's keep praying, "Reveal yourself, vindicate your servants, bring people to repentance, and send the blessings that you promised. Do it for your glory Lord, over and over again."

September 24

Elijah's Discouragement

1 Kings 19:1–5a

We do not wrestle against flesh and blood, but against the rulers, against the authorities, against the cosmic powers over this present darkness, against the spiritual forces of evil in the heavenly places.
Ephesians 6:12 (ESV)

Rather than submit to the clear and powerful message that God gave on Mount Carmel, Jezebel, as the tool of Satan she was, resisted and pledged to continue her vendetta against Elijah. Ahab, who had seen firsthand what God had done, was neutral at best; his inaction showed his lack of godly character and his unwillingness to take a stand for God.

Elijah ran for his life. Even with his prophetic power and close connection with God he was unable to continue the battle. Sometimes going into hiding is an obedient response; Elijah's departure from Israel after announcing the drought had been just that. But flight now was purely out of concern for his own survival, and likely served to diminish Israel's newfound respect for the power of God.

Elijah had just seen the power of God displayed, but now felt alone and powerless in the face of the continuing spiritual warfare. His prayers proved it. He was no longer the bold partner-servant, sure of what God wanted. Elijah's prayers now were pitiful cries for help. It was understandable; great spiritual victories are often followed by spiritual lows, temptations, and depression. It's a familiar problem for those who work hard for the Lord. And some, like Elijah, at least temporarily desert their calling and compromise their previous witness.

The solution is not to deny fear and weakness. It is rather to understand the nature of spiritual warfare and the letdown that can occur so soon after displays of God's power. Despite any feelings to the contrary we may be sure that God has an answer for every trouble and never leaves his servants on their own.

September 25

An Answer for Elijah's Discouragement

1 Kings 19:5b–18

Attend to my cry, for I am brought very low! Deliver me from my persecutors, for they are too strong for me!
Psalm 142:6 (ESV)

God answered Elijah's need rather than his request to die; an angel was sent to give him enough energy to travel on to the mountain of the LORD. There God listened to Elijah's complaints and then began to reveal himself through signs: a storm, an earthquake, and a fire. These were not the revelation of the LORD, but the signs of his coming revelation, which Elijah heard as a gentle whisper. The LORD repeated his earlier question, and Elijah answered with his earlier response. Elijah thought he'd done enough and wanted to retire, if not die. But it was not for Elijah to determine when his work was finished. The LORD was not through with him or with Israel.

In his new commission for Elijah, the LORD revealed both judgment and grace. Because Israel's repentance was superficial, it could not escape the LORD's judgment. Elijah may have hoped for such a reprieve when Mount Carmel resounded with cries of praise to God, but this hope was now taken away.

However, the LORD still had many left in Israel who remained faithful to him. Seven thousand is a significant number, being seven (the number of perfection or completion) multiplied by one thousand (the number representing the whole multitude of those who remained faithful to the LORD). In other words, although Israel as a whole was to suffer judgment, this would not impair God's purposes. He would preserve a remnant of true Israel, the faithful, who would be heir to his covenant and promises.

With this fresh look at the LORD's plans, Elijah became reenergized for service as the LORD's prophet. But he was also given help—Elisha—to be his apprentice and to eventually succeed him as God's prophet to Israel.

September 26

Ahab's Contempt for God's Kindness

1 Kings 20

Do you presume on the riches of his kindness and forbearance and patience, not knowing that God's kindness is meant to lead you to repentance?
Romans 2:4 (ESV)

God had not yet taken the kingship of Israel from Ahab, so it was still possible for Ahab to do better than he had to this point. Or, he could do worse, moving farther away from the LORD until God removed him from office. Today's Scripture tells the story of the path Ahab took.

Israel faced an imminent attack from Syria that worried Ahab greatly. God sent a prophet to tell him that he would give Israel the victory. And God did. Later, when Ben-Hadad threatened Israel again, the prophet returned to give Ahab a similar message. Again, Israel triumphed; God gave Israel the victory so that Ahab would give the LORD the honor he deserved.

Ahab twice saw God's power in delivering Israel from certain defeat. If ever the time was ripe to give himself to full allegiance to the LORD, this was it. But, in sparing the life of the captured king of Syria and offering to make a treaty with him, Ahab opposed God's judgment against this sworn enemy of Israel.

A prophet of the LORD made this clear to Ahab by a question he put to the king. The prophet pretended that he had been in the battle and accused of dereliction of duty. He asked Ahab for mercy. Ahab had no patience for this supposed shirker and condemned him to die. At that, the prophet revealed that Ahab had pronounced sentence on himself, since he had neglected to carry out the command of the LORD with regard to Ben-Hadad.

Ahab became sullen and angry at this judgment of the LORD. It was a telling reaction. If there had been any doubt about Ahab's allegiance to the LORD, it was now erased by his negative response to God's word.

September 27

Ahab, Unfaithful Shepherd of Israel

1 Kings 21

Have they no knowledge, all the evildoers who eat up my people as they eat bread and do not call upon the LORD?
Psalm 14:4 (ESV)

Ahab's unsuitability to shepherd God's people, which had been proven by his unfaithfulness with respect to an avowed enemy of the LORD, would soon be confirmed by his equal unfaithfulness with respect to his own people.

According to the law of the LORD it was wrong for Ahab even to ask for Naboth's inheritance. God had told his people, "The land must not be sold permanently, because the land is mine and you reside in my land as foreigners and strangers" (Lev. 25:23). God had provided each family with land as a permanent inheritance. But here Ahab was, trying to get around God's provisions for even the most humble of his people.

When Naboth answered Ahab with a biblical response, the king reacted with his familiar disregard for what God wanted: he became sullen and angry. His wife Jezebel, the confirmed idol-worshiper and God-hater, affirmed Ahab in his attitude. Although she despised the law of the LORD, she now used it to have Naboth falsely convicted of blasphemy. As a result, Naboth was executed and Ahab got the property he coveted.

In this, of course, Ahab proved himself to be as unfaithful a shepherd with of his own people as he had been with respect to an enemy of God. So Elijah, at God's prompting, called Ahab on it with a word of judgment from the LORD.

At hearing Elijah's words, Ahab finally did the right thing; he repented. This may have been Ahab's first experience with repentance; it is certainly the first that Scripture records. And because of it, Ahab received a measure of grace from the LORD (v. 28). However, only time would tell if Ahab's humility before God would last.

September 28

False Leadership Continues

1 Kings 22:1–9; 2 Chronicles 18:1–8

When I look there is no one; among these there is no counselor who, when I ask, gives an answer. Behold, they are all a delusion; their works are nothing; their metal images are empty wind.
Isaiah 41:28–29 (ESV)

Ahab had humbled himself after his execution of Naboth, but his attitude toward God would be tested in the trouble that was brewing with Aram. Ahab asked for the support of Jehoshaphat, who was allied to him through marriage. The king of Judah answered that he was willing with one stipulation: "First seek the counsel of the LORD" (1 Kings 22:5). It was something that Ahab himself should have thought to do and he readily agreed.

The four hundred prophets Ahab summoned to determine God's will on this matter were, in title at least, prophets of the LORD. But Jehoshaphat was obviously skeptical of their answer because he inquired whether there was not a prophet of the LORD to ask.

The four hundred were not prophets of Baal and Asherah like those who had been vanquished in the contest on Mount Carmel. But, as Ahab knew, neither were they real prophets of the LORD. Their presence in court was merely to give Ahab's desires the stamp of authenticity. Their loyalty to the LORD apparently mirrored Ahab's own—incomplete and fickle at best. In any case, Ahab knew exactly why Jehoshaphat was skeptical of their prediction of success, and he also knew the prophet Micaiah to whom he should turn for a real word from the LORD.

However, Ahab worried that Micaiah would be negative about his plans. Ahab already hated him for the same reason he regarded Elijah as his enemy—both prophets told him the truth about his failures as Israel's king. So it was only with reluctance that he agreed to hear from Micaiah. Despite his previous humility, Ahab was still not inclined to hear about his failures or to truly seek the LORD's will.

September 29

Ahab Reaps what He has Sown

1 Kings 22:10–37; 2 Chronicles 18:9–34

As I have seen, those who plow iniquity and sow trouble reap the same.
Job 4:8 (ESV)

The messenger sent to get Micaiah warned him that he'd be wise to agree with the four hundred prophets who had predicted success for Ahab. But Micaiah, true to form, answered that he was bound to say only what the LORD revealed to him. Then he went on to mouth the words that Ahab wanted to hear: "Attack and be victorious, for the LORD will give it into the king's hand" (1 Kings 22:15).

Knowing that the prophet's words were insincere, Ahab pressed Micaiah for a true answer from God. And he got just the answer he had feared—nothing but defeat would follow his planned course of action. Micaiah also told Ahab that the other prophets were so far from being the LORD's servants that God had put a lying spirit in their mouths.

This was a very bad omen for Ahab, who slapped Micaiah in prison and persisted in the course he had determined to take. Ahab took precautions to avoid the predicted disaster and Jehoshaphat felt compelled to go along with him; he put on the clothes of Israel's king while Ahab wore the clothes of an ordinary soldier so that the enemy would not be able to find and kill Israel's commander-in-chief. It almost worked. Jehoshaphat was mistaken for Ahab and almost killed for it until his pursuers realized their mistake at the last second and let him go.

Jehoshaphat would later be rebuked by another prophet for his cooperation with Ahab (see 2 Chron. 19:2). As for Ahab, all of his precautions could not save his life; it was ended by an apparently random arrow. Ahab died in dishonor because he despised the LORD's leadership as well as the many opportunities he'd been given to change his ways and become a suitable shepherd for God's people.

September 30

Ahab's Epitaph

1 Kings 21:25–26

The wicked...are like chaff that the wind drives away.
Therefore the wicked will not stand in the judgment,
nor sinners in the congregation of the righteous.
Psalm 1:4–5 (ESV)

After the division of Solomon's kingdom, the rulers of Judah (headquartered in Jerusalem) generally received a better report than those of Israel (headquartered in Samaria). However, Judah's record was not consistently good, and Judah was eventually destroyed for disobedience, just like Israel. Nevertheless, Israel's wickedness was typically the greater, and it would be the first to go into exile.

The relative level of wickedness in Israel is seen in part by the final evaluation Scripture gives to its kings. All of Israel's kings tolerated the so-called *sins of Jeroboam* (see 1 Kings 12:28–33; 13:33–34). Scripture repeatedly says that they "did evil in the eyes of the LORD." Some, however, were judged to have done **more** evil in the eyes of the LORD than any of the kings who preceded them. Ahab stands as the preeminent example of this unholy line, as his epitaph indicates (see 1 Kings 21:25-26). That's probably why Scripture devotes so much attention to Ahab—most of the attitudes and actions of his life are testimonies to the things God hates. God gave Ahab many chances to repent and change his ways, and when Ahab did not, God still stuck with his plan to redeem his people and show his grace to the whole world through them.

What a tragedy that Ahab showed such intolerance for what God wanted. By intent or not, Ahab trained his heart and actions to become more and more incompatible with what God loves. It's the very thing, God forbid, that usually happens to those who refuse to take care of the little things that stand in the way of their love for God, instead allowing sin to have its way in their lives. May God help us to be more like Elijah and Micaiah.

October 1

Jehoshaphat's Epitaph

2 Chronicles 19:1–20:30

O our God...we are powerless against this great horde that is coming against us. We do not know what to do, but our eyes are on you.
2 Chronicles 20:12 (ESV)

Jehoshaphat was severely reprimanded by Jehu for his alliance with Ahab. Jehoshaphat also had other errors of judgment in his twenty-five years as Judah's king. Even so, he compares well to Ahab in his readiness to accept correction and serve the LORD. Ahab always tried to have his own way. But Jehoshaphat genuinely sought God's direction and help, not only when he faced Judah's enemies. He also rid the land of idol shrines and appointed godly judges. Unlike Ahab, Jehoshaphat was judged at the end of his life to have done what was right in the eyes of the LORD.

Jehoshaphat's prayer and next actions in the face of the Moabite/Ammonite threat is still a model for the prayers and actions of Christ's people facing adversity.

- He called people from all over Judah to come together and pray; they were as one before the LORD.
- He acknowledged the previously displayed wisdom and power of God, and called upon God to remember that he had promised to hear and answer the prayers of his devoted people.
- He confessed the complete dependence of himself and his people on the saving mercy of the LORD.
- After his prayer he obeyed the LORD's instructions.
- He and his people began to praise God for his answer to prayer even before they witnessed it.
- After the victory, Jehoshaphat led the people in joyful rededication to the LORD.

Afterwards, Judah was given "rest on every side" and the fear of the LORD came upon the surrounding nations. Such rest and such a testimony is what God's people can always expect when they truly depend on the LORD.

October 2

Elijah's Successor

2 Kings 2

On the day I punish Israel for his transgressions,
I will punish the altars of Bethel.
Amos 3:14 (ESV)

Elijah had proved himself to be a genuine and powerful prophet of the LORD, one without equal in Israel. God's other faithful servants might have been excused for wondering what would happen when Elijah died. Would his spirit and his mission be given to another? As it turned out, Elijah would not die, but would be transported directly into the presence of God. Before he departed, however, he chose Elisha as his successor. Elisha wisely asked for and received a double portion of Elijah's spirit.

As with Elijah, Elisha served as the agent of God's messages of grace and judgment for Judah and Israel. A well-known story from early in his ministry emphasizes judgment for those who persisted in disobedience. Elisha, on his way to Bethel, was taunted by some youths from there. The curse he pronounced on them resulted in the injury or death of forty-two of them. To understand this severe judgment, it will help to remember that Bethel at this time was one of two centers of idolatrous worship that had been set up by Jeroboam (see 1 Kings 12:28–33). Also, the insults of these idolaters were not so much affronts to Elisha as they were to the LORD whose name Elisha bore and who had chosen Elisha to take Elijah's place as God's messenger.

Elisha's ministry would not, however, be primarily one of judgment. He also would frequently demonstrate the healing power and mercy of God. His first miracle, healing the water of Jericho, showed God's mercy to his own people. But Elisha would also repeatedly show and tell of the mercy of God to the poor and outcasts, and especially those who were outside of the covenant circle. Elisha's ministry would demonstrate that the love and mercy of God was far more generous than most people imagined.

October 3

The Grace of God Shown to Israel

2 Kings 4

Choose life, that you and your offspring may live,
loving the LORD your God, obeying his voice
and holding fast to him, for he is your life.
Deuteronomy 30:19–20 (ESV)

The Scripture for today gives several illustrations of the power of God's word and of the LORD's intention to bless and prosper his chosen people through the ministry of Elisha.

First was God's help for the widow of one of his prophets. It may be that the LORD's earlier instructions for the care of widows and orphans were not being followed closely enough (see Deut. 24:19–21). For whatever reason, this widow was on the verge of bankruptcy. But, she had not forgotten that all things were possible through God, so she approached his prophet for an answer to her distress. Through the miracle of the endless supply of oil, God provided all the food and money she needed.

Next was a woman who already had plenty of food and money—and was generous with it—but had never been blessed with the child she desperately wanted. She had given up hope by this time, but Elisha blessed her; the result was that she miraculously gave birth to a son. When this boy died suddenly, the LORD used Elisha to perform another miracle—the boy was raised from death.

Crowds witnessed two other miracles of Elisha. In the first of these, the LORD proved his power over life and death by neutralizing the poison that threatened the lives of the hungry prophets. In the second, a few bread rolls were miraculously multiplied to feed a hundred people.

The miracles Elisha preformed, like those later done by Jesus, are testimonies both to the good will of God toward his people and to the truth that it is nothing for the one who created all things to supply every need of those who put their trust in him.

October 4

Rumors of Grace Outside of Israel

2 Kings 5:1–8

Behold, you shall call a nation that you do not know, and a nation that did not know you shall run to you, because of the LORD your God, and of the Holy One of Israel, for he has glorified you.
Isaiah 55:5 (ESV)

Foreigners to Israel were sometimes more aware and more appreciative of the grace and power of God than were God's own chosen people. The Syrian, Naaman, for example, heard of God's work through Elisha from an Israelite slave in his household. His desperate hope for a cure for his leprosy was such that he made arrangements to travel to Israel to see the prophet.

Israel's king, on the other hand, had little appreciation for Elisha or his God, even though the prophet correctly prophesied not long before that Israel would win an important battle against Moab. God used Elisha in other miraculous ways too. But Israel's King Joram was so blind to the display of God's grace to him and his people and had so little regard for the power of Elisha and the God he served that he considered the impossible request of Naaman's king to be a pretext for war.

Hearing of King Joram's dismay, Elisha rebuked him for his ignorance and instructed that Naaman be sent to him so that the power of God might be displayed in the life of this outsider to Israel. Naaman came eagerly, prepared for the occasion with lavish gifts to reward the one who could restore his health. Although he had heard of the grace and power of God, he had no idea that what he sought was unavailable for purchase. Nor did he know that what was about to happen would be such an important testimony for him and for everyone who heard of his experience.

Thank God for faithful servants like Elisha who persist in doing God's will, and for those, such as the slave girl, who aren't afraid to believe in and testify to the work of God.

October 5

Grace is for Outsiders Too

2 Kings 5:9–14

[The LORD] says, "It is too light a thing that you should be my servant to raise up the tribes of Jacob and to bring back the preserved of Israel; I will make you as a light for the nations, that my salvation may reach to the end of the earth."
Isaiah 49:6 (ESV)

Naaman was significantly disappointed and angered when, upon arrival at Elisha's house, he did not even get to see the prophet. Naaman had expected some deference and ceremony at the least. But all he got was a message. "Go take a bath in the river."

General Naaman went off in a rage. His resistance was not unusual. In fact, it's common for the human heart not only to want what it wants, but to want it according to preconceived ideas. People don't mind rigorous procedures to achieve healing or salvation; in fact, most of us rather prefer them. We will endure all sorts of requirements so long as they seem reasonable. But, we're too often reluctant to follow the simple prescription of the Word of God.

Something in Naaman had to die before he could follow Elisha's instructions. He received wise counsel on this from his servants and came to see that he had to give up his pride and submit himself to the instructions of an ordinary and unimportant person. It was only when he did this—when he gave up his rights and obeyed the Word of the LORD through Elisha—that he was healed.

Seven times Naaman had to go into the river—to show that the healing was a work of God. Afterwards his skin became like that of a child. There was no more evidence of open, running sores, numb fingers and toes; he was made whole. It was a physical sign, both to Israel and the world beyond Israel, of the healing power and saving grace that cleanses the bodies and spirits of those who come under the power of the Spirit of God.

October 6

You Can't Buy Grace

2 Kings 5:15–19

He saved us, not because of works done by us in righteousness,
but according to his own mercy, by the washing of
regeneration and renewal of the Holy Spirit.
Titus 3:5 (ESV)

Naaman was overjoyed by his healing. He naturally appreciated the prophet Elisha. But more than that, he appreciated the God of Elisha who had shown that he was without equal in the world. In fact, Naaman said as much and wanted to show his appreciation in the customary way—with a generous payment for services rendered.

What Naaman did not understand, however, was that God is not impressed by worldly wealth. Nor did Naaman know that God takes delight in freely showering grace, not only on his servants, but on outside-of-the-covenant idol worshipers such as Naaman.

God meant to teach Naaman that he could never pay for his grace, but that it was a free gift offered to undeserving sinners. God also wanted Naaman to see that the only place to direct his gratitude was to the one by whose power he had been healed.

That Naaman began to understand these things is signified by his confession that Elisha's God was the one true God and the only one deserving of his sacrifices. To that end, he requested permission to take some dirt from Israel, the land of the people of Yahweh, so that he could bring more acceptable sacrifices when he returned home to Syria, where the worship of Yahweh was unknown.

Naaman was thus given a taste of what God intended for many more outside-of-the-covenant, lost-in-sin people. He would be a sign of God's grace to all such as he, and a message to Israel that they should neither take God's grace for granted nor forget the love God has for strangers and aliens.

October 7

God's Anger over Misrepresented Grace

2 Kings 5:20–27

May your money perish with you, because you thought you could obtain the gift of God with money...Repent, therefore, of this wickedness of yours, and pray to the Lord that, if possible, the intent of your heart may be forgiven you.
Acts 8:20, 22 (ESV)

Gehazi knew the lessons that God wanted Naaman to learn about God's grace. However, in his greed, Gehazi put them out of his mind and secretly caught up with the Syrian to secure for himself some of the wealth that his master had refused to take. For his part, Naaman was happy to comply. He had tried to pay for the healing he had received. Now he got another chance. He saw that Elisha was not that different from other prophets after all—he wanted to take gifts secretly in order to preserve his image as someone who cared nothing for money.

Tragically, Gehazi's greed gave Naaman the wrong idea about God. Naaman now thought, or was tempted to think, that God and his prophets were just like all other gods and their prophets.

We don't know if Gehazi's misrepresentation of God's grace was disastrous for Naaman. But we do know that it was disastrous for Gehazi. The leprosy, which had not been a judgment for Naaman, became a judgment for Gehazi and his descendants. That's the sort of unhappy results sin always has if it is not dealt with properly. Except for the surprising grace of God that sets people free, the sins of the parents become compounded and solidified in the lives of their children and grandchildren.

Such personal consequences are bad enough. But even worse is the compromised witness to the purposes and character of God. Those who are supposed to live for the Lord must never sidetrack or silence the message of redeeming love that can neither be earned nor paid for, but comes freely by the grace of God in Christ Jesus.

October 8

Jonah's Failed Escape

Jonah 1:1–16

Father, I have sinned against heaven and before you.
I am no longer worthy to be called your son.
Luke 15:21 (ESV)

The New Testament often describes the lengths to which God will go so that even those whom others deem most unlikely and undeserving might be brought under the umbrella of his grace. But, there is also ample evidence of this before the time of Jesus. We've just read of Elisha's ministry to Naaman and others who were outsiders to Israel and its covenant relationship with God. Another significant example of God's extravagant grace to outsiders is his call to Jonah to preach to the Assyrians in Nineveh.

Jonah was aghast at the mission that the LORD gave him. He agreed with God's assessment of the evil in that city, but thought that the people there were beyond repentance and unworthy of mercy. So Jonah fled in the opposite direction, running not only from Nineveh but from God himself. In doing so, he left Nineveh in peril and also endangered both his life and the lives of the crew of the ship on which he took passage.

Everyone aboard the ship knew that there was something supernatural about the storm that refused to abate. But only Jonah knew that he was the cause. His failure was not one of unbelief, for he still believed in the LORD. He simply did not agree with God's plan to offer the people of Nineveh a chance to repent. However, as Jonah finally came to understand, it is futile to resist the plans or try to escape the reach of the sovereign LORD.

Jonah knew that his life was forfeit for his attempt to run from God. How can it be otherwise for anyone who stands against God Almighty? We may wonder whether it is worse to live in wickedness and evil, as the Ninevites were doing, or, knowing God, to consciously resist his direction, as Jonah did. But, no wise person will do either.

October 9

Jonah Gets another Chance

Jonah 1:17–2:10

O LORD my God, I cried to you for help, and you have healed me. O LORD, you have brought up my soul from Sheol; you restored me to life from among those who go down to the pit.
Psalm 30:2–3 (ESV)

God could have found a replacement for Jonah. But the LORD is as persistent in correcting the disobedience of those who are in covenant with him as he is in calling new people into covenant with himself. In mercy, therefore, God provided a "great fish" to swallow Jonah and, after three days to deposit him on solid ground, alive and willing to serve according to God's directions.

Jonah prayed in the interim. No doubt he recalled both his own faithlessness and the LORD's faithfulness, and had time to reconsider both the futility of disobedience and the fruitfulness of a life of obedience. The psalms of Israel helped here; Jonah used the words that all of his people had memorized; he asked God for help and testified to the power and goodness of the LORD.

Some people cannot believe that Jonah could have survived such an ordeal. Others think that he actually died and then was raised to life three days later. Either way, this is a story of God's provision and power, and the unswerving dedication God has to do whatever it takes to accomplish his purposes. It may be that Jonah even used the story of his deliverance in his preaching to the people of Nineveh.

Jesus himself later compared what would happen with him to what happened with Jonah (Matt. 12:39–41). Just as Jonah was delivered from the fish after three days, he would be raised to life after three days. Jesus also said that the people of Nineveh, who repented in response to Jonah's preaching, would testify at the judgment to the foolishness of those who refused to repent and turn to God at the message of Jesus, a much greater prophet, and one who provided a much greater salvation.

October 10

Ninevah Gets another Chance

Jonah 3:1–4:4

I am sending you to open their eyes, so that they may turn from darkness to light and from the power of Satan to God, that they may receive forgiveness of sins and a place among those who are sanctified by faith in me.
Acts 26:17–18 (ESV)

Jonah obeyed God's second call to confront Ninevah with the need for repentance, although he was not particularly tactful in doing so. His message seemed designed to irritate and alienate people rather than draw them to his message and his God. But Jonah was not strategizing, as Christians often do today, about how to build bridges of mutually beneficial dialogue. Strategies may sometimes be helpful in evangelism, but the crucial factor is faithfulness to the message that God wants preached. Authorized and effective preaching is always informed and energized by God's Spirit.

Because this was the case with Jonah, his lone voice among the multitudes of people who lived in this vast spiritual wilderness of a city prompted an amazing response. Masses of citizens mourned their wickedness, fasting and donning sackcloth and ashes. Even the king and his court joined in this heartfelt demonstration in the hope that God might turn from the prophesied destruction. And in mercy, he did.

It became clear then that Jonah's obedience to God's second summons to call Ninevah to repentance had been a reluctant one, for the escape of Ninevah from the judgment of God was not to his liking. Jonah offered God a reproach rather than praise: "I knew that you are a gracious and compassionate God, slow to anger and abounding in love, and a God who relents from sending calamity" (Jonah 4:2). Jonah had learned that it was useless to try to escape the reach of the LORD or subvert his will. But he had not yet learned to love what God loved—the reconciliation of sinners and their inclusion in the circle of his grace.

October 11

An Important Lesson for Jonah and Israel

Jonah 4:5–11

I have no pleasure in the death of anyone,
declares the Lord God; so turn and live.
Ezekiel 18:32 (ESV)

Ninevah's repentance didn't last. The book of Nahum records a prophecy against Ninevah, which had reverted to its wickedness within a century. But the final lesson of the book of Jonah is less about what the Assyrians did with the grace they had received than about Jonah's bad attitude toward God's extravagant mercy to outsiders.

Jonah was so disgusted by God's mercy to the Assyrians that he preferred death to the unwelcome prospect of seeing life and prosperity for these enemies. But God reproved him with a question that was very similar to one he'd asked an angry Cain centuries before (see Gen. 4:6). On that occasion, Cain had ignored God's counsel that he should master his anger. On this one, we're not told what Jonah did with his anger, but God schooled him in the foolishness of it by providing, and later destroying, a plant that Jonah loved for the shade it provided.

Jonah may have eventually learned his lesson, but we know that God's extravagant mercy posed a perpetual challenge for Israel. The Pharisees of Jesus's day—in their disdain for outsiders—were rather like Jonah, albeit without his eventual obedience. Even though Jesus took pains to instruct them in what God really wanted, it seems he had little if any success.

Even today, some people who benefit most from the mercy of God fail to appreciate it when God offers that same mercy to those they deem less deserving. Such an attitude not only misunderstands the nature of grace, but also vastly underestimates the debt that all servants of God owe to the gracious work of his Spirit in and for them. God's lesson for Jonah is fully as important for us as it was for Jonah and his people.

October 12

The Day of the LORD

Amos 5

Woe to you who desire the day of the LORD! Why would you have the day of the LORD? It is darkness, and not light.
Amos 5:18 (ESV)

In the years following the ministries of Elijah and Elisha, spiritual conditions in the northern kingdom continued to deteriorate. About 150 years after Solomon's death, God sent Amos, whom he had called from tending sheep, to convey his warnings to those called to be God's sheep.

In his preaching, Amos spoke of a coming day of the LORD. This was not a new concept for the people of Israel, but the popular notion was that the promised deliverer would help God's people by judging the wicked. Every wrong the people had suffered would be put right, every national enemy would be subdued, and the wealth of the surrounding nations would flow into the land. All of this would usher Israel into a wonderful time of abundance and happiness.

However, Amos tells his hearers that the day of the LORD will be the opposite of what they expect; it will be a day of judgment for them. God was sick and tired of an obedience that was confined to religious rituals, sacrifices, and songs. God had seen through the smokescreen of Israel's sacrifices; the plight of the oppressed among them made their sacrifices a lie. What God wanted from Israel was worship accompanied by the integrity of service that promoted justice and righteousness in the land. Because the people were not giving God what he most valued, they would have to go into exile.

The day of the LORD would come within fifty years for the northern kingdom; Israel was conquered and taken into exile by Assyria in 721 BC. Israel's fate is a prescient warning of a final and universal judgment for all who persist in pretend worship and thereby stand in opposition to God and his kingdom.

October 13

The Visions of Amos

Amos 7—9

Whoever will not listen to my words that [the prophet] shall speak in my name, I myself will require it of him.
Deuteronomy 18:19 (ESV)

God gave Amos several visions to illustrate the judgment he planned for Israel because of their failure to repent:

- A swarm of locusts that stripped the land of food (7:1–3)
- Judgment by fire that destroyed the land (7:4–6)
- A plumb line showing Israel to be like a leaning wall, so off balance spiritually that the nation was about to fall over and break apart (7:7–9)
- A basket of ripe fruit that symbolized Israel's ripeness for destruction (8:1–2)
- The LORD standing beside the altar, poised to smash it and let its stones crush the heads of the people (9:1–4).

The last vision in particular speaks of the impossibility of escaping the LORD's judgment. The inescapable omnipresence of the LORD, which Psalm 139 depicts as ultimate comfort for those who love God, becomes a terror for those whom God judges.

The reaction of Amaziah, the official priest of the altar at Bethel, showed Israel's distaste for God's message. Amaziah did not say that the message was wrong, he just told Amos to stop saying such things (7:10–13).

Although the message of Amos did not result in repentance, his news for Israel was not entirely bad. The book concludes with a vision of hope that looks forward to a time after God's judgment against Israel has taken its course—a time when he would restore his people (9:11–15). The picture of wine dripping from the mountains and flowing from all the hills is a picture of God's complete provision and his people's complete satisfaction—a provision and a satisfaction that we now know comes only through Jesus Christ.

October 14

Spiritual Prostitution

Hosea 1:1–2:13

Rejoice not, O Israel...for you have played the whore, forsaking your God. You have loved a prostitute's wages on all threshing floors.
Hosea 9:1 (ESV)

Forty years after Amos's prophecies, political and social upheaval was destroying Israel from the inside, and Assyria was threatening Israel from the outside. God raised up another prophet, Hosea, whom he instructed to marry a prostitute named Gomer.

I can imagine that the people would have seen Hosea's choice of Gomer as wife as either extremely generous or extremely foolish. In their opinion only a saint or a fool would marry a prostitute. But that's what Hosea did—because God wanted Israel to see itself as the prostitute he had married.

Hosea and Gomer had three children, each of whom, we infer from Hosea 2:4, was conceived in adultery, for Gomer was unfaithful to her marriage vows.

- The son named Jezreel signaled that God would vent his anger on the house of Jehu for the massacre at Jezreel.
- The second child was a daughter, Lo-Ruhamah, her name a statement that God would no longer be merciful to the Northern Kingdom of Israel.
- The third child was a son, Lo-Ammi, named to show that the LORD no longer regarded Israel as his people.

The message in this whole sequence of events was unmistakable. The covenant that the LORD had made with Israel was like a marriage relationship in which God and his chosen people pledged their love and commitment to each other. But Israel, like Gomer, had taken other lovers. Gomer's false lovers were the men who paid her money for sex; Israel's were the false gods of the surrounding nations, gods like Baal, who were credited with power over fertility and nature. How could either marriage continue under such circumstances?

October 15

An Invitation to Recommitment

Hosea 2:14–3:5

I feel a divine jealousy for you, since I betrothed you to one husband, to present you as a pure virgin to Christ. But I am afraid that…your thoughts will be led astray from a sincere and pure devotion to Christ.
2 Corinthians 11:2-3 (ESV)

Hosea's hard message to Israel was not the end of the matter. He was compelled to speak of the unrelenting desire of God for a renewal of the covenant (marriage) commitment between God and Israel. There was something in Israel that had to have wanted this too, for the nation remained unsatisfied in its prostitution: "She shall pursue her lovers but not overtake them, and she shall seek them but shall not find them. Then she shall say, 'I will go and return to my first husband, for it was better for me then than now'" (Hosea 2:7).

As a sign of what was possible for his people, God told Hosea to find his adulterous wife and bring her home, restoring her to the covenant relationship into which he had originally entered with her. This was costly, for Hosea apparently had to pay for her release from the one to whom she had prostituted herself.

We don't know for sure that Gomer became a faithful and loving wife after this, but the implication is that she did. And we also infer from Hosea 2:21–23 that the names of her children were changed as well. The name *Jezreel* would now signify contentment, and *No Mercy* and *Not My People* would be renamed *Mercy* and *My People.*

If Israel had listened to Hosea's graphic message, who knows what great mercy God would have shown to that very generation. But it was not to be. Within a few years Israel had become a vassal of Assyria, paying tribute to avoid destruction. A few years after this, the northern kingdom was destroyed, and most of the Israelites who were not killed were sent into an exile from which they never returned.

October 16

Avoiding Destruction

Hosea 4:1–6

Know that the LORD, he is God! It is he who made us, and we are his; we are his people, and the sheep of his pasture.
Psalm 100:3 (ESV)

God's hard message through Hosea could have had different results if only Israel had the sense and the heart to return to its first love. God's people also might never have left their first love if they had cultivated the knowledge of the LORD. Hosea speaks for God when he puts it like this: "My people are destroyed for lack of knowledge."

God speaks here not mainly about more information or understanding, but about the kind of knowledge that exists between husband and wife in a good marriage relationship. To know one's spouse is to be intimate with them. Hosea and Gomer didn't have that. Israel also did not have the kind of relationship with God that would lead to spiritual growth. Without such a close and loving relationship, the marriage of God and his people was as doomed as Hosea's marriage.

Whenever people refuse to be the friends and servants God created them to be—and run off and serve other gods—they die. No life is possible where the intimate relationship between God and people has been cut. Only death can follow spiritual adultery. Such death may be seen both as the LORD's judgment and as the logical consequence of human sinfulness.

Coming to an intimate knowledge of God is a process that requires intention. After the Holy Spirit reaches out to draw us into relationship with God through faith in Jesus Christ, we, by the power of that same Spirit, are empowered to intentionally nurture our knowledge of God. That means continual feeding on the word of God, which directs us away from affairs with other gods and toward a mature and living relationship with the one true God.

October 17

Isaiah Despairs in Seeing God's Holiness

Isaiah 6:1–5

[I saw] one like a son of man...from his mouth came a sharp two-edged sword, and his face was like the sun shining in full strength. When I saw him, I fell at his feet as though dead.
Revelation 1:13, 16-17 (ESV)

In the declining years of the northern kingdom, God called Isaiah to prophesy to both Israel and Judah. This is the account of his call to ministry.

No one except Judah's high priest—and then only once each year—was granted admission into the Most Holy Place of the temple. But in his God-given vision Isaiah is granted a glimpse into that innermost room of the temple, the very throne room of God. This is heaven; it represents the place where God has all authority, the entire universe over which he rules. His robe, his presence, fills the place.

Isaiah is astounded by what he sees (and that to which the angels and the smoke of incense testify)—the glory and holiness of the LORD Almighty. However, it is not grateful astonishment that Isaiah feels, but overwhelming dread. He is horrified by his own uncleanness, which stands out boldly and offensively against the purity and holiness of God. He sees his guilt and that of his people; he sees that he is ruined and responds in hopeless despair saying, "Woe is me!" (in modern language: "I'm damned") knowing that he has no hope of withstanding the justice of God.

Isaiah does not exaggerate; to meet the holy God and see him in all his glory is to be overwhelmed by a sense of personal unworthiness and impurity. Part of Isaiah's terror is that he cannot do anything to make himself worthy to stand in God's presence. What he does not yet know is that awareness of his hopeless state is the necessary first step in becoming able to stand without fear in the very presence of the LORD. Moreover, as it was with Isaiah, so also it is with each of us.

October 18

Isaiah is Cleansed and Forgiven

Isaiah 6:6–7

For by grace you have been saved through faith.
And this is not your own doing; it is the gift of God,
not a result of works, so that no one may boast.
Ephesians 2:8–9 (ESV)

How do the unclean and unworthy become clean and worthy? All too often religion gives some sort of legalistic solution:

- You must light so many candles.
- You must say so many prayers.
- You must deny yourself certain pleasures.
- You must study and learn.
- You must give so much money.
- You must reform your life.

But all of this gets the cart before the horse. These are not ways to become cleansed or worthy; they may be responses to God's grace, but they aren't ways to earn it. The only way to become cleansed is by the initiative of God, as is shown by the way Isaiah became clean and worthy. The burning coal with which the seraph touched Isaiah's mouth is the grace and cleansing fire of God, a fire that wipes away sin and guilt and brings reconciliation with the holy God.

God's presence inevitably shines a light on our own dark and unworthy souls. Isaiah's experience also gives us fresh insight into God's nature and his willingness to make the relationship possible. What a wonderful feeling Isaiah must have had in being cleansed. We who have been reconciled by grace through faith in Jesus Christ don't really have to wonder what it was like; the cleansing, forgiveness, and freedom that we have in Christ is just like that Isaiah received when the seraph touched his lips with the burning coal from the altar. Our cleansing from sin and reconciliation with God is worth more than every other relationship and physical or material advantage that the world can offer.

October 19

Isaiah Answers God's Call

Isaiah 6:8

I appeal to you therefore, brothers, by the mercies of God, to present your bodies as a living sacrifice, holy and acceptable to God, which is your spiritual worship.
Romans 12:1 (ESV)

Isaiah knew that God's question: "Whom shall I send? And who will go for us?" was directed at him. He wouldn't have dared answer it before, guilty and dirty as he was before God; he was too busy lamenting what he thought would mean his death. But after his forgiveness, after his purification, Isaiah saw that God was calling him to a task for which he'd previously been unqualified, and he accepted the challenge: "Here am I. Send me!"

As unique in some respects as Isaiah's call was, it is not unique as an example of how God works, because God's self-revelation always comes with an implicit invitation. First, the guilty and impure are invited to accept God's cleansing and forgiveness. After this comes God's invitation to join him in his work.

There can be no valuable service to God without God's cleansing, given to us today by grace through faith in Christ Jesus. Then, however, "Here am I. Send me!" is the inevitable response of all who have come to God in true faith. Reluctance to answer God's call to a life of service, whether or not it is as clear and specific to us as it was to Isaiah, is not humility but disobedience.

Except for Jesus and his angels, not one of God's servants has served him perfectly. But our imperfections and inadequacies must never be an excuse for ignoring God's call to a life of intentional service to him. It is possible to waste our lives making excuses, if not for our sinfulness, then for our inabilities. But God can and will use each person he has redeemed. A good beginning for each day is to ask the Lord to open our eyes to the opportunities he puts before us. Beyond that we must ask for the wisdom and courage to respond as God directs.

October 20

Isaiah's Commission

Isaiah 6:9–13

[Our parents] disciplined us for a short time as it seemed best to them, but [God] disciplines us for our good, that we may share his holiness.
Hebrews 12:10 (ESV)

It's not clear whether Isaiah's commission as God's spokesman was to show just how hard-hearted and worthy of judgment God's people were, or to encourage them to repentance. This ambivalence is also seen in the gospel accounts of Jesus's use of this quotation from Isaiah.

- Mark's account (4:12) indicates that God's intention is the former: the preaching of God's word serves to show just how worthy of judgment hard-hearted people are.
- Matthew's account (13:10–13) indicates that God's desire is the latter: the preaching of God's word is meant to penetrate hard hearts and bring people to repentance.

God clearly intends both consequences. Jesus was given both the ministry of revealing God's judgment against wickedness (Mark's emphasis) and the ministry of revealing his infinite mercy to those who responded to his message in repentance and faith (Matthew's emphasis). In fact, God's judgment of sin recreates the possibility of life in harmony with him.

Isaiah, similarly, had a dual mission from God. God's chosen people mostly closed their hearts and minds to his prophetic message. Despite his lack of success, however, Isaiah knew that he was to keep preaching until the end to make clear the inevitable results of disobedience. But, Isaiah's work was not entirely disappointing; he also understood that what he had experienced in his encounter with God was what the LORD wanted for all of his people. He knew that God would eventually make it happen too—God would give a remnant a different way to go into the future, a way that involved freedom from the guilt of sin and a life of trust in God and wholehearted service to him.

October 21

Ahaz and Hezekiah

2 Kings 16:1–4; 18:1–7a

The righteous hates falsehood, but the wicked brings shame and disgrace.
Proverbs 13:5 (ESV)

The response of God's people to Isaiah's ministry is illustrated in the contrasting ways two kings of Judah reacted to God's messages. They were father and son—Ahaz and Hezekiah. Over the next few days we'll look at their fears, the gracious invitation each received from God though Isaiah, their differing responses, and the consequences of their decisions. Take note, first of Scripture's summary of their lives:

- Ahaz "did not do what was right in the eyes of the LORD his God." He is contrasted to David, far from perfect, but a man after God's own heart. Ahaz was more like the kings of Israel, careless about the worship of the LORD and imitating the worship practices of the adjoining nations.
- Hezekiah "did what was right in the eyes of the LORD, just as his father David had done." Late in his life God judged him for unseemly pride in his strength and possessions (see Isa. 39). However, for his overall trust and obedience, Scripture commends him as the best king of Judah since David.

Second Chronicles 29—31 gives more detail about the ways that Hezekiah demonstrated his faithfulness:

- He repaired the temple, reconsecrated it and Judah's priests, and called for appropriate offerings to be made.
- He led his people in the celebration of the Passover, which had long been neglected.
- He approved the destruction of shrines of worship to false gods and made provision for the priests of the LORD to be supported in their service.

Both Ahaz and Hezekiah were called to lead the people in the service of the LORD. But only one honored the LORD and became a blessing to himself and his people.

October 22

Ahaz's Fear and God's Counsel

Isaiah 7:1–9; 2 Chronicles 28:5–6

[The LORD has come] that we, being delivered from the hand of our enemies, might serve him without fear, in holiness and righteousness before him all our days.
Luke 1:74–75 (ESV)

Ahaz, king of Judah, was very worried about two kingdoms to the north, Aram (Syria) and Israel. He had good reason to be: the armies of these nations had inflicted heavy losses upon the armies of Judah.

But Ahaz had also seen signs of God's grace. After one devastating loss, Oded, a prophet of the LORD, secured the release of the people that Israel had taken captive together with the plunder they had taken from the people of Ahaz. Oded accomplished this by reminding Israel of their kinship with the people of Judah and of their call to serve the same God.

A while later, however, Judah again came under attack from the allied armies of Aram and Israel. In response, Ahaz and his people were shaking in their boots, worried that Jerusalem itself would be conquered. Ahaz considered asking for help from the major power of the world at that time—Assyria. Before he did so, however, God sent Isaiah to tell Ahaz not to rely on Assyria, but to stand firm in faith and trust the LORD for deliverance. With Isaiah was Isaiah's son Shear-Jashub (meaning: *a remnant shall return*)—his name meant to be confirmation to Ahaz that God would take care of his people.

Ahaz did not have much practice in serving the LORD or standing firm in faith. Nor did he have much appreciation for Isaiah. But once again he was reminded that those who threatened him were themselves under the control of the Sovereign LORD. It's a reminder that all of us still need in deciding how to respond to the things that frighten us. If we don't stand firm in our faith, we will not stand at all.

October 23

Ahaz's Response and Its Results

Isaiah 7:17–25; 2 Kings 16:7–18;
2 Chronicles 28:20–25

Zion shall be redeemed by justice, and those in her who repent, by righteousness. But rebels and sinners shall be broken together, and those who forsake the LORD shall be consumed.
Isaiah 1:27–28 (ESV)

Ahaz remained uncomfortably silent before Isaiah; he had already decided not to trust the LORD, but to trust his own instincts instead. The book of Isaiah implies the result, but we find out from Kings and Chronicles that despite the word of God to him, Ahaz went ahead with his plan to ask Assyria for help. Help is not free, however, and along with his request Ahaz sent along silver and gold from both his palace and from the temple of the LORD. Also, instead of true worship, he continued to build altars to idol gods, provoking the God of his ancestors to anger.

God's anger did not reveal itself right away for, with the help of Assyria, both Syria and Israel were driven out of Judah. Isaiah's second son was not two years old (see Isa. 8:3–4) before what Isaiah had prophesied had come true. Neither of the countries that Ahaz had feared was any longer a threat to Judah.

But then, just as Isaiah had prophesied, Assyria turned on Judah and treated it as an enemy. Fortunately for Ahaz, this trouble did not come in his lifetime; it happened thirty-four years after Isaiah first came to Ahaz, and after Ahaz's son Hezekiah succeeded him as king of Judah.

But disaster, sooner or later, is the inevitable result of preferring one's own counsel to that of the LORD. Some people, like Ahaz, seem to get away with wickedness and not even be called to account in this life. But his people suffered from his lack of godly leadership and he himself is remembered as one who did not do what was right in the eyes of the LORD. His life was a testimony to the truth of Romans 6:23: "The wages of sin is death."

October 24

Hezekiah's Fear and God's Counsel

Isaiah 36:1–37:13; 2 Kings 18:17–19:13

Abide in me, and I in you. As the branch cannot bear fruit by itself, unless it abides in the vine, neither can you, unless you abide in me.
John 15:4 (ESV)

The aqueduct of the Upper Pool, on the road to the Washerman's Field was the setting for the meeting between the Assyrian commander and Hezekiah's representatives. It's the same place where, thirty-four years earlier, God sent Isaiah to Hezekiah's father with the message that Ahaz should not depend on Assyria for deliverance from his enemies but should trust in the LORD.

Ahaz had refused, putting his trust in Assyria instead. Now, the so-called ally whom Ahaz had hired to fight his enemies had turned against Judah and conquered many of its cities. With Jerusalem itself being threatened by Assyria's army, Judah was in more trouble than ever.

To this point Hezekiah had been a different kind of king than his father; he had tried his best to serve the LORD. But what would he do now that his enemies were so very near and so clearly powerful? Would he continue to trust the LORD, or would he believe Assyria's message: "Be very afraid of us; no one can rescue you."?

Hezekiah did not know what would happen. He had seen the fulfillment of Isaiah's prophecy that the LORD would use Assyria to execute his judgment on Israel and Syria (Isa. 8:7–8). But he also knew of God's determination to deal with Jerusalem and its images as he had dealt with Samaria and its idols (Isa. 10:10–11). In his distress he tore his clothes, donned sackcloth, and went to the temple to pray.

It was then that God sent Isaiah with a message suitable, not only for Hezekiah but, for all time and for all servants of the LORD—the message not to be afraid of the one who contradicts the LORD's message and blasphemes him.

October 25

Hezekiah's Response and Its Results

Isaiah 37:14–38; 2 Kings 19:14–37

There is salvation in no one else, for there is no other name under heaven given among men by which we must be saved.
Acts 4:12 (ESV)

Hezekiah had consistently demonstrated his character through his actions to promote the service of the LORD throughout Judah. But Hezekiah showed his intention here too in the silence of his representatives in the face of Assyria's threats (Isa. 36:21). This was not like the prior silence of Ahaz—a stubborn intention to go against God. It was rather a signal of Hezekiah's intention to resist the threat from Assyria by continuing to trust the LORD.

Hezekiah's consistency in seeking the will and favor of the LORD in prayer is another indicator of his intention to keep trusting God. Hezekiah would not always be so selfless in prayer (see Isa. 38—his prayers on the point of death). But the prayer recorded in today's Scripture shows only concern for the LORD's honor.

That, by the way, is a wonderful way to pray. God does not reject prayers for our own welfare, but he desires that our main goal, even if it means present distress for us, is that we and people everywhere will know his authority over every person and kingdom, and will come to know and serve him alone as the one true God.

Assyria came to know God's authority even if they did not join in service to him. Sennacherib's retreat in disgrace and later murder by his own sons demonstrates that no worldly might is sufficient to prevail against the LORD. "So the LORD saved Hezekiah and the people of Jerusalem from the hand of Sennacherib king of Assyria and from the hand of all others. He took care of them on every side" (2 Chron. 32:22).

Hezekiah benefited personally from this deliverance. But it's clear that the regard in which others held him was really a testimony to the LORD's power and purposes.

October 26

Signs from God and for Him

Isaiah 7:10–17; 37:30–32

Let your manner of life be worthy of the gospel of Christ, so that...you are standing firm in one spirit, with one mind striving side by side for the faith of the gospel, and not frightened in anything by your opponents. This is a clear sign to them of their destruction, but of your salvation...from God.
Philippians 1:27–28 (ESV)

People who know that God wants their undivided loyalty often want a sign—especially in times of trouble—that things will turn out all right. God invited Ahaz to trust him but Ahaz had already decided to trust Assyria and so refused a sign from God.

God gave him one anyway—telling of the coming birth of an *Immanuel* who would not reach manhood before the kings Ahaz feared would lose their power. This prophecy would be doubly fulfilled, once in the lifetime of Ahaz, but ultimately and more completely in the life of Jesus. The promised *Immanuel* (God with us) would, in name and person, signal the presence of God.

Hezekiah also received the promise of a sign from God. He saw God's provision of food for his people as a sign of the LORD's presence and care. It was confirmation of his decision to trust the LORD.

It is interesting that although doubting and frightened people usually want immediate signs from God, the signs he gives, like those given to Ahaz and Hezekiah, are often seen only in retrospect. They were called to trust and obey; only later would they see their trust vindicated.

God's faithful people repeatedly find this to be true. In times of trouble we often see only dimly what we later see clearly, that God was with us and helping us all the while. Furthermore, it's as we persevere in faithfulness and trust that we ourselves may become signs for God. We may be privileged, as Isaiah himself was (Isa. 8:18), to become living signs that point not only to God's judgment of sin, but also to his mercy for sinners.

October 27

God's Love for His Children

Isaiah 49:14–16

As a father shows compassion to his children,
so the LORD shows compassion to those who fear him.
Psalm 103:13 (ESV)

Consider the strength of feeling behind the LORD's invitation to both Ahaz and Hezekiah to trust in God. Jesus would later compare his own desire to love and protect God's people to the solicitous actions of a mother hen toward her chicks (Matt. 23:37). But Isaiah uses an even stronger simile, comparing the love of God to the love that mothers have for the children whom they have birthed and nursed and nurtured.

God's love even goes beyond this for, impossible as it may seem, a mother can forget her child. Jeremiah tells of people being in such desperate straits and so starving that they killed and ate their own children (Lam. 4:10). I can't imagine that. Even less can God imagine forgetting his own children. As Isaiah indicates, God has tattooed his children on the palms of his hand.

Hosea similarly points out the strong ties that bind God to his people: "It was I who taught Ephraim to walk, taking them by the arms; but they did not realize it was I who healed them. I led them with cords of human kindness, with ties of love. To them I was like one who lifts a little child to the cheek, and I bent down to feed them" (Hosea 11:3-4). As parents feed their children and teach them to walk, kiss their wounds better, love them and lead them along; that's how God treats his children.

All of this conveys a strength of feeling that leads one to sacrificial action on behalf of another. It's that which led God to send his only Son to make the supreme sacrifice, both for the sake of those he called his chosen people, and for enemies who would embrace God's offer to adopt them. That also tells us how much God was pained by the rejection of Ahaz and pleased by the trust of Hezekiah—and how much he desires our own trust.

October 28

Revival under Josiah

2 Chronicles 34—35

I dwell in the high and holy place, and also with him who is of a contrite and lowly spirit, to revive the spirit of the lowly, and to revive the heart of the contrite.
Isaiah 57:15 (ESV)

Hezekiah's son Manasseh succeeded him as king of Judah, but did not follow his father's example. Manassah rebuilt idol shrines throughout the land and did much evil in the eyes of the LORD. Later in his life Manasseh repented and humbled himself before the LORD, but he could not undo all the effects of his rebellion.

Revival in Judah would wait until the reign of Manasseh's grandson Josiah, who, as a young man, began to seek the God of his father David. At age twenty Josiah began to destroy the altars and high places of Judah's idol worshipers and put to death the false prophets and priests.

A few years later Josiah began to repair the temple of the LORD. In the process, Hilkiah the priest found the book of the Law of the LORD that had been given through Moses. When Josiah, previously ignorant of its contents, heard it read, he became frantic and tore his royal robes in dismay at how far he and his people had departed from God's law. He sought a word from the LORD through the prophetess Huldah. She returned with a message of God's judgment against his people; albeit judgment that God would mercifully delay until after Josiah's death.

Josiah redoubled his efforts to show the LORD that he and his people were determined to live for God with all their hearts. He removed all the false gods throughout the land. Once the people repented, Josiah guided them in joyful celebration of the Passover and the Feast of Unleavened Bread. The rededication of Josiah and his people also showed in their lives after the celebration. Eventually God would carry out his judgment, but a generation was saved from it by repentance and revival.

October 29

Jeremiah and the Demise of Judah

2 Chronicles 36

I will send sword, famine, and pestilence upon them, until they shall be utterly destroyed from the land that I gave to them.
Jeremiah 24:10 (ESV)

Jeremiah began his prophetic ministry during the reign of Josiah and continued for about forty years, until after the fall of Jerusalem and the deportation of many of God's people to Babylon.

Jehoiakim, who succeeded his father Josiah after a three-month reign by his brother, radically departed from the pattern Josiah had set, rejecting the service of the LORD for pagan practices. Jehoiakim's reign was marked by oppression, dishonesty, violence, and the shedding of innocent blood; he even dared to put a prophet of the LORD to death. But Jeremiah did not cater to Jehoiakim. He made clear that if the people did not follow God's law and listen to his prophets then God would make them and Jerusalem an object of cursing among the nations (Jer. 26:4–6).

Jeremiah was often ridiculed and persecuted for his message. One time Jehoiakim had the audacity to burn the scroll containing the words that the LORD had given Jeremiah to bring to the king (Jer. 36:22–26). Jerusalem fell to Nebuchadnezzar not long after.

Jeremiah told Zedekiah, whom Nebuchadnezzar put on the throne as his puppet governor, that it was God's will that he not resist Nebuchadnezzar. Instead, it was time for the people to submit to God's judgment, repent of their faithlessness, and once again learn to trust God. But Zedekiah and his leaders rebelled, and then witnessed Nebuchadnezzar's destruction of Jerusalem and the temple of the LORD. Afterwards, Zedekiah was forced to watch the murder of his sons and then was taken in chains to Babylon. It was the low point in the history of God's people, now exiled for disobedience from the land God had given them to inherit and in which he had promised to care for them as his servants and partners.

October 30

Jeremiah's Tears and Hope

Jeremiah 20:7–18; 31:31–34

This I call to mind, and therefore I have hope: The steadfast love of the LORD never ceases; his mercies never come to an end; they are new every morning; great is your faithfulness.
Lamentations 3:21–23 (ESV)

Jeremiah had a difficult life. He was lonely, unpopular, often sad, and doubtful of God's ways. He was ridiculed, falsely accused, imprisoned, and regularly disappointed by the sins of his people. He sometimes resented the call of God on his life, even cursing the day he was born and taking issue with his mother for bearing a man so opposed by everyone (see Jer. 15:10).

Yet, in everything, Jeremiah proved to be the LORD's faithful servant. His life itself was a testimony to the coming devastation that would follow God's judgment on his people. That's why he'd been forbidden several things permissible for others (Jer. 16:1–9):

- marriage and children—because of coming troubles,
- showing sympathy at funerals—as a sign that God had withdrawn his pity from his people,
- feasting and celebration—because of the coming end to joy and gladness in the land.

Jeremiah's message was not entirely without hope, however. He spoke of the unfailing love and compassion of the LORD, and the LORD's great faithfulness. And he looked forward to a new covenant that God would make with his people and a time when his law would be in their minds and on their hearts.

Jeremiah's hope would ultimately find fulfillment in the life, death, and resurrection of Jesus, whose life had similarities to that of Jeremiah's, both in his sufferings and in his trust and hope in God. Although both men had many reasons to give up, they remained faithful to their God-given calling: Jeremiah as a witness to his generation and ours, and Jesus as the one in whom all sins are forgiven and all of the promises of God are fully realized.

October 31

Ezekiel's Call and Mission

Ezekiel 2:1–3:17

O men, how long shall my honor be turned into shame?
How long will you love vain words and seek after lies?
Psalm 4:2 (ESV)

The Babylonians exiled many Israelites, among them, Ezekiel, the twenty-five-year-old son of a priest and a member of Jerusalem's aristocracy. It was the second deportation of Jews into Babylon. The first had occurred about seven or eight years before, and included Daniel and his friends, who ended up in Nebuchadnezzar's court.

About five years into Ezekiel's captivity he experienced "the hand of the LORD upon him." The vision threw him on his face in astonishment at the glory of the LORD and served as the prelude to his call to ministry. Ezekiel was to speak on God's behalf to a nation of rebels, a stubborn people with a history of transgression and rebellion. In the symbolic language of Scripture (see Ezek. 2:8) the people had failed to open their mouths and eat the words given them by God. This failure was the cause of their current condition. Even so, the exiles had not learned their lesson and turned again to the LORD.

By contrast, Ezekiel did eat the word of the LORD and found it sweet. He would be compelled thereafter to speak that word clearly and forcefully to the disobedient people of God. The people probably would not listen, but Ezekiel was to give his message anyhow. The LORD would make him as stubborn for the truth as the people were stubborn against it.

Ezekiel was overwhelmed by the glory of the LORD and the responsibility God had given him to be a sentinel or watchman for God's chosen people. But he would be faithful to his calling, conveying in both symbolic actions and words the glory of the LORD, the magnitude of the peoples' rebellion, and the future God had in mind for those who answered his call to repentance.

November 1

The LORD Leaves His Temple

Ezekiel 8:3b–6; 9:3a; 10:4,18–19; 11:22–23

I will make my dwelling among you, and my soul shall not abhor you. And I will walk among you and will be your God, and you shall be my people.
Leviticus 26:11–12 (ESV)

From the beginning of his work with Abraham and his descendants, God's intention was to recapture a sense of the paradise that existed in the beginning—when he was dwelling in all his holiness with the people he created. The above passage from Leviticus is just one of many Scriptures that attests to this.

The tabernacle, and later the temple of Israel, served as the primary symbol of God's presence with his people. This was confirmed immediately following Moses's completion of the tabernacle when the glory of the LORD came to fill it (Ex. 40:34–38). A similar thing happened upon the completion of the temple by Solomon (2 Chron. 7:1–3). The presence of the holy and glorious God with his sinful but sanctified people was the main thing that distinguished Israel from its idol-serving neighbors.

The most difficult parts of Ezekiel's message concern the disdain God's people had for the privileges and obligations that attended their life with God. Ignoring these resulted in their separation from God's presence, as dramatically pictured in Ezekiel's vision of the departure of the glory of God from his temple.

First, Ezekiel describes the impossibility of reconciling the idolatry of Israel with the glory of God. Then he recounts the departure of the glory of the LORD from the temple, the very place that signaled God's presence in Israel. The people might well have recalled these words from Moses's final sermon: "On that day I will become angry with them and forsake them; I will hide my face from them, and they will be destroyed" (Deut. 9:12). Ezekiel's message is that, but for the grace of God, the exile means a total rejection of Abraham's descendants.

November 2

How Can God's People Live in Exile?

Daniel 1:1–8

How shall we sing the LORD's song in a foreign land?
Psalm 137:4 (ESV)

The fall of Jehoiakim marked the beginning of the end for Judah, an end that would come a few years later when Nebuchadnezzar returned to destroy Jerusalem and the temple. Already now, his removal of the precious articles from the temple in Jerusalem to his own idol temple in Babylon was particularly offensive.

This, together with the loss of their homeland, put Daniel and the other Jewish exiles back into a situation similar to what their ancestors had experienced in Egypt—before God had given them his law, a homeland, and a temple that represented his presence with them. Even as a young man, Daniel understood that the struggle between himself and Babylon was much more than a story of personal and national disaster; it was a war between God and sinful humanity, between good and evil; it was cosmic spiritual warfare.

Daniel knew right from the start that he had to resist becoming fully at home with the religion and culture of Babylon. He and his friends could do nothing about their new names, which honored Babylonian deities; it seems that they tried to cooperate as much as possible with their captors. But they tactfully took a conscientious stand against the food they were given. At least some of this food would have been from animals that were ceremonially unclean or else not prepared according to Hebrew dietary restrictions. Besides that, the first portion of such food was typically offered to Babylon's idols.

Daniel and his friends were not where they wanted to be. But they were determined to remain faithful to the LORD. Their attitude and conduct illustrates the faithfulness and integrity that most of God's people lacked—a lack that had earned God's judgment and brought them into exile.

November 3

The Beginnings of a Life that Mattered

Daniel 1:9–21

One who is faithful in a very little is also faithful in much, and one who is dishonest in a very little is also dishonest in much.
Luke 16:10 (ESV)

A life of faithfulness to God does not necessarily require a refusal to concede anything to those who live by another standard. It rather requires the wisdom to know what compromises must be resisted and to know how to avoid unnecessary hostility in the process of resistance. Jesus put it like this to his disciples: "I am sending you out like sheep among wolves. Therefore be as shrewd as snakes and as innocent as doves" (Matt. 10:16).

When Daniel's request for a different diet was denied by the chief official, Daniel went to the chief's subordinate to propose a test whose failure would pose little risk to him. The man agreed, and in time Daniel and his friends passed the test; they were noticeably healthier than the young men on the royal diet.

Besides this, Scripture says, God gave Daniel and his friends knowledge and understanding so that they were ten times better than everybody else. This was not just a supernatural endowment, although there is some of that in the ability Daniel had to interpret dreams and visions. Knowledge and understanding usually comes to those who combine hard work with a wisdom that comes from a life of obedience to the LORD.

The superiority of Daniel and his friends is a hint of great things to come. But the last verse of the chapter gives another hint too. Daniel, whom many would try to destroy in the years ahead, would outlast both the king and the kingdom that captured him and tried to bend him to their will. He would live to see the edict allowing Israel's exiles to return to their own land—a foretaste of the release from spiritual captivity that is found in Jesus Christ and that will be consummated at the end of time.

November 4

The Source of All Wisdom

Daniel 2:1–24

The LORD gives wisdom; from his mouth come knowledge and understanding; he stores up sound wisdom for the upright; he is a shield to those who walk in integrity.
Proverbs 2:6–7 (ESV)

Dreams were very important in Nebuchadnezzar's culture; they were thought to be messages from the gods. Understanding them was key to achieving or maintaining power. So Nebuchadnezzar wanted some true wisdom about what his dream meant.

This was a problem, for Nebuchadnezzar knew that his so-called wise men weren't all that wise, and that a lot of the wisdom they gave him was merely what they knew he wanted to hear. He determined, therefore, to have his advisors first tell him what he had dreamed and then give him its interpretation. It was an impossible task and put his advisors under the sentence of death.

When Daniel first heard about this decree, he did not have the answer the king wanted either. He and his three friends had been pronounced ten times wiser than all the king's wise men, but they had no more knowledge than Nebuchadnezzar's wise men about the dream. However, they did know the God who has all knowledge and power and they went to him in prayer. It was not clear to them what the LORD would do, but they knew that their only hope was in him. Therein lay the source of their wisdom.

Because of their prayers, God gave Daniel a vision of the dream and its interpretation. This is only the first of many times we are taught this lesson in the book of Daniel: God responds to those who truly pray. He even does the impossible at times. He does not always give the hoped-for answer as he did with Daniel, but he always has an answer that meets the needs of his people and his purposes. In this case God had much more work for Daniel and his friends—work that would testify of the glory of God both to Babylon and to the other exiles.

November 5

The Enduring Kingdom

Daniel 2:25–49

You, O LORD, reign forever; your throne endures to all generations.
Lamentations 5:19 (ESV)

The great statue of Nebuchadnezzar's dream, as Daniel related and interpreted it for him, represented his powerful kingdom and three others to follow it. Although Daniel did not name any but the first, we now know that the Babylonians (gold) would be followed in succession by the empires of Medo-Persia (silver), Greece (bronze), and Rome (iron). The statue's feet and toes seem to represent another form of the fourth kingdom (iron and clay), but there is less agreement about what this represents.

What is unmistakable, however, is what happens to all of these kingdoms of the world. Daniel speaks of a final kingdom—a rock cut out by divine hands—that crushes all the others, and ends up filling the earth. This kingdom, Daniel tells Nebuchadnezzar, will never be destroyed.

Nebuchadnezzar realized immediately that Daniel's ability to see and interpret what he had dreamed was because the dream had come from Daniel's own God. The king therefore honored the LORD as superior to every other god and king. He showered gifts and important responsibilities upon Daniel and his friends in deference to the God they served.

This God, of course, is the one who establishes the final and enduring kingdom. Christ, the stone that the temple builders of this world rejected and refused to build upon, was not sent just to destroy everything in his path, but to prepare a place and a people for God's eternal rule. Those who now serve him are no more powerful than were Daniel and his friends, who could do nothing but pray and live as God wanted them to. But all who are wise will align themselves with the one who has all the power, for God's kingdom will overwhelm and outlast every one founded on earthly might and principles.

November 6

Delusions of Grandeur

Daniel 3:1–18

God chose what is foolish in the world to shame the wise;
God chose what is weak in the world to shame the strong.
1 Corinthians 1:27 (ESV)

Evidently enough time had passed since Daniel had been honored and his God praised as "the God of gods and the Lord of kings" that Nebuchadnezzar could scarcely remember the anxiety that his dream had brought him. But he could hardly forget the giant statue with its head of gold. Perhaps that's where he got the grandiose idea to build an enormous statue meant to represent and praise his greatness and command the worship of his people.

A great religious feast and festive music celebrated the occasion of the statue's dedication. But there was a dark side to the celebration too: the burning, fiery furnace. The furnace showed the weakness of the very kingdom that the statue was built to celebrate. For the king's power was the power of fear and intimidation, without which his kingdom would not stand.

Apparently Daniel was not present at the time, but his three friends, now with important positions in government service, refused to compromise their devotion to the LORD by worshiping Nebuchadnezzar's image of gold. They might have rationalized that they could do what the king wanted and still not lose their faith. But they declined to bow, even after Nebuchadnezzar gave them another chance, and after he reiterated the penalty of death for disobedience.

Shadrach, Meshach and Abednego didn't refuse with the fatalism familiar to devotees of many religions, but in the faith that God would deliver them if it was necessary for the fulfillment of his purposes in Babylon. But, even if God did not deliver them, as they told the king, they could not compromise their allegiance to the LORD they served. Their message was clear: "Only God himself is worthy of the honor of receiving our worship."

November 7

God's Answer to the Prayer of Azariah

Daniel 3:19–30

And this is eternal life, that they may know you the only true God, and Jesus Christ, whom you have sent.
John 17:3 (ESV)

We may be sure that Daniel's friends persisted in prayer to God throughout their trouble. And we may be sure as well that their prayers were not primarily self-centered, but focused on the fulfillment of God's purposes and the promotion of his honor (see v. 18). The apocryphal book, *The Prayer of Azariah*, testifies to this focus. Although it is not part of the canon of Scripture, the prayer of Azariah, who had been given the Babylonian name of Abednego, is consistent with the focus of biblical prayers.

Azariah praised God's justice and lamented the sins of his people in departing from God's ways. Although he and his friends were being punished for their failure to join in the idolatrous worship of Babylon, Azariah recognized that there was little difference between this worship and the previous idolatry of his own people, which had resulted in their exile. He knew that what the LORD wanted at that moment was the same trust he has always wanted, and the same result—that God's people and people everywhere would come to see and praise God's sovereignty over all nations.

Daniel's friends undoubtedly wanted to live through their ordeal, but their primary focus was for the glory of God to be revealed. God answered both of these prayers. He delivered them from the fire without even the smell of smoke on them, and the king applauded God's answer to his pretension, saying, "No other god can save in this way." What's more, the story of this deliverance has inspired many Christians since then to stand up for their faith. Although not all have escaped torment and death, they have taken comfort in the sure knowledge that, as followers of Jesus, they have received something much greater—eternal deliverance from the fires of hell.

November 8

Nebuchadnezzar's Testimony

Daniel 4

"God opposes the proud but gives grace to the humble."
Submit yourselves, therefore, to God.
James 4:6b–7a (ESV)

Babylon was the most impressive city of its time, and much of its splendor was attributable to Nebuchadnezzar. So he probably would not have wondered about whom the majestic tree of his dream represented; it was himself. His wise men could have confirmed that too. But it was not the size and strength of this tree that made him afraid and his wise men silent about its meaning. It was the cutting down of the tree and the binding of its stump and roots, together with what happened to it afterward.

It was up to Daniel to tell the king that his royal authority, great as it was, would be taken from him. Along with this, Nebuchadnezzar would even lose his mind, becoming like an animal until he acknowledged the absolute sovereignty of Daniel's God.

If Nebuchadnezzar believed Daniel's words at first, he soon forgot them as his successes continued, and it was only after a year had passed that what Daniel said came true. Then the king experienced years of debasement and insanity before he came to recognize and renounce the pride that had kept him from understanding the true power behind his success. Nebuchadnezzar's restoration began only when, as he put it, "I raised my eyes toward heaven."

For Babylon's king, and for everyone else, there's a connection between looking to heaven and escaping the insanity of pride. It is not without reason that Christian tradition views pride as the original and most serious of all sins. Every other sin starts in the forgetting, ignoring, or rebelling against God's sovereignty. Nebuchadnezzar learned this—his testimony at the end of his ordeal is a psalm-like hymn of praise to God, to whom no one and nothing can compare.

November 9

The Writing of God

Daniel 5:1–9

[Jesus] answered, "It is written, 'Man shall not live by bread alone, but by every word that comes from the mouth of God.'"
Matthew 4:4 (ESV)

The events of this story occur more than twenty years after Nebuchadnezzar's death. Belshazzar was co-regent with his father Nabonidus, who was leading Babylon's forces against Cyrus and the Persian army. Whether Belshazzar was overly impressed with the might of Babylon, or simply too enamored of its pleasures, he seized the occasion to have a great banquet. At some point in the drunken revelry, he decided that it would be amusing to drink from the sacred cups taken from the LORD's temple. Although Belshazzar had heard of Nebuchadnezzar's humiliation at the hand of God, he did not fear to disrespect God in this. He had no inkling that God would accept his implicit challenge.

Belshazzar and his guests sobered quickly, however, when the fingers of a disembodied human hand suddenly appeared to write an incomprehensible message on the wall. It was the writing of God. The effect was staggering; the king went white as a sheet and his legs became too rubbery for him to stand. This was the first time Belshazzar had encountered God's writing. His terror at it was undoubtedly reflected in the faces and attitudes of all the other partygoers.

Thank God that his writing is not always so perplexing; what he writes is accessible to those who seek him. Proverbs 14:6 says: "The mocker seeks wisdom and finds none, but knowledge comes easily to the discerning." Thank God as well that his writing does not always proclaim such judgment and result in such terror; those things are for those who disrespect or defy God. But for those who seek him, "All Scripture is God-breathed and is useful for teaching, rebuking, correcting and training in righteousness" (2 Tim. 3:16).

November 10

God's Message for Belshazzar and Us

Daniel 5:10–30

Stay awake, for you do not know on what day your LORD is coming.
Matthew 24:42 (ESV)

Upon the queen's advice, Belshazzar called for Daniel and offered him great rewards to interpret the supernatural writing on the wall. Daniel was not interested in the prizes, but he complied, criticizing Belshazzar for several things:

- Even though Belshazzar knew about the humbling of Nebuchadnezzar, he had not learned from it (v. 22).
- He deliberately defied God, using the temple articles for his own purposes (v. 23).
- He persisted in worshiping idols instead of the LORD (v. 23).

Belshazzar received no direct communication from God. Yet, God held him accountable for the truth that had been revealed to him. God's word to him was as follows:

- *Mene:* "Your time is up. I give everyone a certain allotment of time; yours is up."
- *Tekel:* "I have weighed your attitude, words, deeds, heart, and life on the scales of my perfect justice and have found you to be standing in opposition to me."
- *Peres* (the singular of Parsin)*:* "It's time for your reward. You have lived your life as if you believed yourself to be God, so I'm taking your life and your kingdom away from you."

Scripture's conclusion is brief and pointed. It doesn't say whether Belshazzar scoffed or worried or had regrets after hearing Daniel's message. That was beside the point for him because judgment had been passed. It's a lesson for each of us. God numbers days, weighs hearts and deeds, and prepares rewards for every person on earth. Only if our desire and our future is tied up with God, then numbered days, weighed hearts and deeds, and negative rewards are not a matter for worry, for God's kingdom will endure, and the writing on our walls will say, "You're part of it."

November 11

Daniel Meets Opposition with Prayer

Daniel 6:1–10

Since we belong to the day, let us be sober, having put on the breastplate of faith and love, and for a helmet the hope of salvation...Pray without ceasing.
1 Thessalonians 5:8, 17 (ESV)

Daniel distinguished himself in the service of Darius by his capability and by his honesty. In fact, he was something of a thorn in the flesh to the other government officials because of his unusual integrity. Unlike Daniel, these officials were much more concerned about power than about worship. Their scheme to bring Daniel down was borne more from envy and greed than from religious convictions. They feared that Daniel's upcoming promotion would hamper their own ability to keep gaming the system. As a result, they concocted a plan to frame Daniel, a plan that involved his habits of prayer and devotion to the worship of God.

When Darius was approached by the administrators and satraps, he probably believed that they really were interested in seeking out possible traitors to the kingdom. But it also appealed to his pride and sense of rightness to have his people pray to no one but him for the next month. So, fooled by the plotters, Darius gave the plan his unalterable stamp of approval.

How much there was invested in this plot against Daniel. It was even more than the plotters themselves realized. Daniel's service to God in a land of foreign rulers and gods had been accomplished only through a life of prayer. Indeed, prevailing in his task of spiritual warfare was impossible except through continuing prayer. Daniel knew that the edict that the king had been enticed into giving struck at the heart of Daniel's ability to keep serving the LORD. Therefore, he refused to compromise and went on praying as usual. Prayer is indispensable for those who are truly engaged in the service of God.

November 12

The Law Is Twisted to Promote Injustice

Daniel 6:11–17

We know that for those who love God all things work together for good, for those who are called according to his purpose.
Romans 8:28 (ESV)

The laws made to ensure the well-being of the state and its citizens sometimes end up detrimental to the common good. No matter how well-designed laws are, they're not invulnerable to the schemes of evil people. What John Adams, second president of the United States, wrote in a letter to the officers of the Massachusetts militia in 1798 might be said to people in our day: "We have no government armed with power capable of contending with human passions unbridled by morality and religion…Our Constitution was made only for a moral and religious people. It is wholly inadequate to the government of any other.
The Works of John Adams (Boston, 1854), vol. 9, pp. 228-229

If Adams was correct, then even if godly people succeed in their fight to honor and display standards like the Ten Commandments and the Constitution, this will not automatically help citizens to become more peaceful and law-abiding. This is not to say that we should abandon the fight for faithfulness to the Law of God and the national documents that to some degree are based on it, but people really need a change of heart before good laws will do what they're designed to do.

So it was that Daniel's enemies found a way to use the law to hurt one whom the king regarded as a friend, and not even the king could do anything about it. It appeared that evil had won the day, and the participants in the drama celebrated or lamented according to their beliefs. But we mortals are too often premature in both celebration and lament. How often we rejoice in some achievement only to see it come to nothing. And how often we lament injustice only to see God turn it to good. We too easily forget that the sovereign LORD will always find a way to work for the good of those who love him.

November 13

Out of the Lion's Den

Daniel 6:18–28

It is my eager expectation and hope that I will not be at all ashamed, but that with full courage now as always Christ will be honored in my body, whether by life or by death.
Philippians 1:20 (ESV)

I don't know whether Daniel slept or not, but I'm quite certain he spent a more restful night than the king. Daniel surely prayed for his own deliverance, and God answered with the miracle of an angel to shut the mouths of the lions. Yet, the greater miracle was that what most concerned Daniel was not his own safety, but that the LORD would be honored and glorified in this situation.

That's just what happened. Darius decreed that everyone should fear and revere Daniel's God. How that must have encouraged the faithful worshipers of God scattered throughout that world. How that must have renewed their hope and confidence that God had not forgotten them, but would complete the coming salvation that Ezekiel and other prophets had spoken about.

May God help all of his people to be so faithful, so steadfast in putting him first, and so given to lives of prayer. For God is the source of all our strength and hope for now and for the future. As we keep looking to Christ we may be sure that no matter what opposition is arrayed against the LORD and his people, it will end up like those who opposed God's man, Daniel.

We may hope and pray for the conversion of the opposition rather than their destruction. That is just the reason that Christ came to earth—to reconcile such enemies to God, as happened with the apostle Paul himself (see Rom. 5:10) and the Christians in Colossae (see Col. 1:21). But there is also the warning of Hebrews 12:25—"See to it that you do not refuse him who speaks. If they did not escape when they refused him who warned them on earth, how much less will we, if we turn away from him who warns us from heaven?"

November 14

The Four Beasts of Daniel's Dream

Daniel 7:1–8, 15–25

Every spirit that does not confess Jesus is not from God.
This is the spirit of the antichrist.
1 John 4:3 (ESV)

The second part of Daniel's book records four visions he had over a period of about fifteen years. In them are many symbols, phrases, and numbers that are difficult to understand. However, although we may not be able to understand many of the details, the visions have a message for us.

Daniel's vision of four beasts seems to be similar to Nebuchadnezzar's dream of the great statue. But the way Daniel tells the story, the last kingdom in this vision was considerably more terrifying than the fourth kingdom of Nebuchadnezzar's dream. Most interpreters think this beast represents ancient Rome or Syria. The last of the ten kings of Syria was Antiochus Ephiphanes, who rose to his position by subduing three of the other kings. He especially seems to fit the description in that he was a great boaster, even bragging that he was God's equal.

Even so, this beast may also represent a coming world ruler who will similarly speak against the Most High God, oppress God's people, and in his madness, even dare to change the laws that God has ordained and that God alone has the power to change.

To a certain degree we already see this in today's world; in many respects, traditional morality has been turned on its head. Our world has many antichrists who use their power to oppose the LORD and his people. But perhaps you can imagine this trend getting much worse with an ultimate Antichrist, totally sold out to Satan and devoted to overcoming the Most High God and his people (see 1 John 2:18, 22; 4:3). It was enough to deeply trouble Daniel, and it is enough to trouble us as well—we who try to live our lives as much as possible according to God's revealed will. Thank God there's more to Daniel's vision.

November 15

The Victory of the Ancient of Days

Daniel 7:9–14, 26–28

And [God] put all things under [Christ's] feet and gave him as head over all things to the church, which is his body.
Ephesians 1:22-23 (ESV)

Even while the little horn of the last beast (the Antichrist) was still boasting of his ability to withstand God, Daniel saw in his vision the place of authority over the universe and the Ancient of Days sitting on the throne ready to render judgment. He was attended by an unnumbered throng of angels. The apostle John later provided a similar description (see Rev. 20:12) and said that all of the dead were judged by how they had lived, as recorded in the books. But Daniel saw merely the judgment of the beasts.

God's judgment shows that civilization is not on some inexorable upward trend in which things get better until humanity achieves utopia. Rather, God's people, whom we know from the witness of the New Testament are expanding to include previous enemies of God, are finding increasing opposition from those who stand against God. The rift between gospel and anti-gospel is growing. But God's judgment marks the beginning of the end for all who oppose him.

The first three beasts are deposed by God but allowed to live for a time while the fourth is killed and destroyed. In their place "one like a son of man" (a reference to Christ himself) was given all authority and the right to receive all worship. This may be a vision of the end of time but, in a real sense, Christ already rules and what happens today is part of what results in his final victory.

The unmistakable message of the vision, despite the fear that it produced in Daniel, is that the Most High God is in control, even when his opposition seems most successful. God's people, therefore, may be sure of ultimate victory; the power of God himself stands behind his promises and those who live by them.

November 16

Getting Ready for the Antichrist

Daniel 11:21–12:3

Who is the liar but he who denies that Jesus is the Christ? This is the antichrist, he who denies the Father and the Son.
1 John 2:22 (ESV)

Daniel's vision predicts the rise to power of Antiochus IV Epiphanes, ruler of Syria from 175 to 163 BC. Most of the ancient rulers before him were not overly concerned to change the religion of those they conquered, but Antiochus demanded conformity of belief. The Jews had more trouble than anyone with this demand, and therefore endured the most persecution.

Verses 30 and 31 speak of the vendetta of Antiochus against the religion of the Jews—capped by his installation of a statue of the Greek god Zeus in place of the altar. In the so-called Maccabean rebellion that followed, thousands of Jews were slaughtered. But eventually Antiochus was overcome and the temple was cleansed.

This might be just another interesting story, except for verses 36 and following, which describe a coming person who carries the pride, violence, and blasphemy of Antiochus to the extreme. He, it is believed, is the Antichrist, who will bring an unprecedented time of suffering for the righteous (see 12:1). Yet, his end will come (11:45) and God's true people will be delivered (12:1b) together with the righteous dead who will be raised to everlasting life (12:2–3). But others—those whose names are not written in the book of life—will rise to be condemned, sharing the fate of their leader.

This vision given to Daniel is important for God's people to remember, not so we can uncover all of the details of God's plans for the end days of the kingdom of this world, but so we can understand and remember the purpose and end of history. In this way we can prepare to live in such difficult times without losing our way or succumbing to the lures or threats of deceivers small or big. The wise will learn and adjust their lives accordingly.

November 17

The Stimulus for Effective Prayer

Daniel 9:1–3

This is the confidence that we have toward [God], that if we ask anything according to his will, he hears us.
1 John 5:14 (ESV)

This part of Daniel's vision is especially valuable to help us see one way that God calls all of his people to be involved in the agenda of his heavenly kingdom. I speak of prayer. Not all prayer is effective in spiritual warfare like that Daniel faced and which we will face until the end of time and God's final victory. So we must know what stimulates and characterizes effective prayer.

What stimulated Daniel was examining the events of his day in the light of the Scriptures. The particular Scripture that caught his attention was Jeremiah's prophecy that the exile of Israel would last seventy years. The seventy years, Daniel discovered, was just about up. It was that very truth that motivated him to plead with God for the fulfillment of God's promise.

The beautiful thing about Daniel's prayer is that the issue at stake was the LORD's cause. Daniel didn't have much to gain personally from a return to Jerusalem; he was too old. But he had his mind on greater things. He knew that the exile of God's people had brought the LORD's stated purposes into question. God had set apart his people as his special possession and to be a testimony to the nations of the way life was supposed to be lived. So Daniel knew that asking God to show his saving grace and complete what Jeremiah had prophesied was a prayer sure to be answered.

For us too, prayer is not just to tell God what we want. God does allow and even encourage us to ask him for things, with the understanding that it is our goal to conform our will to his. But, more than this, prayer that is inspired by and consistent with Scripture is the way we cooperate with God to bring his plans and purposes into reality.

November 18

The Content of Effective Prayer

Daniel 9:4–19

Thus says the One who is high and lifted up, who inhabits eternity, whose name is Holy: "I dwell in the high and holy place, and also with him who is of a contrite and lowly spirit, to revive... the lowly and... the contrite."
Isaiah 57:15 (ESV)

Daniel began his prayer with confession. He knew that his people were in exile because they had ignored and resisted God. Even though Daniel did not personally commit these sins, he took responsibility for confessing them on behalf of his people.

What had started out as sins of neglect had led to active rebellion against God. Soon, not even God's special messengers, the prophets, were taken seriously. Daniel made no attempt to transfer blame. He knew that although the Babylons of the world will not escape their own responsibility, shifting blame misses the lesson that God wants to teach his people. God wants us to see that evil rewards always follow sin. Confession of sin, therefore, is always the first step in helping people regain wholeness and make God's agenda their own.

After Daniel asked for forgiveness for himself and his people, he asked for deliverance and restoration. He was convinced now—after confession—that God would regard the restoration of Jerusalem as a matter of his own honor. The Almighty God is the only one who can protect his honor and he always does it, for he cannot be unfaithful to his promises, especially where unconfessed sin no longer stands in the way. God has placed his name on the heads of those whom he has redeemed and he will not treat his name lightly.

In our day too, we need to take care of our own relationship with God through regular confession of sin and repentance. Then we may pray confidently for the restoration and revival that God has promised his people, and that will make us a blessing to our world.

November 19

God's Answer to Effective Prayer

Daniel 9:20–23a; 10:12–13

They will call upon my name, and I will answer them. I will say, "They are my people;" and they will say, "The LORD is my God."
Zechariah 13:9b (ESV)

It may be that God sometimes acts apart from prayer, but we don't see much evidence of that in Scripture. Quite the opposite, we see in Daniel's case what is often implied: God acts in response to godly prayer, and he does so immediately. Gabriel tells Daniel, "As soon as you began to pray, an answer was given." The messenger of chapter 10 confirms that: "Since the first day…your words were heard." To be sure, Daniel had to wait for God's answer and to receive what he prayed for. God sent Gabriel immediately, but we aren't told how long it took him to get there. In the case of the messenger of chapter 10 it took three weeks of spiritual warfare.

There's a connection between prayer and what happens in heaven. Communications between God and his faithful servants are so important that the demon princes of Satan will do all they can to break the connection, even waging war against the angel messengers of God. Our part in all this begins as we become broken and repentant before God on account of our sin. Everything flows from that—all restoration, all victory, all life. God always responds to repentant prayer, and from what we see in Daniel, it seems he responds quickly, even immediately.

As long as Satan and his partners remain active on earth, there will be hindrances and delays in the delivery of God's answers. Continuing prayer, then, is our way of cooperating with God to make sure his answers get through. It is certain that God will accomplish what he wants to accomplish and that all his promises will be fulfilled. All the same, knowing this should lead us to pray. It did for Daniel, and it must do so for all God's people however long this spiritual war continues.

November 20

Some Exiles Return Home

Ezra 1—3

When the LORD restored the fortunes of Zion, we were like those who dream. Then our mouth was filled with laughter, and our tongue with songs of joy.
Psalm 126:1–2 (ESV)

A beginning of the answer to what Daniel had prayed for in the first year of the reign of Darius the Mede was seen within two years, in the first year of Cyrus, king of Persia. (Darius was either co-regent with Cyrus or reigned for only a year or two.)

The land that the exiles went back to was much poorer than the one they had left even though they returned with the blessing of Cyrus and articles from the temple. Many of Judah's cities had been torn down and most of the residents lived in villages and rural areas. Various non-Jewish tribes had also taken up residence in the land and would not easily give up their claims.

The spiritual challenges were even larger. Would these few returning exiles be able to reestablish the true worship of God in this land, which retained only a fragment of its former glory? Or would they compromise with their new neighbors and assimilate into the culture?

The priestly leadership of Israel seemed to have a good grasp of the dangers and possibilities the returnees faced. One of the first things they wanted to do was begin rebuilding the temple and reestablishing the sacred feasts and sacrifices of the LORD. They understood that only as their lives centered on the law of God and his presence with them would all God's promises be fulfilled and their rightful status and inheritance be achieved. They were intent on avoiding the sins that had sent their forebears into exile. It was the very thing for which the prophets had longed—that God's people might have learned their lesson from God's judgment through the Babylonians, and never again dishonor the LORD by idolatrous compromise.

November 21

The Returning Exiles Endure Opposition

Ezra 4

Have mercy upon us, O LORD, have mercy upon us,
for we have had more than enough of contempt.
Our soul has had more than enough of the scorn of
those who are at ease, of the contempt of the proud.
Psalm 123:3–4 (ESV)

The returning exiles (mainly from the tribes of Judah and Benjamin) had their hands full with the dual work of making a living for themselves and rebuilding God's temple. Their neighbors offered to help rebuild the temple saying that they also desired to serve the LORD. This offer came from the Samaritans, who were the result of intermarriages between Jews who had been left behind at the time of exile, and their idol-worshiping neighbors.

However, the leaders of Israel recognized the self-interest in the offer of the Samaritans and the threat they posed to the viability of the community. The Samaritans used golden calves in worship, the very same idolatry that had contributed to the exile of God's people from the Promised Land (see 2 Kings 17:24–41). They also denied the importance of Jerusalem as the holy city of God, and had selected a more convenient site as substitute—Mt. Gerizim. This would still be a significant bone of contention in Jesus's day (see John 4:20). Israel's leaders, therefore, refused the offer of help; they didn't want anything to hinder their effort to worship God as he desired. The returning exiles were determined to realize the full benefits of their inheritance from him.

Israel's neighbors did not take the rejection well. They harassed the settlers and hired lobbyists to plead their case to Cyrus, alleging that the Israelites were rebuilding the rebellious city of Jerusalem. It was a half-truth that resulted in a stop-work order from Cyrus. To the returning exiles, who wondered before whether they could ever again be the people God intended, this was a major setback.

November 22

The Need to Put God First

Haggai 1—2

Under the law almost everything is purified with blood, and without the shedding of blood there is no forgiveness of sins.
Hebrews 9:22 (ESV)

For more than a decade, work on the temple remained at a standstill, although the people made some progress in other areas of reconstruction. Even so, they were repeatedly frustrated in their rebuilding efforts. Poor harvests kept them from experiencing the God-blessed plenty that they hoped to have in this new chapter of God's work with them.

The word of the LORD came to Judah's leaders through the prophets Haggai and Zechariah. Haggai gave them God's message explaining their poor harvests—they had failed to complete the rebuilding of the temple. He said, "What you brought home, I blew away…because of my house, which remains a ruin, while each of you is busy with your own house" (Hag. 1:9).

The temple represented God's presence with his people. It was the only authorized place to offer the sacrifices that atoned for the sin of the people and made them clean enough to live in the presence of God. This was no arbitrary condition, but an essential one, although that requirement would one day be satisfied by the one-time sacrifice of Jesus on the cross. The apostle Peter puts it like this: "For Christ also suffered once for sins, the righteous for the unrighteous, to bring you to God" (1 Peter 3:18).

Zerubbabel, the governor, and Joshua, the high priest, made no excuses for their negligence, but rather put the people back to work rebuilding the LORD's temple. In turn they received the LORD's assurance that they would be able to measure the increase in material and other blessings from that day forward. Today, too, all those who put the LORD first will surely see blessings multiplied in their lives.

November 23

Proper Worship Is Restored in Judah

Ezra 5—6

I know the plans I have for you, declares the LORD, plans for welfare and not for evil, to give you a future and a hope.
Jeremiah 29:11 (ESV)

In the second year of Darius the Great, Haggai received the LORD's instructions that his people should get back to work on his temple. By God's grace they got permission for this and also financial help from Darius. Far from being worried about the earlier warnings of rebellion, Darius believed that he would be blessed by the prayers of the Jews for his well-being.

With this help, the Israelites completed the temple in four years, and once again offered sacrifices to the LORD in Jerusalem according to the provisions of the law of God. They also observed the Passover and Feast of Unleavened Bread, confessing that it was God's power that had convicted the king to assist them in this work of the LORD.

To be sure, this temple was only a transitional version of a more glorious one to come. Zechariah foretold a future descendant of David who would build the LORD's temple (Zech. 6:12–13). Surprisingly, he would be both king and priest, unlike any of the kings of ancient Israel who preceded him.

That's just what happened too. God maintained his covenant with David through fifteen successors to the throne until the exile and through the years after the exile until the coming of Jesus, who was of David's line. As a priest of Almighty God, Jesus offered the priestly sacrifice for sin—himself (see Heb. 10:12). And then, having overcome death by his resurrection, he ascended into heaven from where he rules as king over the whole world, working to create a suitable dwelling place for Almighty God. This, by God's will, is not a building but a people. In Christ you, too, are being built together to become a dwelling in which God lives by his Spirit (see Eph. 2:22).

November 24

Esther Becomes Queen

Esther 1—2

Seek the welfare of the city where I have sent you into exile, and pray to the LORD on its behalf, for in its welfare you will find your welfare.
Jeremiah 29:7 (ESV)

Although some of the Jews had been allowed to return to Judah and reestablish a foothold in the Promised Land, many more remained in exile in Persian-controlled lands. Among these were Mordecai and his cousin and ward Hadasseh, whose Persian name was Esther. They lived during the time of Xerxes, son of Darius the Great.

Although there was no official policy against the Jews at this time, it was safest not to stand out as a Jew. Even so, Mordecai and Esther feared the LORD, and Esther had been taught from childhood about God's will for his people.

Esther came to the king's attention after he had deposed his own queen for insubordination. Because Esther won his favor more than any other candidate, he made her his new queen. It was a prestigious position for such an outsider, although no one knew of her Jewish ancestry. Xerxes may not have cared about this anyway, but it mattered to some other people in the kingdom, and Esther's secret turns out to be important for the story.

Esther was in a position of some power, although, as she knew from what had happened to the previous queen, that power was totally dependent on the continuing favor of the king. So it was that she was well-positioned to pass on the news of a conspiracy against the king that Mordecai overheard one day.

Even though the name of the LORD is never mentioned in this-book, it is clear that Mordecai and Esther had the integrity expected of those devoted to observing the law of God. As part of their duty to God, they sought the welfare of the authorities that God had placed over them.

November 25

Haman's Vendetta

Esther 3:1–4:3

The kings of the earth set themselves, and the rulers take counsel together, against the LORD and against his Anointed.
Psalm 2:2 (ESV)

One day, Mordecai got into trouble with Haman, one of the king's officials. Haman had taken full advantage of his status, expecting everyone to bow down to him when he passed by. Everyone obeyed except Mordecai who, just like Daniel and his friends, saw God alone as worthy of such honor. Besides this, Mordecai knew that Haman was a descendant of the Amalekites, who had tried to destroy God's people in the days of Moses and who remained a threat in Saul's day.

That wasn't merely a struggle between two nations; the Amalekites had acted as Satan's agents in an attempt to destroy both Israel and God's plan for the world. After this, God himself gave the command that his people should "blot out the memory of Amalek from under heaven" (Deut. 25:19). As a faithful follower of God, Mordecai could not honor a sworn enemy of God.

The result was predictable; Haman became enraged. Learning that Mordecai was a Jew, Haman determined to seek revenge against him and all his people. To that end he misrepresented the threat they posed to the king. Haman was correct that the Jews had different customs than Xerxes's other subjects, but he lied about them being disobedient and disloyal to the king. But, the king trusted Haman that it was not in his best interest to tolerate the Jews. Xerxes told Haman to do as he pleased with them.

What Haman wanted to do was the very same thing that his ancestor Agag had wanted to do in the time of Moses and Joshua: kill all the Jews. The news of Haman's order was a terrible blow to Mordecai and the Jews throughout the kingdom. They mourned not only for what this meant personally, but for what it meant for all God's promises.

November 26

Esther Risks Her Life for Her People

Esther 4:4–5:14

Do not fear what you are about to suffer...
Be faithful unto death, and I will give you the crown of life.
Revelation 2:10 (ESV)

Esther was deeply distressed by the news of the king's order. Still, she was reluctant to put her life on the line by informing the king what Haman's order meant to her and her people. But Mordecai would not accept her excuses. He undoubtedly had God's sovereignty in mind when he admitted that relief and deliverance could come from another place. Yet, he was sure that this truth did not relieve Esther of her responsibility. He believed that if anyone was in a position to do some good—such as Esther was—then she ought to seize that opportunity, even at the risk of danger to herself.

Mordecai did not know for sure if Esther would be able to help the Jews. Nor did he know if she might get into trouble by attempting it. But he did tell Esther that perhaps God had arranged things so that she was in a position to save her people. With that, Esther agreed, asking only for fasting and prayer support for the ordeal ahead.

In the meantime, Haman raged all the more against Mordecai and his people. He made plans that were opposite to those Esther was making.

When God's people take a stand for him and his kingdom, it is never safe; it will even incite opposition. But we do well to remember Mordecai's point of view and Esther's faithful response, as well as her prayerful preparation. It is not for us to say how God might act through us, even if we feel unqualified for such service or threatened by the potential results. We need only to be obedient in using our positions and responding to the opportunities God puts before us. When we do this, we can be certain that, whether we live or die, the LORD's cause will be advanced.

November 27

God's Judgment and Salvation

Esther 6—10

Do not be deceived: God is not mocked, for whatever one sows, that will he also reap. For the one who sows to his own flesh will from the flesh reap corruption, but the one who sows to the Spirit will from the Spirit reap eternal life.
Galatians 6:7–8 (ESV)

Esther's efforts were successful, and wicked Haman and his supporters got what they deserved. Not only were the lives of God's people spared, the Jews also received the king's permission to form a militia to protect themselves against attack. It was a great victory for the Jews of Persia and became the occasion for a celebratory feast that continues to this day (Purim).

Today we may be a little conflicted by this story. On the one hand, we rejoice whenever the good and innocent prevail over the evil and guilty. We like to see the power of evil people taken away and enjoy hearing about the rewards that came to Esther and Mordecai. We applaud the protection from racist abuse that the Jews came to enjoy. On the other hand, we cringe at the violence and wholesale killing that accompanied the victory of God's people. It may seem too much like unhealthy revenge.

However, we should understand just what was at stake. This was yet another episode in the spiritual warfare that began with Satan's aspiration to make himself like the Most High God and Satan's subsequent fall from heaven (see Isaiah 14:12–14 and Ezekiel 28:12–18).

For God's righteousness to prevail, evil must be judged, and for God's beloved people to be saved, all those who persist in following the ways of Satan must be condemned. We may be grateful, therefore, that by God's grace his final judgment is postponed (see 2 Peter 3:9) so that more of those who are now witting or unwitting tools of Satan may have the opportunity to repent and come to God through Christ for salvation.

November 28

God's Sovereign Power

Psalm 2

O LORD, God of our fathers, are you not God in heaven? You rule over all the kingdoms of the nations. In your hand are power and might, so that none is able to withstand you.
2 Chronicles 20:6 (ESV)

The book of Esther does not refer to God, but he is clearly the one who saved the Jews from their enemies through Mordecai and Esther. What happens here is a good illustration of Psalm 2: Although the high and mighty of the earth conspire to establish their own standards and power at the expense of the LORD and his people, God's sovereignty over them is undeniable.

God laughs at the presumption of those who oppose him. No matter how solid they appear, none of these people, ideals, or governments will last. They threaten and boast but, even while they expand their territory, their foundations are being undermined. For God has installed his son as king already and is even now making the nations an inheritance for Christ. The claim to power of God's opposers is as fragile as pottery struck by iron.

Psalm 2 does not, however, just announce the defeat of all who oppose the LORD; it also calls everyone to repentance and faith. It invites the rulers of the earth and all others who oppose the Sovereign God to be wise and turn to serve him instead of opposing him. In this way they will find blessing in place of the judgment that overtakes all who persist in rebellion.

The conversion the Psalmist had in mind is not to a faith that functions only in private or in company with others of like mind. Nor is it a faith ignorant of direct and personal communication with the LORD. It is rather a living faith, applicable to all of life's situations and problems. It is a faith that takes seriously God's call to wholehearted love and service. It is also a faith, although this psalm does not mention it, which is evangelistic, broadcasting God's call for everyone to serve him and rejoice in his rule.

November 29

Ezra's Return from Exile

Ezra 9:1–10:17

You shall not intermarry with [idolaters]...for they would turn away your sons from following me, to serve other gods. Then the anger of the LORD would be kindled against you, and he would destroy you quickly.
Deuteronomy 7:3–4 (ESV)

More than a decade following the events described in Esther, Ezra, a priest and expert in God's Law, led another contingent of Jews back to their homeland. In this they had the approval and financial support of the king of Persia (Ezra 7:13–16).

With their new attention to the law of God, the returnees soon came to realize that they had violated God's law against marrying idol worshipers. This very thing had been a major factor in Israel's downfall. (Consider King Solomon, who had appeased his foreign wives by building temples for their gods, and whose own heart was led astray in the process, and King Ahab, who wasn't too pure in the first place, but whose marriage to Jezebel had ensured disaster for himself and his people.)

God's prohibition had less to do with ethnicity than with the religious practices of the foreigners. In fact, those who put away their idolatry and worshiped only Yahweh were regarded as part of the covenant people of God. Rahab, the former Canaanite prostitute from Jericho, and Ruth, the former idolater from Moab, are two examples.

The decision of Ezra's community was that foreign wives had to be sent back to their families of origin. Perhaps some avoided this through conversion; for those who did not, we can only imagine the resulting family disruption and hardship. This is not what we would do today. Although the Apostle Paul counseled against being unequally yoked with an unbeliever (1 Cor. 6:14–15), he also advised against divorce in such cases (1 Cor. 7:12–14). But the returning exiles' decision in this matter is a sign of how intent they were on following God's law.

November 30

Nehemiah's Prayers for God's People

Nehemiah 1

Thus says the LORD God: I will gather you from the peoples and assemble you out of the countries where you have been scattered, and I will give you the land of Israel.
Ezekiel 11:17 (ESV)

Nehemiah was a Jew, still serving the LORD as a member of the exilic community in Susa. He knew of the return of Ezra's contingent to Jerusalem thirteen years earlier and was always eager to hear how they were doing. He was in a position to hear such news, for he lived at court as a cupbearer for the king.

Nehemiah heard, to his distress, that the people in and around Jerusalem were having a lot of trouble; they hadn't been able to rebuild their lives. The great gaps in Jerusalem's walls and its burned gates left the people vulnerable to attack. This distressed Nehemiah, for it was his great hope that his people would once again enjoy the blessings of God in the Promised Land. In his grieving he devoted himself to a season of fasting and prayer.

Notice these features of Nehemiah's prayers:

- They showed humility and his recognition of the need for God's forgiveness for himself and his people.
- They were unselfish; he thought of God's honor and the threat to God's promises. He knew that Jerusalem's broken walls were a sign of the broken Kingdom of God. But he also prayed long and hard that God would restore his people to their rightful place for his glory.
- They did not put limits on God's timing or methods. Nehemiah kept praying, waiting, and believing, knowing that God would answer when the time was right. He was also open to God using him, and he made himself available to God.

Nehemiah's prayers would not only be effective for his day; they still serve as an excellent model for our own prayers. Such God-centered prayers honor God and can expect his reply.

December 1

Wholehearted Dependence and Trust

Psalm 123

The sacrifice of the wicked is an abomination to the LORD,
but the prayer of the upright is acceptable to him.
Proverbs 15:8 (ESV)

This psalm expresses the kind of attitude Nehemiah had when he came to God with his concerns for the troubles of his brothers and sisters back in the Promised Land and for the sad state of Jerusalem's walls. We don't know for sure that Nehemiah knew this psalm, but the dismay he felt over the harassment and ridicule doled out by Israel's enemies is certainly reflected here. Nor was Nehemiah's concern merely for himself and his people; it was for the honor of the Lord of heaven whom they represented.

This psalm makes clear that all authority resides with the one whose throne is in heaven; there is no higher authority than God. On the other hand there is probably no one more dependent or lacking authority than slaves, who have no life of their own. In ancient times slaves were typically not allowed to carry weapons, even for self-defense. They did not dare to respond to insults or violence without permission; they had no defense unless their master would protect and defend them.

When this psalm was written, it was the custom for household slaves to stand with their hands crossed on their chests and their eyes fixed on their master, alert for the smallest sign of his desires. But the slaves of this psalm look for something more than orders; they look and hope for mercy, for relief from the contempt and ridicule they have suffered because of their enemies.

Psalm 123 combines an expression of faith in God with an attitude of complete dependence on him. In doing so, it vividly contrasts this attitude with the arrogance, pride and supposed independence of those who are not the LORD's servants. This psalm, therefore, remains an appropriate prayer for any of God's people today who find their ways blocked by spiritual opposition.

December 2

Nehemiah's Prayers Are Answered

Nehemiah 2:1–10

Beloved, if our heart does not condemn us, we have confidence before God; and whatever we ask we receive from him, because we keep his commandments and do what pleases him.
1 John 3:21–22 (ESV)

One day, after Nehemiah had persevered in prayer for some time, God opened the king's eyes to notice that something was troubling Nehemiah. When the king asked him about it, Nehemiah became very afraid; the king had never spoken personally to him before. But he did not second guess his conviction that this was God's answer to his prayers, and Nehemiah told the king what he'd been praying for. Afterwards, the king authorized him to travel to Jerusalem and supervise the rebuilding of its walls.

Some people don't believe that prayer actually does any good. They say, "Go ahead and pray if it makes you feel better. But don't tell me it really changes things. Do you actually think that you can get God to change his mind or pay special attention to your requests? Don't be silly. Prayer is like talking to yourself; if it has any effect, it's because of the power of positive thinking at work."

But that's not the message of Scripture. Nor is it the truth that long experience has taught God's people. The Bible says, and God's people have learned, that prayer does change things. In fact, every work of God's power through me and you has to begin with prayer. Nehemiah's story is a case in point.

Like Nehemiah, we may dare to approach God in unselfish and obedient prayer, asking in confidence for things that we know are on God's heart, because our God, using those who approach him and many other resources at his disposal, does change things for the advantage of his kingdom and the praise of his glory. He alone deserves the credit, but we may be agents of his saving grace through our prayers and the obedience that follows them.

December 3

The Walls Rebuilt Despite Opposition

Nehemiah 4:1–23; 6:15–16

God is our refuge and strength, a very present help in trouble.
Psalm 46:1 (ESV)

Nehemiah wept when he first received word about the sad state of the political and spiritual center of his people. His concern was not only for Jerusalem's broken-down walls, but also for the other difficulties of the retuning exiles. His first priority, however, was to rebuild the walls. In the ancient world, city walls provided protection from one's enemies. Also, the rebuilding of Jerusalem's walls would be a powerful symbol to both God's people and their enemies of the protection and approval of the LORD.

Given the opportunity to return and supervise this project, Nehemiah rounded up materials and laborers and started to work. He knew that this would not be accomplished without opposition. Two of the opposition leaders were Sanballat, governor of Samaria to the north, and Tobiah, governor of the area across the Jordan to the east of Jerusalem. They likely saw a stronger Jerusalem as a threat to themselves and so used both political connections and physical intimidation to stop the rebuilding.

But Nehemiah persisted, convinced that he was doing the work of God. He managed to get almost everyone involved in the rebuilding project, some in the actual work and others standing on guard to protect them. Both men and women contributed, and the wall was completed in only fifty-two days.

This was only one step in the reestablishment of God's people in the Promised Land. But there could now be renewed attention to other areas of neglect in the service of the LORD. One problem Nehemiah had already addressed during the rebuilding (ch. 5); he convinced the richer citizens to stop charging the poor interest on their debts and to stop seizing their property. It was an important step in Israel's commitment to obey God's laws.

December 4

New Attention and Response to the Law

Nehemiah 8:1–9:3

If they confess their iniquity and the iniquity of their fathers…
then I will remember my covenant with Jacob and…
Isaac and…Abraham, and I will remember the land.
Leviticus 26:40, 42 (ESV)

A few days later, the people assembled for the reading of God's law. They had seen God's hand in the re-building of Jerusalem's walls; now they gathered to hear what more the LORD required. This hadn't been done for a long time; it was a significant symbol of their intention to not mess up this new opportunity with God.

What followed can only be attributed to the powerful work of the Holy Spirit, for the people listened attentively for six hours as God's Word was read. They heard how God had called them to be a nation devoted to serving him. They heard about all the miracles and mighty acts God had performed for them. And they heard again about God's commands given through Moses, commands to which they knew they had not paid adequate attention.

What Israel chose to do in response to the reading of God's Word was crucial, because the very problem with their ancestors, the problem that had caused their exile, was what Scripture repeatedly refers to as hardheartedness. The people had often ignored God's law, and when this was pointed out to them by prophets, still, usually refused to repent and change their ways.

But these Israelites wept for their sins; in their conviction, they didn't care how they looked to their neighbors. They were sad for so long that Nehemiah had to tell them to stop grieving and go have lunch: "Do not grieve, for the joy of the LORD is your strength." So they rejoiced, and in the following days listened again and again to the word of the LORD and again joined their hearts in confession and praise. Afterward they bound themselves in writing to live according to the law of God and not neglect their offerings for God's temple and his priests (Neh. 9:38).

December 5

Sabbath Keeping

Nehemiah 13:15–22

In your hearts honor Christ the Lord as holy,
always being prepared to make a defense to anyone
who asks you for a reason for the hope that is in you.
1 Peter 3:15 (ESV)

The Sabbath day had lost its special significance in Nehemiah's time and culture. But Nehemiah saw that the solemn promises made by himself and his people required attention to the proper observance of the Sabbath. Nehemiah promoted that by policing commercial activities on that day. But, of course, he had no way to ensure that his people would also honor God's intention for the Sabbath in their hearts. Only doing that would really keep Nehemiah's people from repeating the sins that had led their nation into exile.

Israel would not do so well in future years; by Jesus's day, instead of using the Sabbath to remember God's deliverance of them, the Jews were misusing it as a day in which they tried to deliver themselves through a legalistic adherence to Sabbath laws. The Pharisees were more conscientious about protecting the Sabbath against violations than about promoting it as a God-given means to revive the minds and souls of God's people.

Jesus used words and deeds to show his people another way to keep the Sabbath. The types of deeds that were consistent with God's Sabbath work of delivering Israel from Egypt were works of mercy such as healing the sick and raising the dead.

Today, Christians typically use Sunday instead of Saturday as their main day for worship. Even so, honoring God's intentions for the Sabbath involves using this day, not mainly to escape work and devote oneself to leisure but, to re-center ourselves on God, in whom we may both work and rest. In fact, this is what helps us to anticipate the eternal Sabbath, when both work and play will be just the way God wants it to be.

The Coming Messiah

Psalm 110

God exalted him at his right hand as Leader and Savior, to give repentance to Israel and forgiveness of sins.
Acts 5:31 (ESV)

Ezra and Nehemiah did their best to help the returning exiles live and worship in ways consistent with the law of God handed down through Moses. They wanted to make sure that the chosen people of God never again indulged in the sort of idolatry and other disobedience that had led to God's judgment at the hands of Assyria and Babylonia.

We don't know much about what happened after the time of these leaders. Except perhaps for a few words from the prophet Malachi, the Old Testament record ends with Nehemiah's work. Scripture is silent about the next four hundred years—until the angelic announcement of the imminent birth of John the Baptist as recorded by Luke.

By this time, Israel had become subject to Roman rule, and, judging by what we know of the Pharisees of Jesus's day, legalism in worship practices had become entrenched. This was not universal, for there were still some who fit Jesus's description of the kind of worshipers the Father seeks—those who worshiped "in spirit and truth" (see John 4:23). But what legalists and true worshipers had in common was their anticipation of a Messiah, foretold by the prophets, who would restore Israel to its former glory and fulfill all of God's promises to Abraham.

In the final days of this year we'll look at just a few of these prophecies, mainly from the book of Isaiah. But take note first of Psalm 110, which has the distinction of being the psalm most referenced in the New Testament. Even before Jesus's birth, it was regarded by the post-exilic Jewish people as predictive of a Messiah who would be both king and priest. What none of them realized, however, was just how great this Messiah would be.

December 7

The Mountain of the LORD's Temple

Isaiah 2:2–4

Nations will fear the name of the LORD,
and all the kings of the earth will fear your glory.
Psalm 102:15 (ESV)

Isaiah was dismayed about the evil in his country and in Jerusalem, the so-called city of peace. He wrote, "See how the faithful city has become a prostitute! She once was full of justice; righteousness used to dwell in her—but now murderers" (Isa. 1:21).

However, Isaiah speaks of a coming day in which things will be different, in which "the mountain of the LORD's temple" will be raised to a clear position of superiority above all other kingdoms, systems and organizations. Isaiah is speaking about the kingdom of God, for which Jerusalem and the centrally located temple of the LORD were the primary symbols. One day, Isaiah continues, people will recognize that God's way is the best way—that the LORD and his servant-people have a quality of life that cannot be found anywhere else. People will flock from all nations and races into God's Kingdom where they too can live by God's law, at peace with former enemies.

Isaiah's hearers might have wondered a bit about this second part of the promise. After all, God had emphasized for so long the necessity for Israel to remain separate from its neighbors so the Israelites would not be contaminated by pagan religions. But the reason to avoid such mixing would disappear in God's kingdom, for only those who were willing to submit themselves to the LORD would join God's cause.

Isaiah doesn't use the term "Messiah," but he makes clear that the coming descendant of David—whom we know to be Christ Jesus—will be anointed by God. Christ has now come and is making God's kingdom everything that God intends it to be—a place where people can be blessed by the LORD, ruled by him and living in harmony with their neighbors.

The Light of Life

Isaiah 9:1–7

Your kingdom is an everlasting kingdom,
and your dominion endures throughout all generations.
Psalm 145:13 (ESV)

In this passage Isaiah looks toward the future and describes its events with a certainty that belongs to actions already completed. In a time of despair Isaiah speaks the word of God about the child to be born as if he already sits on the throne that will be his. This son of David is a great light to people walking in darkness. This is the darkness of sin in which not only the Gentiles, but God's own people have been walking. They "call evil good and good evil [and] put darkness for light and light for darkness" (Isa. 5:20). The light will be for both Israel and the Gentiles—to open eyes that are blind, to free captives from prison and to release from the dungeon those who sit in darkness" (see Isa. 42:6-7).

Even now, Isaiah says, the burdensome yoke, oppressive rod, and battle boots are destined for burning. This is because the child to be born will bring God's deliverance. Like all children he will have humble beginnings, but he will be divinely powerful.

- He is Wonderful Counselor—with infinite wisdom.
- He is Mighty God—first manifest as a very human child, but one with a divine character.
- He is Everlasting Father—like other kings, a father to his people, but with an everlasting kingdom.
- He is Prince of Peace—bringing an endless rule of justice and righteousness and peace.

By all human accounts, it was a highly improbable scenario that Isaiah pictured. However, as we look back on events that Isaiah could only anticipate, we see that it did happen with the birth of a child who later claimed with the full authority of God himself, "I am the light of the world. Whoever follows me will never walk in darkness, but will have the light of life" (John 8:12).

December 9

The LORD Our Righteousness

Isaiah 11

Behold, the days are coming, declares the LORD, when I will raise up for David a righteous Branch, and he shall reign as king and deal wisely, and shall execute justice and righteousness in the land. In his days Judah will be saved...And this is the name by which he will be called: "The LORD is our Righteousness."
Jeremiah 23:5–6 (ESV)

Isaiah identifies several marks of the coming Messiah, marks that have since been fulfilled in Jesus.

- His ancestry: At the time of the exile, little more than a "stump of Jesse" remained. But from that stump—David's line—would arise a shoot (or what Jeremiah called a branch) to carry out the desires of the LORD. (See the genealogies of Jesus in Matthew 1 and Luke 3.)
- His source of help and quality of character: He would give undivided devotion to the LORD and have understanding, wisdom, and power by his Spirit. (Matt. 3:16–17; 7:28–29; Luke 2:40)
- His righteous judgments: The punishments and mercies that followed his wise decisions would be absolutely correct and just. (John 7:24; Mark 12:41–44)
- Life in his kingdom: There would be perfect peace and safety in the messianic kingdom. The complete fulfillment of what Isaiah pictured awaits the second coming of Christ. However, many New Testament passages speak of the future in store for us and the life to which we should now aspire. (Luke 1:67–79; John 14:27; Rom. 14:17; 2 Tim. 2:22; Rev. 21:3–4)
- The citizens in his kingdom: A remnant of Abraham's descendants, redeemed from physical and spiritual exile, would be included. Also, people from other nations, seeing the beauty of his glorious kingdom, would flock to become part of it. (Luke 2:30–32; Acts 13:47–48; Rom. 10:13; Eph. 3:6; 1 Tim. 2:3–4)

December 10

Comfort for God's People

Isaiah 40:1–11

[God] will dwell with them, and they will be his people, and God himself will be with them as their God. He will wipe away every tear from their eyes, and death shall be no more, neither shall there be mourning, nor crying, nor pain anymore, for the former things have passed away."
Revelation 21:3–4 (ESV)

Isaiah 40 has long been a favorite passage of Christians, especially since it was immortalized in the opening movements of Handel's *Messiah.* The first verses proclaim comfort to God's people who feel forsaken. Certainly, the exiles would have felt forsaken by God. They had lost the land and the temple that had marked them as God's chosen people. But Isaiah proclaims an end to God's punishment for sin; it has been paid for.

In a sense, however, Israel's exile was an inadequate payment; Romans 3:21–26 tells us that full and complete forgiveness of sin comes only through Jesus Christ. So those who have come to him in faith have much better grounds for comfort than even Isaiah knew about. The end of God's punishment for sin goes hand-in-hand with his return to live in covenant harmony with his people. Isaiah proclaims that God's coming must be prepared for. In his day that required a life of ongoing repentance and devotion to the law of the LORD. But Matthew 3:1-12 applies this passage to John the Baptist, whose vigorous calls for repentance just before Jesus began his ministry paved the way for Jesus's fuller revelation of the comfort and glory of the LORD.

Isaiah had a glimpse of the power, reward, and comfort that would come with the end of Israel's exile. But he proclaimed something much greater than he probably knew—a tender shepherd and powerful teacher, healer, and king who would rise from death and ascend to rule, but whose authority would be fully realized only with his return in glory at the end of time (see John 1:4–7; 22:12–15).

December 11

The Servant of the LORD—Part 1

Isaiah 42:1–8

The LORD to Moses: *I will raise up for them a prophet like you from among their brothers. And I will put my words in his mouth, and he shall speak to them all that I command him. And whoever will not listen to my words that he shall speak in my name, I myself will require it of him.*
Deuteronomy 18:18–19 (ESV)

Although God designed the whole of his creation for service to him, humans are called to the special task of being his caretakers (see Ps. 8:4–6). However, Scripture also speaks of a special few whom God calls "my servant," among them, Job (Job 42:7–8), Moses (Num. 12:6–8), and David (1 Kings 11:34–39). Israel is also given this designation by Isaiah and Jeremiah, for example, Isaiah 44:21—"Remember these things, Jacob, for you, Israel, are my servant. I have made you, you are my servant; Israel, I will not forget you."

This brings us to Isaiah 42, the first of four "servant songs" about a specially enabled and faithful servant who is supported, chosen, and delighted in by God, and also fully enabled by his Spirit to bring justice to the nations. This servant is called in righteousness, walks hand-in-hand with the LORD, and is made to be both a covenant for Israel and a light for the Gentiles—all of this so he can act as God's agent to open blind eyes and proclaim freedom for those held captive in darkness.

In a limited sense, this servant is the nation of Israel. Already in his call to Abraham, God promises to bless all peoples on earth through him. Walter Kaiser says that this finds confirmation in "the sentiment of Psalm 67: May God be gracious and bless us fellow Israelites…so that the nations may look on us and say that what Aaron prayed for, by way of God's blessing, has occurred…Accordingly, may the rest of God's purpose come to pass as well, that in the blessing of Israel all the nations of the earth might be drawn to receive the message of God's salvation as well." "God's Purpose for Missions in the Old Testament" p 31.

December 12

The Servant of the LORD—Part 2

Isaiah 42:1–8

Many followed [Jesus], and he healed them all
and ordered them not to make him known.
This was to fulfill what was spoken by the prophet Isaiah.
Matthew 12:15-17 (ESV)

God's intentions for Israel were relayed to it by Moses in Exodus 19:5–6, "Now if you obey me fully and keep my covenant, then out of all nations you will be my treasured possession. Although the whole earth is mine, you will be for me a kingdom of priests and a holy nation." This hope was still held out to God's people by Zechariah (8:13, 23): "Just as you, Judah and Israel, have been a curse among the nations, so will I save you, and you will be a blessing…people from all languages and nations will…say, 'Let us go with you, because we have heard that God is with you.'"

Some faithful people did act as God's kingdom of priests and holy nation. And some foreigners were drawn to the LORD because of it. However, the nation as a whole did not do well, and the fulfillment of God's purposes would wait for the arrival of one special offspring of Abraham, "Christ" (Gal. 3:16).

That the definitive "my servant" of Isaiah is Jesus is confirmed, among other places, by these verses:

- Matthew 12:18–21, which repeats Isaiah 42:1–4.
- John, whose repeated announcement of Jesus as the light of the world confirms Isaiah 42:6.
- Luke, whose record of the words Jesus used to begin his ministry echoes those in Isaiah 42:7 and 61:1–2.

Another important thing to note about Isaiah's servant of the LORD is what the New Testament says time and again about the service God expects from his redeemed people. Paul applies Isaiah's words about God's light for the world to himself and the church of Christ: "I have made you a light for the Gentiles, that you may bring salvation to the ends of the earth" (Acts 13:47).

December 13

"My Servant"—Rejected and Condemned

Isaiah 52:13–53:12

I am small and despised, yet I do not forget your precepts.
Psalm 119:141 (ESV)

This Old Testament Scripture probably gets more use than any other during the season of Lent. I invite you to read it for the next three days, noting the various aspects of Isaiah's prophecy and the New Testament accounts showing fulfillment in Jesus.

The rejection and condemnation to be endured by the one God calls "my servant" is made explicit in Isaiah 52:14 and 53:3, 7–9. Referring to this and similar prophecies, Jesus himself predicted his coming abuse and death to his disciples: "We are going up to Jerusalem, and everything that is written by the prophets about the Son of Man will be fulfilled. He will be delivered over to the Gentiles. They will mock him, insult him, spit on him; they will flog him and kill him" (Luke 18:31–32). The testimony of all the gospels is that this is just what happened to Jesus.

There is also the matter of the silence with which Jesus met the accusations against him, just as Isaiah foretold. Jesus did not defend himself to any of these authorities:

- The high priest (Mark 14:61)
- Pilate (Matt. 27:12–14)
- Herod (Luke 23:8–9)

Jesus was silent in spite of his innocence of all charges. And by that innocence, Jesus fulfilled yet another part of Isaiah's prophecy. His accusers, despite looking hard for charges to bring against Jesus, could find none and so invented false charges (see Mark 14:55–57). Other Scriptures also testify to the innocence of Jesus:

- 2 Corinthians 5:21 calls Jesus "him who had no sin."
- Hebrews 4:15 attests to the sinlessness of Jesus in facing his temptations.
- 1 Peter 2:22 affirms, "He committed no sin, and no deceit was found in his mouth."

December 14

"My Servant"—Penalty Bearer for Sin

Isaiah 52:13–53:12

The next day [John] saw Jesus coming toward him, and said, "Behold, the Lamb of God, who takes away the sin of the world!"
John 1:29 (ESV)

The sacrificial system in Israel was established by God so that the guilt of sin could be taken away and fellowship with God restored. One of many relevant passages is Leviticus 17:11, "The life of a creature is in the blood, and I have given it to you to make atonement for yourselves on the altar..." Isaiah clearly identifies the servant as chosen by God, like a sacrificial lamb, to bear the penalty of the sins of others (Isa. 53:4–6, 10a, 12b).

Jesus identified this as his task: "The Son of Man did not come to be served, but to serve, and to give his life as a ransom for many" (Matt. 20:28). The sacrifice Jesus came to make was much more effective than any previous sacrifice, however. A multitude of New Testament Scriptures affirm this; a few of these will suffice to help us understand how great a gift Jesus has given us.

- "We have now been justified by his blood" (Rom. 5:9).
- "God made him who had no sin to be sin for us, so that in him we might become the righteousness of God" (2 Cor. 5:11).
- "Christ redeemed us from the curse of the law by becoming a curse for us" (Gal. 3:13).
- "God was pleased...to reconcile to himself all things...by making peace through his blood, shed on the cross" (Col. 1:19–20).
- "He suffered death, so that by the grace of God he might taste death for everyone" (Heb. 2:9).
- "The blood of Christ [will] cleanse our consciences...so that we may serve the living God!" (Heb. 9:14).
- "You were redeemed...with the precious blood of Christ, a lamb without blemish or defect" (1 Peter 1:18–19).
- "He himself bore our sins in his body on the cross...by his wounds you have been healed" (1 Peter 2:24).

December 15

"My Servant"—Raised and Exalted

Isaiah 52:13–53:12

After making purification for sins, [God's Son] sat down at the right hand of the Majesty on high.
Hebrews 1:3 (ESV)

Isaiah prophesied that the servant of the LORD would not only be despised and rejected and give his life as atonement for the sin of others, he would also "be raised and lifted up and highly exalted" (Isa. 52:13). Isaiah 53:10b–12a confirms this and also labels those who have experienced his healing and peace as "offspring."

Central to the gospel are the teachings that sin must be punished and that it has been punished once for all by Christ's death on the cross. But, Christ's sacrifice would have been inadequate if he had remained dead. Paul says, "If Christ has not been raised, your faith is futile; you are still in your sins" (1 Cor. 15:17).

It's very significant that the overwhelming testimony of Scripture is that Christ has been raised from the dead, and has been exalted to sit at the right hand of God in heaven. Philippians 2:9–11 says, "God exalted him to the highest place and gave him the name that is above every name, that at the name of Jesus every knee should bow, in heaven and on earth and under the earth, and every tongue confess that Jesus Christ is Lord, to the glory of God the Father." Paul repeats this theme often—among other places in Ephesians 1:20–23.

Christ's resurrection assures us that those who have come to Christ in true faith will also live with him; death no longer has mastery over us (see Rom. 6:8–9). Peter also speaks of "an inheritance that can never perish, spoil, or fade…kept in heaven for you…until the coming of the salvation that is ready to be revealed in the last time" (1 Pe. 1:4-5). In the meantime (see Romans 8:34) we are assured of Christ's ongoing prayers for us. We have life now, and the promise that life will continue for the infinite future! What more could anyone want?

December 16

How Will the LORD Make Himself Known?

Isaiah 64:1–4

Christ Jesus, who, though he was in the form of God, did not count equality with God a thing to be grasped, but emptied himself, by taking the form of a servant, being born in the likeness of men.
Philippians 2:5b–7 (ESV)

Despite what Isaiah said about the humility and suffering of God's special servant, it is the hope that he expresses in this passage that dominated Israel's view of the coming Messiah. One day the LORD would rend the heavens and come down to rescue his people from the hand of their oppressors, putting an end to all doubt about who was sovereign over all the nations of the world. Isaiah attributed the fact that God had not already done this to the sins of God's people. But one day, Isaiah hoped and prayed, the LORD would no longer hold himself back.

If we are honest, isn't it often our hope, too, that the LORD will show his power on behalf of those who do his will? There is too much blasphemy, idolatry, and injustice; if only the LORD would dramatically intervene to save the innocent who are so often oppressed. Mostly, however, such a revelation of the LORD's authority will have to await his coming at the end of time. Meanwhile, far more often than not, God acts in quiet ways that become apparent only to those who are waiting and looking for him.

The eventual arrival of the promised Savior is a case in point. By Luke's account Jesus's birth was a humble affair. But, to reveal it, angelic birth announcements were made to two rather unlikely couples living at this transition point of history. Zechariah and Elizabeth, both descendants of Aaron, were old and childless. The other couple was engaged but not yet married—Joseph and Mary, both of the royal line of David, but with little of his status and none of his power. These two couples were humble and ordinary people, but their pregnancies were anything but ordinary, for both were impossible by all human accounts.

December 17

The Forerunner of Jesus Announced

Luke 1:5–25, 57–79

Behold, I send my messenger, and he will prepare the way before me.
And the LORD whom you seek will suddenly come to his temple;
and the messenger of the covenant in whom you delight,
behold, he is coming, says the LORD of hosts.
Malachi 3:1 (ESV)

Zechariah was alone in the Most Holy Place, privileged that day to burn incense before the LORD. Suddenly Gabriel appeared to him announcing that God was answering his prayers with the coming birth of a son. Zechariah didn't believe it, which is interesting since that's what he'd been praying for. Perhaps, as we do at times, he was praying without expecting an answer from God. He started to believe, however, when he was not able to speak.

No doubt Zechariah thought much over the months of Elizabeth's pregnancy, astonished that God would bless them so. At the time of the baby's circumcision and naming, he confirmed Elizabeth's statement that the child would not be named after his father or a relative as was customary, but would be called John. By then he was fully convinced that this miracle child was chosen by God to prepare the world to receive the coming Messiah.

It was then that the Holy Spirit gave Zechariah insight about what God was doing. Most of Zechariah's song of response passed over the role that his own son would play—calling people to repentance. Instead, he sang of the coming Messiah and the salvation he would bring. No doubt Zechariah saw the coming salvation as the fulfillment of centuries of God's work with his people. In keeping with the expectations surrounding the coming of the Messiah, Zechariah probably thought less about the suffering the Messiah would undergo than he did about the power of the LORD that would be displayed on behalf of his people. Finally, God's people could do something they'd never been able to do with consistency, "serve him without fear in holiness and righteousness."

December 18

Gabriel's News and Mary's Song

Luke 1:26–56

God to Abraham: *In your offspring shall all the nations of the earth be blessed, because you have obeyed my voice.*
Genesis 22:18 (ESV)

One of the key truths in this passage is the angel Gabriel's witness to the divinity of Mary's coming child. He says, "He…will be called Son of the Most High" (Luke 1:32). The term "Most High" is another name for God as verse 35 shows: "The holy one to be born will be called the Son of God." Gabriel says that this divine son is not only the legitimate heir to the throne of David, but that he will keep his position forever as head of an eternal kingdom. This makes him the ultimate fulfillment of God's promise to David in 2 Samuel 7:12–16.

When Mary responded that she did not understand how she, as a virgin, could give birth to such a child, Gabriel told her about the divine conception. He also told her of Elizabeth's equally impossible pregnancy. With that, Mary believed the angel's message, a message that was confirmed soon after in her visit to Elizabeth, who recognized her own baby's kick as a Holy Spirit inspired response to the presence of the mother-to-be of Jesus.

Mary was so moved, both by the power of God at work and by its manifestation in an insignificant person such as herself, that she broke out in song—one that we've come to know as the Magnificat. She asserted that what God was doing in her was such a blessing that all generations to come would testify to it. Mary was right; we are astonished that Almighty God was so gracious, not only to her, but to us in our insignificance, and that he has blessed us with a Savior. What else can we do but what Mary did—worship? Our great God deserves it, and that worship also helps us keep first things first in our short and too often frustrated and tired lives. Recognizing God's work in Christ is the key to a life of meaning and joy.

December 19

The Genealogy of Jesus—Part 1

Matthew 1:1–17

It is too light a thing that you should be my servant to raise up the tribes of Jacob and to bring back the preserved of Israel; I will make you as a light for the nations, that my salvation may reach to the end of the earth.
Isaiah 49:6 (ESV)

Matthew prefaces his announcement of Jesus's birth more mundanely than Luke—with a genealogy. It shows that Jesus could trace his ancestry back to Abraham, and also that he was of the special tribe of Judah and the royal line of David—the very line from which God had promised to provide a Savior for his people. Beyond that, there are a couple of amazing things about the first series of names in this genealogy (vs. 1–6). One is the growth of Israel from one idol worshiper, Abraham, whom God called to worship him, and to believe that God would make him and Sarah into a great nation. God did just that, despite the ways that Abraham and his descendants so often failed to cooperate.

Also amazing is the inclusion in Matthew's genealogy of four women, which was quite unexpected at that time.

- Tamar had been the Canaanite wife of a son of Judah, and then became a neglected widow until she tricked her dead husband's father into making her respectable.
- Rahab had been a prostitute of Jericho, who helped Israel's spies and later married an Israelite.
- Ruth had been one of the detested Moabites; Boaz married her to preserve the line of Elimelech in Israel.
- Bathsheba, wife to Uriah the Hittite, had been forced into King David's bed and later became his wife.

No human would have chosen these people to be part of the bloodline of Jesus, but the LORD used each one, thus demonstrating his continuing grace to Abraham's descendants and anticipating his revelation that his saving grace is not only for Abraham's descendants, but for people from every race and nation of the world.

December 20

The Genealogy of Jesus—Part 2

Matthew 1:1–17

Righteousness and justice are the foundation of your throne;
steadfast love and faithfulness go before you.
Psalm 89:14 (ESV)

Frederick Dale Bruner, in his excellent commentary on Matthew, sees the second and third sections of Matthew's genealogy of Jesus, as highlighting God's justice and faithfulness.

Section two (vs. 6b–11) names the ancestors of Jesus from the glory days of Israel under David and Solomon to the time Judah was humiliated in the exile to Babylon. After Solomon, the kingdom was divided and the decline that began in Solomon's later years continued until both kingdoms had been exiled in punishment for their rebellion against the LORD. In this part of the genealogy, Matthew leaves out three names and changes a couple of others (Asa to Asaph and Amon to Amos), probably to emphasize how close the people's sins came to erasing God's promise to David's house. (Both Asaph's psalms and the prophecies of Amos emphasize God's judgment for his peoples' sins.)

Section three (verses 12–16) takes God's people through the years of exile from the Promised Land and God's temple in Jerusalem. Then, even after some exiles were allowed to return and rebuild the temple, their lives were never what they hoped they would be. Scripture is silent about the four centuries between the times of Nehemiah and Malachi to the first of the New Testament Scriptures. Yet, even here, when God seemed most distant, he was at work preserving the royal line of David in preparation for the birth of Jesus. God is faithful.

In sum, Matthew uses Jesus's genealogy to emphasize in turn, the mercy (Matt. 1:1-6), the justice (Matt 1:7-11), and the faithfulness (Matt. 1:12-16) of God, who has worked out his sovereign purposes throughout the generations so that Jesus might be born as the fulfillment of all God's promises to Abraham.

December 21

God's Ways Are Not Our Ways

Matthew 1:18–20, 24–25

For my thoughts are not your thoughts, neither are your ways my ways, declares the LORD. For as the heavens are higher than the earth, so are my ways higher than your ways and my thoughts than your thoughts.
Isaiah 55:8–9 (ESV)

According to God's law and tradition, an engaged woman and man were not to come together as wife and husband until their marriage. Joseph knew he hadn't been with Mary; that's why her pregnancy was humiliating for him. And since Mary had obviously violated the engagement, divorce was the appropriate response for Joseph.

Joseph had the right to end the engagement publicly so that no shame would fall upon him. Yet, innocent Joseph was prepared to take some of the social shame and personal guilt for the failed engagement upon himself. He decided to give Mary a letter of divorce quietly. In other words, he chose to act mercifully, going beyond the legal requirements.

Before he could take any action, however, an angel of the Lord appeared to righteous Joseph to tell him that the child in Mary was conceived by the Holy Spirit. Joseph believed, and so had to rethink what righteousness required. He saw that even the most rigorous and merciful human righteousness had to submit to the Holy Spirit's work. Because of the better saving righteousness of God, Joseph changed his mind about the divorce.

What had looked shameful and embarrassing to Joseph turned out to be the world's salvation; God's ways are not our ways. In a very similar way, the self-denial and confession of sin and submission to Jesus Christ that is so shunned by the world turns out to be the way that people come to perfect freedom. So then, everyone who would follow God needs to be open to re-education by his Spirit. After all, God's ways are not our ways and his thoughts are not our thoughts.

December 22

There Is Something about That Name

Matthew 1:21

God has not destined us for wrath,
but to obtain salvation through our Lord Jesus Christ.
1 Thessalonians 5:9 (ESV)

Matthew records the angel's instructions to name the divine child "Jesus" (meaning "Yahweh Saves"). No doubt other boys at that time also bore that name; it was not unusual to have names that showed loyalty to the LORD. Matthew's own name was derived from a Hebrew name meaning "gift of Yahweh" and John's from one meaning "Yahweh is gracious." But as the angel makes clear, Jesus will do more than testify to God's salvation; he himself will be God and he himself will save. Whom will Jesus save and from what will he save? He will save **his people**, from **their sins**.

This was in part a message for the Jews; Jesus would preach saving grace to them and give his life in sacrifice for their sin. But Jesus would take his salvation message to non-Jews also—to all who would receive his message about the kingdom of heaven and the humility required of its citizens and then deny themselves, take up their cross, and follow Jesus (see Matt. 16:24).

Jesus's salvation was not to be the political liberation that many people expected, but the liberation of people from the power and bondage of their own sins. As Matthew and the other gospels make clear, as desirable as political liberation might be, Jesus wants people to look at their own sins rather than focus on the sins of others.

Matthew goes on to say more about how Jesus accomplishes his mission—that it is the Holy Spirit who brings people to repentance and cleanses through baptism. And the same Spirit also gives these repentant and cleansed believers the power to change, assurance of salvation, and the privilege to be disciples of Jesus and evangelists for his kingdom. This is all part of what will happen through the life of this Jesus.

December 23

Jesus Is Immanuel—"God with Us"

Matthew 1:22–23

The Word became flesh and dwelt among us, and we have seen his glory, glory as of the only Son from the Father, full of grace and truth.
John 1:14 (ESV)

With this second name, Matthew tied what God was doing through Jesus to what he did in Isaiah's day (Isa. 7:14) and even before that, throughout covenant history. God's actions were all designed to result in the birth of this savior. The second name also testifies that God saves by getting up close and personal with the people he is saving. God saves us by being "God with us."

Although the claim that God is with us is not unique to Christianity, others who make this claim have quite a different idea than the Scriptures proclaim. For example, idol worshipers believe that their gods are with them in visible form and can be carried from place to place. Other people believe that humanity itself is divine; *Emmanuel's Book* was written by a woman who claimed to be in contact with a spirit who called himself Emmanuel, and who used her as his voice to the world. This Emmanuel didn't deny Christ or criticize Christianity, but he changed the biblical message to say that "Christ wants to help everyone to a realization of their own divinity."

At the other extreme is Islam, which teaches that Allah is too transcendent to be with us. Some tenets of Islam are similar to those of Christianity; we agree, for example, that God is not subject to laws of space and time and that he alone is worthy of worship. But, contra-Christianity, Islam contends that humans were not created in God's image, that God would never humble himself to become human, and that salvation is merit-based.

Christians thank God that Jesus (*God Saves*) is Immanuel (*God With Us*) and that his coming to earth makes it possible for sinful humanity to live, now and forever, in the presence of the holy, holy, holy Lord God Almighty.

December 24

Jesus Fulfills God's Promises to Abraham

Genesis 12:1–3; 15:4–5, 18–21; 17:1–8

"Abraham believed God, and it was counted to him as righteousness." Know then that it is those of faith who are the sons of Abraham. And the Scripture...preached the gospel beforehand to Abraham, saying, "In you shall all the nations be blessed." So then, those who are of faith are blessed along with Abraham, the man of faith.
Galatians 3:6–9 (ESV)

Matthew's assertions about Jesus's ancestry and purpose show that Jesus fulfills all of the promises given in God's covenant to the first of his chosen people, Abraham:

- That he would have many descendants.
- That God would provide a home for them.
- That the whole world would be blessed by his offspring.

These promises were partly fulfilled within a few hundred years:

- Abraham's descendants were the twelve tribes of Israel.
- They settled in Canaan and prospered there until disobedience separated them from God and eventually led them into exile.
- They became a blessing to the world, probably seen most clearly in ancient times during Solomon's reign.

Ultimately, however, the promises were fulfilled in one special descendant of Abraham—Jesus Christ—who gave up his life as a sacrifice for the sin of the world.

- Fulfilling the "many descendants" promise, Jesus, although he never had any biological children, has untold millions of adopted children, all those who believe in him and serve him as their Savior and Lord.
- Fulfilling the promise of a home in which to flourish, Jesus invites all people to find rest in him and live as God's children in the power of the Holy Spirit.
- Fulfilling the promise that Abraham's offspring would be a blessing to the world, we have Christ's body—his church—the members of which are to bless the world by living as citizens of Christ's kingdom and sharing the gospel of God's grace.

December 25

Who Is Jesus to You?

Matthew 1:21–23; Luke 2:29–32

And this is eternal life, that they know you the only true God, and Jesus Christ whom you have sent.
John 17:3 (ESV)

When Simeon, by the power of the Spirit, recognized Jesus as God's answer to the longing of his soul, he was ready to die in peace. Are you? Will you be among the opposition to God that is destroyed with Satan or among those who live forever with Jesus who said: "I am the way and the truth and the life. No one comes to the Father except through me" (John 14:6)?

Belief is the way one comes to God through Jesus. "Whoever hears my word and believes him who sent me has eternal life and will not be judged" (John 5:24). To believe is to agree to what Scripture says about Jesus and what he came to do. But it also has to result in a life of obedience; obedience, albeit imperfect, is proof of true belief. Those who put Jesus's words into practice are like the wise man who built his house on the rock (Matt. 7:24).

Please understand, obedience cannot earn salvation. "For it is by grace you have been saved, through faith—and this not from yourselves, it is the gift of God—not by works, so that no one can boast" (Eph. 2:8–9). However, all who really receive this gift will pursue obedience with the help of God's Holy Spirit.

True servants of Christ will act responsibly with the gifts God has entrusted to them (see 1 Cor. 4:2): caring for God's world, being responsible and generous with their material blessings, demonstrating faithful love in marriage and family, showing concern for the material and spiritual welfare of neighbors, and so on. They also know that the Christian life is not a solitary affair, but that God calls us to be part of a visible community of worship and work so that both alone and together with other members of Christ's church, we closely follow Jesus, loving God above all and our neighbors as ourselves.

December 26

Isaiah's Vision of the New Jerusalem

Isaiah 62

The one who conquers, I will make him a pillar in the temple of my God...and I will write on him the name of my God, and the name of the city of my God, the new Jerusalem, which comes down from my God out of heaven, and my own new name.
Revelation 3:12 (ESV)

The new name that Isaiah prophesied for God's people meant they would have a new status as a sign of God's favor. This is confirmed by the imagery of verse 3 which calls God's people a glorious crown of splendor for the LORD. As we now know, that wouldn't happen for a long time. As desperate as their situation was already, God's covenant people would go farther downhill before they would see the light of God's fulfillment.

Yet, the promises would hold, and fulfillment would come. With the benefit of hindsight and the perspective of the New Testament, we see that Isaiah's prophecy of a Savior (verse 11) was fulfilled in Christ. God's kingdom has been established as supreme by Christ's life, death, resurrection, and ascension. And ever since, people of every nationality and race have come to serve in God's kingdom, drawn to each other by the same bond of love that draws all of them to God through Jesus Christ.

The signs of Christ's victory are seen, among other places, in the radical changes brought about in the lives of many sinners who have come to faith in Christ. One redeemed drunkard, being hassled by his former drinking buddies about his belief that Jesus turned water into wine, said, "I've seen him do something just as great; in my house he turned whiskey into furniture."

God did not rest until his promises came true in Jesus. But there's more to come. The kingdom of God is still growing. God will not rest until his ridiculed, hated, and even persecuted people are vindicated. He will not stop until his light erases the darkness and everything is just the way he wants it to be.

December 27

A Sign of Hope

Ezekiel 37:1–14

In [Christ Jesus] you also are being built together into a dwelling place for God by the Spirit.
Ephesians 2:22 (ESV)

One of the better known visions of Ezekiel is of a desolate valley full of the dry bones of the dead. It was a visual metaphor of the condition of the people of God in exile, spiritually stagnant and despairing. Although some recognized their spiritual need, they were dead to any hope of spiritual vitality. They (Ezekiel included) certainly knew that they could do nothing to escape their condition. But then God asked Ezekiel an interesting question: "Son of man, can these bones live?"

The obvious answer was "No; no way." How could these lifeless, gnawed on, mixed-up bones find their mates and reattach, resupplied with the ingredients that make up healthy organisms, and once again live? They could not. And more to the point, there was no way that the people of God could live again. They were either dead or in exile, with their government, their holy city, their temple, and their civilization destroyed. There was no way they could live again. Except that with God all things are possible. So Ezekiel cautiously but reverently confessed that only the LORD knew what he was able and willing to do.

God then commanded Ezekiel to speak the word of the LORD to those bones. He obeyed and saw the bones join together to form skeletons and then live again. It was an echo of the creation when "The LORD God formed a man from the dust of the ground and breathed into his nostrils the breath of life (Gen. 2:7).

The obvious message was that although Judah was under judgment, dead, and without hope, God would, by his Spirit, call them back to life and service to him. It's the same message God wants his people to get today. Judgment and death aren't the last word for those whom the Lord has called to be his own.

December 28

God's Everlasting Covenant of Peace

Ezekiel 37:15–28

"For the mountains may depart and the hills be removed,
but my steadfast love shall not depart from you,
and my covenant of peace shall not be removed," says the LORD.
Isaiah 54:10 (ESV)

Ezekiel's prophecy was initially fulfilled after seventy years of exile, when some people were allowed to return home. That's when Israel came back to life as a nation. But it was fulfilled in a more complete way in Jesus Christ. When Christ came, the life and hope of the Jewish people was as dead as it had been in the exile. Not many of them expected the self-sacrificing and humble Messiah that God sent; that's why they, with the help of their Gentile masters, ended up killing Jesus on a cross. But it was that very murder and God's reversal of it on Easter that gave, and continues to give, life to people who are the spiritual equivalent of old, dried-out bones. It's these people, born-again Jews and Gentiles alike, who make up what the apostle Paul calls "the Israel of God" (Gal. 6:16).

The book of Acts is nothing less than the story of God putting flesh on dry bones, then breathing life into them, and doing it all over the then civilized world. The continuing spread of the gospel today into new language and people groups is the same thing, a fulfillment of Ezekiel 37.

There are still many people who feel like dried or drying bones, and some too, who have lost their way—although they may not recognize it—and who can't or don't want to find their way out of the deceit of sin. God's message of hope cannot be heard by those who are full of themselves, but only by those who have the honesty to admit that they are dead without God. Wherever people come to the end of themselves, look to Christ for help, and receive his Spirit, this is where dry bones become living souls—souls in everlasting community with God and also with all who have found life in him.

December 29

The LORD Returns to His Temple

Ezekiel 43:1–12

Jesus told the merchants and money changers: *"Do not make my Father's house a house of trade." His disciples remembered that it was written: "Zeal for your house will consume me."*
John 2:16–17 (ESV) (see Psalm 69:9)

Ezekiel's visions culminated in a temple that would surpass what the Babylonians destroyed. This temple would be fully as large as David's kingdom. Moreover, foreigners would be included so long as they had become part of God's new community—those circumcised in flesh and heart (Ezek. 44:5–9). The new temple and all who ministered in it had to be holy, free of the contamination that plagued worship in Solomon's temple and land prior to the exile.

This temple was originally Paradise itself. After that fell apart, God made plans to restore the communion that was there.

- The first significant advance in that was with the moveable tent of meeting with its different courts and places for sacrifice and furnishings—all in service to God.
- Next came Solomon's temple, a permanent structure that improved on what Moses had built.
- But all along, God's presence was greater than a mere building; God wanted his dwelling place to be the whole of Jerusalem—the city of God. And the temple would be more than a city too; it would be a people—Israel, the people of God, living by God's laws for life, and with the LORD in their midst.

So the zeal for God's house that consumed the Psalmist, and Jesus after him, was really an intense desire for God's people to experience the reality of his presence with them. Ezekiel's vision, too, was of a pure and holy communion between God and his people, a communion in which the glorious God would live forever among a priesthood and a people cleansed from evil. Hence Ezekiel's conclusion: "And the name of the city from that time on will be: THE LORD IS THERE" (Ezek. 48:35).

December 30

The Life-giving Presence of God

Ezekiel 47:1–12

Solomon's prayer at the temple dedication: But will God indeed dwell on the earth? Behold, heaven and the highest heaven cannot contain you; how much less this house that I have built!
1 Kings 8:27 (ESV)

In Ezekiel's vision, the return of the LORD would recapture the glory of the paradise God originally created for us. Although the venue had changed from garden to city, the essential thing was the presence of the LORD. It's the very same essential that Jesus conveyed through his words and deeds. He didn't want people to get hung up on the symbols of a connection with God only to have the real connection escape them. The temple pointed to the reality of this connection. Jerusalem, also, was a holy city as long as it contributed to the connection with the Father that Jesus had. Even Israel itself was a worthless nation if it did not represent and model the Kingdom of God where there was harmony between God and his creatures.

As Jesus preached, and in harmony with Ezekiel's vision, when the LORD returns in all his glory to fill his temple it will be for the benefit of those who are truly devoted to him; there will be an inheritance for them all. (Galatians 6:16 calls them the *Israel of God.*) Ezekiel also saw a vast life-giving river flowing from the temple and transforming the wilderness. (It sounds very much like God's creation of "new heavens and a new earth" (Isa. 65:17-25) and also the new heaven and new earth of Revelation 21:1.)

The book of Ezekiel begins with a vision for a people who have lost their land and temple through sin and rebellion. And it ends with a vision of the LORD returning in glory to a new temple in Jerusalem to reside in the midst of his people once again, never to leave them. This is the life that now belongs to those who are in Christ and which will be completely realized when Christ comes again. Until then, we can do nothing more important than heed Ezekiel's call to be faithful to our Savior and Lord.

December 31

The Eternal Presence of the LORD

Micah 4:1–5

For you are a people holy to the LORD your God.
The LORD your God has chosen you to be a people for his treasured possession, out of all the peoples who are on the face of the earth.
Deuteronomy 7:6 (ESV)

We are in the last days Micah speaks about, although not yet at the point where the LORD reigns unopposed and his people enjoy the fullness of his peace. But in Christ we have come closer than all of the faithful under the old covenant to that better country for which they longed (see Heb. 11:16). The sacrificial system that God used to postpone our punishment for sin has been done away with once and for all by the sacrifice of our eternal high priest, Jesus Christ. By one sacrifice Jesus removed the curtain that kept us separate from God (see Heb. 10).

So, unlike the faithful Israelites who couldn't even think of going into the Most Holy Place, you, if you are right with God in Jesus Christ, may live in it. You wear the robe of Christ's righteousness and bear on your soul the seal of God, which reads: "Holy to the LORD." Along with the clothing, you see the Bread of the Presence in God's every provision for you. The Golden Lampstand is the light of Christ in your life and in our world. In fact, you're even part of the lamp whose light drives away the world's darkness; what feeds the flame are the gifts of the Holy Spirit. And the incense is the prayers of God's people, arising morning and evening before the throne of God, all of which he uses to accomplish his purposes.

As you live in the presence of God, let it show. As Moses, fresh from meeting God, continued to reflect his glory (Ex. 34:29)—so can you. If you live in God's presence, it can't help but show, not for your glory, but for God's. Finally, remember this sure hope: what you experience on your best days, in your closest walk with God, is just a shadow of what heaven will be. Then "we will walk in the name of the LORD our God for ever and ever" (Mic. 4:5).